TO BE
DISPOSED
BY
AUTHORITY

IRAQ ABLAZE

This book is dedicated to Samir Kassir, a very dear friend and prominent journalist who was described by many of his colleagues as the most vociferous and bravest advocate for human rights and democracy throughout the Middle East. He paid his life as a price for that when a bomb was planted under his driving seat in Beirut on June 2, 2005 by the enemies of such values.

It is also dedicated to the children of Iraq and Palestine who are hoping for a better future and safer environment in which to grow up.

IRAQ
ABLAZE

INSIDE THE INSURGENCY

ZAKI CHEHAB

I.B. TAURIS

LONDON · NEW YORK

Published in 2006 by I.B.Tauris & Co Ltd
6 Salem Road, London W2 4BU
175 Fifth Avenue, New York NY 10010
www.ibtauris.com

ISBN: 1 84511 110 9
EAN: 978 1 84511 110 6

A full CIP record for this book is available from the British Library

Typeset in Baskerville
Printed and bound in Great Britain by MPG Books, Bodmin, Cornwall

Contents

THE PAST SHAPES THE FUTURE

Traveling from Beirut to Baghdad on the *Flying Carpet*, a small, nineteen-seat passenger plane, was an unnerving experience. Two hours into the flight, in a turboprop Metro SW4 commuter aircraft, the pilot asked us to prepare for landing at Baghdad International Airport. We then circled high above the airport for about fifty minutes. The seasoned passenger next to me explained that there was a risk of being shot at by insurgents living in the area close to the airport. The pilot maintained a high altitude until he received word from the control tower that it was safe to attempt a steep landing.

A few minutes before we exited the plane, the pilot told us that the airport had been under missile attacks and that a previous flight had been forced to return back to Jordan. I was already beginning to understand what was awaiting me in Iraq.

What saddened me that day, January 24, 2005, as I returned to Baghdad to cover the first democratically held elections in the country for decades, was the culture of bribery that had flourished in my absence. I had to pay the head of customs to allow my bags through. My Iraqi companion thought nothing about handing over the fifty U.S. dollars, a considerable amount by local standards. He told me that if I questioned them, my passage would definitely be delayed, if not made miserably difficult.

The atmosphere was tense. The few passengers who were arriving or departing had to travel along the highway that connects the airport with the city of Baghdad–now known as the "Road of Death." Our car was one of few on the road, and our driver confirmed the news given by the pilot, that the airport had been targeted shortly before our arrival. A few bombs, planted by insurgents, had exploded on the side of the road, killing and injuring a group of patrolling American soldiers. Little wonder then that you rarely encounter smiling-faced American forces. You find tense, wary soldiers who have seen many comrades injured or killed in action. The average number of coalition forces killed ranges between three and five daily.

Car engines littered the roadside–a visual reminder of the regular suicide bombings. Our driver, who makes this journey daily, was incredulous that the coalition forces hadn't succeeded in securing this vital route–a mere twenty-minute drive from Baghdad. The brief trip reinforces the daunting challenges faced by American commanders and the newly built Iraqi security forces to make the country safe and secure.

My interest in Iraq began thirty-nine years ago, when I was eight years old and living in a refugee camp in South Lebanon that was administered by the United Nations Relief and Works Agency. In a local shop within Bourj Al Shamali camp, where I grew up with my three brothers and four sisters, I bought an out-of-date magazine, new ones being too expensive, and saw pen friends advertised. I was keen to have a pen pal, as we had little contact with the outside world. I chose to correspond with a boy my age who was from a town called Al Fallujah in Iraq. We stayed in touch for over four years, exchanging letters, photographs, and stories.

Thirty-five years later, in June 2003, I visited Fallujah for the first time when it became headline news because of the violent confrontations there between U.S. forces and resistance fighters. I was determined to look for the pen friend I had last heard from when I was twelve. All I could remember was his name and the school he used as an address to correspond from. So, in Fallujah, the town of mosques, I decided to ask in one of those mosques if they knew of his whereabouts. The Imam gave me an address that turned out to be correct, and I came face-to-face with my former pen friend for the first time. He, too, was able to recall my name and the address at my camp in Lebanon where he had sent his schoolboy news. As we caught up on the intervening years, I became aware of his support for the fledgling resistance. My gut feeling was that he was a member of one of the groups.

More than a year after our first encounter, I wanted to fulfill my promise to meet up with him again when I returned to the country to cover the elections. I engaged the help of an Iraqi intermediary named Othman to try to locate my friend, as it was no longer safe to travel on my own by road to Al Anbar province, in which Fallujah is one of the main towns. Even though I am an Arab, traveling outside the capital of Baghdad is as dangerous for me as it is for any other person. By now there had been several kidnappings of European journalists, foreign workers with Arab nationalities such as Lebanese, Egyptian, Moroccan, and Syrian, as well as countless Iraqis. All had fallen prey to the highway kidnap gangs, who either pass their victims on up the chain of gangs for ransom or kill them. No one is immune.

The news from Othman was that my pen friend, a doctor, was no longer consulting from his clinic, and his home was boarded up. His neighbors explained to my intermediary that the Americans had arrested his five sons, and he, too, was wanted. Three sons were being detained in Al Anbar jail, one in Basra, and the youngest boy, sixteen-year-old Abu Bakr, was being held in the now famous Abu Ghraib prison near Baghdad. Determined to find my friend again, I asked Othman to leave my telephone number with any of my friend's neighbors who would agree to help. Finally, I received a call. The caller told me that my friend had been granted a visiting pass to see his youngest son in Abu Ghraib prison, and that he would come and find me at my hotel in Baghdad after the visit.

His huge smile was still there, but his anger was barely contained as he explained that his sons—an engineering graduate, a doctor, a dentist, a medical student, and his sixteen-year-old, who was a secondary school student—had been arrested on false information that had been passed to the American forces, accusing the young men of sympathizing with the resistance. A friend of his had told him that if he paid twelve thousand American dollars, an American commander would be willing to intervene and release them. He smiled ironically and shrugged his shoulders. His eyes expressed his sadness at this new reality, at this new Iraq.

This book takes an unsparing look at this new reality.

CHAPTER ONE

INSIDE THE INSURGENCY

My first encounter with the so-called Iraqi resistance took place during the stifling heat of June 2003. Saddam Hussein's regime had fallen two months earlier. I met with Kamel, Mohammed, and Abdul Khader at a farm close to the city of Al Ramadi, the capital of what is referred to as the Sunni Triangle.

In the shimmering late afternoon sun, the city seemed to be on edge. I stepped out of the car at the entrance to the main market, called Souk Al Muktar–a Friday market that was now a flourishing gun souk since the fall of the regime. I was told not to worry if I heard explosions. Before they were purchased, all manner of weapons and ammunition could be tried and tested in the makeshift firing range a strategic distance away.

People clamored toward me when they discovered I was a journalist. They started to vent their anger about the United States and its coalition forces, which by that time had already claimed hundreds of civilian lives. I was shown banners draped over the walls of the Abdul Malik Mosque, otherwise known as the Grand Mosque, that listed the names of those who had recently been killed by American forces in the area. That day, the citizens of Al Ramadi were gathered at one of the large mosques in the city to mourn the death of Omar Sadek Mukhaiber, who had been killed the previous evening by U.S. forces. Mukhaiber, twenty-nine years old and recently married, was unarmed and driving a civilian car on his way to the ice-making factory owned by his parents. He had failed to stop at a checkpoint, but there had been no signs warning him or other drivers of the danger they were approaching. His death could not be justified or excused, and the anger of the people was overwhelming. It was deaths like these that were galvanizing rapidly growing local resistance groups against what they now considered as a hostile occupation.

A man in his thirties, whom I had seen earlier in the mosque, introduced himself as Kamel and asked if I was interested in seeing for myself the spot where the young man had been shot. By the time we arrived, a few people had gathered and formed an angry mob. One of them was especially keen to make his threats of revenge heard, warning that resistance fighters were armed and ready to fight. I asked if it would be possible to interview any of the fighters. Kamel stepped in once again and invited me to meet his local militia. At that time they were unknown and newly organized, but today their activities make international news. Kamel told me that the group operated from the suburbs of Al Ramadi.

We had intended to make the seventy-mile journey back that night along the road from Al Ramadi to Baghdad, which was being attacked daily by the resistance as well as by street gangs. My Iraqi driver, Abu Hassan, took me aside to warn me that we should leave the city before darkness fell. The Americans had imposed a 10:00 PM curfew, and anyone traveling after that time risked being shot. That was the moment I became conscious of the danger of being in this area, both for myself and my driver. It was over an hour's drive back to Baghdad, and along with the U.S. curfew there was the added risk of being targeted by thieves who had become active on this busy road linking Baghdad to the Jordanian and Syrian borders.

Determined not to turn down the opportunity of meeting Kamel's group, I decided to remain in the area rather than return to Baghdad as planned. Asking if there was a hotel where we could spend the night, Kamel reprimanded me, as is the Arab way, saying it would be an insult if we stayed anywhere else but his home. Abu Hassan was still anxious and was emphatic that he must go home to his family in Baghdad to sleep, as he hadn't told them he wouldn't be returning for the night. He promised to drive back to Al Ramadi to pick me up the next morning, so we arranged a rendezvous in the main square in the center of the city and he left.

As Abu Hassan was quite meticulous about the upkeep of his car, I found myself making unfavorable comparisons as I clambered into Kamel's ancient Chevrolet, with its torn seats and over-flowing ashtrays. We drove past the Euphrates River, flanked by a deserted American checkpoint on one side and a heavily guarded entrance on the other. My fellow passenger was introduced as Abdul Karim, a taciturn, shaven-headed man, about Kamel's age, with the thick moustache typically sported by the men of this region. Steering with one hand, Kamel waved his cigarette hand toward one of Saddam Hussein's many palaces and explained that it was now the headquarters of the American forces in Al Ramadi, who had renamed it Camp Blue Diamond. This was the temporary new home of the third Armored Cavalry Regiment from Fort Carson, Colorado. Camp Blue Diamond was constantly under attack either from drive-by shootings or from 62-millimeter mortar shells fired from the surrounding farms. Such attacks were happening almost every day.

We passed fields of tomatoes and eggplant, shaded by heavily laden date palms, and Kamel, an amusing and practiced joke-teller, kept Abdul Karim and me entertained during the journey. He explained how during the nineteenth century Al Ramadi had become wealthy due to its strategic location as a staging post along the lucrative camel caravan route from Baghdad to the countries of the Levant–Palestine, Lebanon, and Syria. He told stories about the passing villages, which are locally known by the names of the principal tribes that lived there. After twenty minutes or so, we turned off the main road and headed for a small village. Worried that his family might be curious about a stranger arriving at their home for the night, Kamel asked whether I would mind saying that we were old friends who hadn't seen each other for some time, in case his brothers or father started asking awkward questions. I reassured him, and we parked the car on one of the side roads to give me time to hide my camera, and then said our good-byes to Abdul Karim. We drove on to farmland that had about fifteen houses scattered around it, all belonging to Kamel's relatives. No one else was traveling the road that evening, but we could hear the drone of an American helicopter buzzing overhead.

Earlier in the day, American forces had laid siege to a nearby village. Their mission was to arrest the Imam of the village mosque, after accusing him of inciting his worshippers to join the Islamist jihadi groups fighting to liberate their country. Kamel described how the U.S. forces used loudspeakers demanding the Imam surrender. An Iraqi sniper from the edge of the village shot one of the American soldiers who was positioned behind his machine gun in a Humvee. The soldier later died.

With my camera safely concealed, we drove on to Kamel's house within the farm compound, which was protected by an iron gate and high walls–typical of this region and Arab society in general. Privacy is important, and houses are built in such a manner that the occupants, particularly the women, cannot be seen by their neighbors. In his thirties and married with two children, Kamel shared the house with his parents and two older married brothers. He went ahead to forewarn his family that there would be a guest for the night. The women were at home alone, and they set about preparing the reception room, known as the *diwaniya,* where male relatives, guests, and members of tribes who are traveling relax to chat and sip coffee or mint tea.

Kamel's brothers and father then arrived and invited me to join them for evening prayers. Apologetically, I said that I didn't pray, and while they were arranging their prayer mats, I went out into the garden, noticing how uncannily quiet it was—no sounds of war, just the mosque and the voices of shepherds calling to their goats. By the time I returned to the house, dinner was laid out on the floor over a brightly colored plastic sheet. The meal was a traditional Iraqi dolmas—vine leaves stuffed with vegetables and rice and served with fresh yogurt and pomegranate sauce. The discussion was not about the war but about the bad news in the market that day. Kamel's nephew had taken some of their produce to sell, but the prices were down dramatically as a result of high unemployment.

Citizens of the Al Anbar province are proud of the fact that they belong to some of the most influential tribes in the country, and they have a reputation for producing tough leaders. Traditionally they worked as civil servants or were part of the army—many of them reaching positions of power within these institutions. The dissolution of the army and civil service after the fall of the regime, along with their subsequent loss of power and income, had festered discontent.

Kamel suggested we go outside again to enjoy the garden and talk out of earshot of his family. He explained that he had been a former police officer and had lost his job when the regime fell. Now his time was spent organizing his group, whom I was hoping to interview. He reassured me that one of the fighters, Abdul Khader, who was in charge of our rendezvous, was on his way.

We sipped green tea and talked about the deteriorating security situation in the country. It was now unsafe to go out after dark in Baghdad or travel the main roads that connected Iraq's major cities. We were interrupted by whistling, shortly followed by the appearance of Abdul Khader, who was obviously one of Kamel's extended family but was careful not to alert the rest of Kamel's household of his presence. Kamel asked him to wait for a few seconds. He discreetly picked up the bag containing my camera, and we left through a back gate from the house that led out to the fields. Thankfully, the moon was nearly full and provided us with light. We were nervous about American patrols passing by with their searchlights, and Kamel ordered us to follow directly behind him and without talking. Eventually we arrived at a small house at the far end of the farm. Kamel knocked gently on the door. Inside were five men between the ages of twenty and forty, their heads wrapped in Iraqi headscarves that revealed only their eyes, and wearing an assortment of clothing from tracksuits to galabias.[1] I was introduced to a man named Mohammed, whom Kamel described as the leader. He apologized for not introducing me to the others, saying there was no point in giving false names.

I was invited to sit with the men on a mattress on the floor, surrounded by weapons—hand grenades, pistols, AK-47 machine guns, RPG-7s, and a small 62-millimeter mortar. I have to admit I was nervous. There was the possibility of a tip-off, which could lead to a confrontation with the patrolling American forces. With the area under strict curfew, I was already breaking the law. The fighters may have been dressed in assorted civilian clothes, but from their covered faces and budding arsenal there was no mistaking their intentions. These particular fighters were not Baathist remnants. On the contrary, they defined themselves as nationalists and blamed Saddam Hussein for bringing Americans into

Iraq. They hoped that the capture of Saddam by allied forces would sever the links between Saddam and the resistance movement once and for all.

The room was lit by a single kerosene lamp, as the electricity supply had gone out during one of the regular power cuts. Some members of the group reported to Mohammed about the movements of American forces that day in the surrounding area. These intelligence reports provided details as to the average number of American soldiers in each convoy entering the road leading to this suburb of Al Ramadi and how regular the patrols were. They asked about a particular police station. Mohammed replied that more observation was needed for both targets–the American convoys and the police station. As the electric lights flickered back on, Mohammed formally welcomed me to their gathering on behalf of the group and invited me to start my interview.

I asked him when the idea to set up an organization to resist the Americans had first arisen. He replied that it began immediately after the arrival of the U.S. forces into the country: "We started this national front with ten people. We then opened it up to more people, and with the help of the faithful and those who believe in our cause, we have expanded to the extent that we have bases or cells all over Iraq.

"People join us from all walks of life. Those who cannot fight support us financially. We don't have any connections at all with Saddam's regime. We are well trained, as most of us took part in the Iran-Iraq War, but occasionally young recruits ask us for training. We tend to hold training sessions when we get together as a group so that each one of us knows how to use the weapons of other members in case something happens to them. We have bases in Basra, Mosul, Baghdad, and in five towns in Al Anbar province:[2] Al Qaem, Haditha, Anah, Hit [pronounced "Heet"], Fallujah, and Al Ramadi. There is plenty of coordination going on between these different groups and bases."

"So do you have connections with any other resistance groups fighting the Americans?" I ventured.

"Before, we had no links with them, but now we do. Some groups have Islamic backgrounds, some used to belong to the Baath Party, others used to be members of Fedayeen Saddam [Saddam's "Men of Sacrifice"], but we are an independent, national organization. Sometimes when we have an operation to carry out and we need additional help in specific areas, such as supplying us with logistics or hiding some of our members after attacks, then we do coordinate with other groups."

Operation Desert Scorpion, Peninsular Strike, Operation Ivy Serpent, and the oddly named Operation Soda Mountain were launched by the Americans in the early days to crush the nascent resistance. But the situation escalated.

Abu Musab Al Zarqawi, the ruthless Jordanian militant known for beheading kidnapped victims, established a strong base in Fallujah, close to Al Ramadi, where I first encountered members of an insurgency group. Zarqawi rose through the ranks of Al Qaeda and was honored by Osama bin Laden with the title "Emir of Al Qaeda in the Country of Two Rivers" (referring to the Tigris and Euphrates rivers). Bin Laden's "Man in Iraq" succeeded in recruiting hundreds, if not thousands, of Iraqi followers, together with several hundred fighters from other Arab countries such as Syria and Saudi Arabia, Sudan and Yemen.

To overcome this escalating opposition force, American troops attacked Fallujah city and the surrounding areas on November 7, 2004, destroying most of the houses in the city and forcing its inhabitants to seek refuge in makeshift camps or in school buildings that had been deserted by students and teachers.

I wanted to know how the resistance dealt with large-scale offensives against them. Mohammed answered, "If you want to attack a target, and the target is small, you have to make greater efforts to reach it, but if the target is larger, it becomes easier to find. Therefore, the more American forces there are in our area, the easier it is for us to single them out and attack them."

"Many Iraqis I have spoken to in Baghdad are saying that the resistance is killing more Iraqi civilians than even American or coalition soldiers. What do you say about that?" I asked.

"I don't agree," Mohammed quickly replied. "Iraqis who are being killed by our fighters are collaborators with the Americans—translators or Iraqi police carrying out missions on behalf of the coalition forces."

"So what kind of attacks do you expect to carry out in the future?"

Mohammed's response was immediate: "All kinds, and we will use every means available to us."

The interview ended in the early hours of the morning. There was no mistaking the intensity of their commitment to their cause, which was the liberation of Iraq from its current occupiers. Mohammed asked me if he could read a statement for broadcast. At the time, it was the first televised statement from a group that was being collectively referred to as the "Iraqi resistance." The message was addressed to: "President George Bush and his allies" from: "The National Command Front." It read as follows:

We made a promise to our people to send the bodies of your soldiers home, one after the other in response to the random terrorist attacks which are being carried out by the American forces where innocent people get killed and the elderly humiliated. We have made a promise to God that the attacks which we will carry out in the future will be more painful and much heavier than the attacks which have already taken place. And with the help of God, and the noble members of the resistance, who have no connection or any affiliation to the former regime of Saddam Hussein, we will succeed.

Once again we call upon you, if you are serious about looking after the safety of your soldiers, to leave our country immediately, or we will take revenge for every Iraqi killed or humiliated and every house ransacked. You should know that the Iraqis are now well aware of the big lie you have told them that you are here to liberate Iraq from dictatorship.

The statement over, Mohammed ordered his men to prepare themselves for their next mission. "You are welcome to film it," he said. I wasn't sure if he was joking, but Kamel saved the situation by saying that we should return to his house before any member of his family worried about our absence. Kamel and I retraced our steps through the fields. We passed a woman, whom Kamel greeted, but he made sure that I was partially hidden from her view to avoid awkward questions. The night was sultry, and as we arrived at the house, he asked whether I would like to sleep outside, reassuring me that there were no mosquitoes.

As I slept under the stars, the eerie silence of the night was interrupted only by American patrols and their helicopters hovering from time to time, and the barking of the farm dogs when the patrols came too close. When I later recalled that evening, I realized that I was actually in a battlefield. My hosts were fighters who were engaged in daily assaults against American troops. Professionally, I felt a sense of elation to be the first to film these men whom President George Bush promised to "root out and destroy." But I was deeply concerned that someone might discover what I had learned from these militants. Not only had I been out and about during curfew hours with men whose intention was to kill military personnel of the coalition forces, but I also had information concerning their identity and whereabouts that would be extremely sensitive for the Americans.

I woke with the movements of the early morning household

preparing for prayers and was surprised to see Kamel's father wearing a police uniform. Kamel explained that his father had no idea about his activities as a member of the resistance. His older brother was a former army officer whose position was made redundant after the regime fell. He knew about Kamel's clandestine life and was okay about it, but it was kept secret from both his father and other brother in order to protect them. This precaution was taken in case the resistance cell was discovered and its family members arrested by the occupying forces.

We ate a farm breakfast of homemade cheese yogurt and fried eggs while sitting in the front garden, which was just warming up in the early morning sunshine. After thanking my hosts for their hospitality, I prepared to leave with Kamel, who cautioned me to keep out of sight. We drove for about twenty minutes as far as Saddam Hussein's palace, and from there crossed the bridge over the Euphrates River and into Al Ramadi.

We continued past different government offices, including the regional council, the governate, and the police headquarters. All were under American control or protection. However, that didn't prevent the people employed by these departments from being sympathetic to the resistance. For most, getting rid of the occupying forces was their uppermost concern.

In the main souk of Al Ramadi, while waiting for my driver to arrive from Baghdad, I went to buy a newspaper from a stall that was surrounded by local men wearing traditional dishdasha robes and kuffiyeh headdresses. I probably stood out as a foreigner, or perhaps I was recognized as a journalist who had been there the previous day, but a serious-looking youth approached me offering to sell me a videotape. He claimed that the tape contained footage of an attack against American forces that had been filmed by a member of the resistance. As I talked to the young man, an American convoy drove by. U.S. flags fluttered from the antennas of their Humvees, and helmeted soldiers wearing wraparound goggles trained their machine guns in readiness. I could see that the convoy had made Kamel nervous, so I wound up my conversation with the video seller by asking how much he wanted for his tape. Without a beat, he said, "Two hundred U.S. dollars." Unsure of the content of the unseen tape and the exorbitant price, I left empty-handed.

Relieved at the safe return of my driver, I suggested to Kamel that he park his old Chevrolet and transfer to Abu Hassan's newly washed and vacuumed car. Kamel was keen for me to visit a sheikh from the Al Dulaimi tribe who lived in Samarra.[3]

"Why are the Americans being attacked?" The sheikh asked. He then proceeded to answer his own question. "It's because they humiliate people—breaking down gates and doors to enter homes, and beating and handcuffing husbands in front of their wives and children. It all leads to bitterness and hatred, and so people resort to violence to take revenge." There is no underestimating the significance of honor in Arab society. It is not an outdated concept but rather an important code of respect by which people conduct their daily lives. I reminded the sheikh of the punishments meted out by the previous regime: "It's better to be humiliated by an Iraqi than at the hands of strangers and infidels."

In the sheikh's *diwaniya* a man joined us and, discovering I was from the media, introduced himself as a mujahid named Abdul Salaam, who freely admitted to being a member of the Islamic resistance. I asked him what he thought about the calls for jihad (holy war) issued by Saddam Hussein, who was then on the run. These were in the form of videotapes passed to Arabic television stations before the deposed leader was arrested. He answered, "They used to lie that they had carried out his wishes in order to milk more money out of him." Indeed, it's widely known that many of Saddam's loyalists used to resort to lying in order to curry favor with him and then claim his reward. Abdul Salaam continued, "We carry out operations with the help and support of our nation, and I can assure you that with Allah's will, America will be defeated as other superpowers have been defeated." He was referring to the Soviet Union's withdrawal from Afghanistan, and his answer gave a clear insight into the mentality of the resistance. "American forces didn't come here to overthrow Saddam Hussein but to crush the Iraqi people. Iraq is for Iraqis, but now we are an occupied country. What's happening is shameful and immoral. Talk to people anywhere in the country, and they will tell you that the U.S. forces smash down doors with no respect for whoever is inside. They take money, attack people, and rob whatever the government has in order to get their hands on Iraq's wealth. So that's why we must defend our great Iraq, where we were born and for whom we are prepared to die."

A tall, strongly built man in his early sixties had been listening intently to our conversation, stroking his large moustache. He introduced himself as Sheikh Saleh and launched into his story. He, too, belonged to the Islamic movement that was burgeoning in the Samarra area. With some pride he told me he had taken part in attacks against American forces after they made their headquarters in his town. Many of his comrades were his age or even older, fighting alongside their teenage grandchildren. "With the help of God, we are going to win, and the resistance will succeed in forcing the Americans to withdraw—just like they did from Vietnam. We have large supplies of weapons, and we are well-trained." Sheikh Saleh laughed when he recalled that the Americans always attributed attacks against them as being carried out by Saddam loyalists.

That comment by Sheikh Saleh reminded me of a call I had received at the Palestine Hotel in central Baghdad in mid-June 2003. It was from Hazem Al Samarrai, an Iraqi friend of mine who owns a bookshop in central London and had traveled to Iraq with me the previous month on the first civilian flight to operate from London to Baghdad after the war officially ended. Also on the flight was Sharif Ali bin Al Hussein, a cousin of King Faisal II, who was killed along with almost all the royal family in a palace coup massacre in July 1958. Sharif was just two years old at the time and was immediately taken out of the country. He was making an emotional return to live in Iraq as the first member of the royal family to do so since his family was murdered.

Hazem was calling from his satellite telephone to tell me he was on his way to his hometown, Samarra, and had just come across an ambush carried out by insurgents of an American convoy. He insisted that if I got there in less than half an hour, I would be able to get footage of the burning wreckage. I called my cameraman and my driver, Abu Hassan, and we rushed to the scene, where hundreds of local people and passersby were watching a Humvee tank and a military truck in flames. As well as the heat of the flames, the temperature that blazing June day was soaring over 122 degrees Fahrenheit. Witnesses surrounded us to explain that a group of insurgents had been hiding at the side of the road and had attacked the Humvee from behind with an RPG-7 and rocket launcher until it caught fire. Two of the insurgents had then followed the truck on a bike and lobbed a gasoline bomb toward it. Helicopters soon arrived, hovering low to disperse the crowds, who were giving cover to the insurgents to enable them to flee the area. The fire was eventually brought under control and the victims of the attack airlifted out.

Samarra, the sheikh's town, is similar in size to Al Ramadi. It lies in a fertile valley sixty miles north of Baghdad, on the banks of Iraq's Tigris River. It is now a dusty-looking town, but the golden cupola and blue-tiled dome of the two shrines that dominate the city are reminders of its former glory days when it was the seat of the Muslim caliphate. Samarra was one of the few Sunni-dominated areas that suffered under Saddam Hussein's rule, because the town and its tribes were regional rivals to Saddam's hometown of Tikrit.

The sheikh continued to explain why Samarra had paid a heavy price: "Many high-ranking officers, tribal leaders, and active members of the Baath Party were executed or imprisoned because of their refusal to step into line with Saddam's policies. It was well known that Saddam hated our town to the extent that he deprived us of even the most basic services a town needs for survival."

I asked him if there was any kind of coordination between the different resistance groups—especially when it comes to carrying out attacks. "There are brothers who give the orders," he said. "And for sure, a lot of coordination takes place if the operation happens to be in areas where other cells of resistance belonging to the Islamic party—my party—operate. But we also join together with mujahideen belonging to other groups who have cells active in a specific area."

Commenting on criticism directed toward the resistance for targeting police stations or convoys in crowded are as where many civilians had been killed, Sheikh Saleh said warnings are circulated in Baghdad and other cities, telling Iraqi citizens to stay away from occupation forces and armored tanks. "This way our fighting cells can carry out their martyr operations without harming civilians. However," he added, "we will not feel guilty if any of our citizens who collaborate or work with the Americans get killed."

Driving back to Fallujah from Samarra, we chose to travel the old road that goes on to Jordan and Syria in the east. Impressive villas line the roadsides, and you can see large oil containers that Saddam's regime gave to various villages to buy their loyalty to overcome the hardships caused by UN sanctions that had been in place since 1990. Leftover military hardware from the Al Habaniya airbase served as further visual reminders of times past. Abandoned MiG fighters and helicopters indicated what was once an important airbase but had now been abandoned by the

Americans, who had built fortified fences and tall observation posts. We felt apprehensive driving on this road. Because of the proximity of the U.S. base, drivers invariably got caught behind long, slow-moving U.S. convoys. In order to escape from such an obvious target for any resistance fighters along the road, it was tempting to drive fast to overtake the convoy. Many people have lost their lives this way after being caught in the crossfire.

Fallujah, on the eastern bank of the Euphrates, is the second largest city in Al Anbar province after Al Ramadi and is known dually as the "city of mosques" or the "city of tribes." There are reported to be close to two hundred mosques in the city and surrounding villages, and some of the most important tribes in Iraq make their homes here. Most of the mosques were established by Fallujah's rich upper class, who amassed their wealth long before the Baathist rule. This wealthy population emerged because the city is built on fertile land. The word *fallujah* means "green land" in Arabic, and over the centuries, the area's inhabitants reaped their rewards. During the UN trade embargo against Saddam Hussein, oil smuggling to the accessible markets of Jordan and Syria provided a lucrative income. The government turned a blind eye to these illegal activities, which were carried out between tribes associated with Saddam and high-ranking officers of the military.

Fallujah is a very conservative city, and its religious schools and scholars are renowned beyond the borders of Iraq. During Saddam Hussein's time in power, Fallujans bombed cinemas, which the regime had encouraged to flourish, and blew up shops selling alcohol, music, and videos—similar to the manner in which the Taliban operated in Afghanistan. In his last decade of power, the dictator embarked on a religious campaign, in contrast to his previous secular stance. He encouraged people to find God and amended the Iraqi flag to include the words *Allah Akhbar!* (God is great). But the idea backfired, because within this more religious environment, the Islamist Salafis, a very strict Islamic sect, were able to flourish. The Iraqi government attempted to quell this religious uprising by closing down their mosques and expelling any soldiers and officers in the army who belonged to this sect. Once Saddam Hussein's regime fell, the resistance came not only from the Salafis but also from among the tribes.

On April 28, 2003, members of the Eighty-second Airborne Division opened fire on a demonstration in Fallujah, killing fifteen people. One of the elders in Fallujah told me what happened. The trouble started when a female teacher protested to a U.S. marine about their school having been transformed into a military base. It appeared that the exchange got out of hand, and the marine forced the woman to lie on the ground. This angered her students and other young men who had been watching, and a fight started. Shots rang out and resulted in the death of the teacher, several students, two Iraqi males, and an American soldier. Some of those who witnessed the scene claimed that the soldier must have been killed by American fire, as the Iraqi men had no weapons in their hands.

Following afternoon prayers on the same day, the mourning families walked past the scene of the shooting, chanting, *"God is great! God is great!"* and calling for revenge. An American soldier opened fire and seventeen more died. The Americans wouldn't allow the bodies to be collected until that evening, which meant they were buried without the traditional mourning ceremony. In retrospect, although the incident barely registered in the Western media, this confrontation was the spark that fanned the flames of the Fallujah insurgency movement.

When a member of a tribe is killed, it is tradition to avenge that death. In this atmosphere, calls for jihad—particularly after Friday prayers—became commonplace. The Americans arrested Sheikh Jamal Shakur, the Imam of Fallujah's Grand Mosque, along with members of his family. The town's inhabitants were outraged, and pictures of the Imam bearing slogans asking the Americans to free him were daubed all over the city. His followers openly spoke of revenge attacks, not just because of the arrest of the sheikh, but because American soldiers had entered the mosque wearing their military boots—a shocking insult in Islam.

Weapons were available to everyone, and most Iraqis are well trained in using them. Those who actually carried out the attacks were young Islamists. But ex-regime members or Saddam Hussein loyalists would come out into the streets, noisily demonstrating and waving Saddam Hussein placards as if to take the credit.

This clash between American forces and the locals of Fallujah was unlike others in the Iraq war. It was more of a tribal war than a resistance force. The Americans' lack of understanding about the complicated traditions and customs of the area, combined with the poor treatment of the tribes by the troops, created a flashpoint—Fallujah's inhabitants had been pushed over the edge. In turn, American commanders wondered why they were receiving such a negative reaction even though they thought they were offering help—repairing schools, providing water pumps, opening clinics, and so on.

Past regimes in Iraq, even before that of Saddam Hussein, had an unwritten understanding with tribal leaders that allowed them certain authority and autonomy in their fiefdoms. When the Americans came under fire, their response was to arrest whoever they came across instead of consulting the head of the tribe responsible. The incident in Fallujah turned whole tribes against the Americans. Four members of the Abu Al Bourissa tribe were killed by American forces during confrontations in the city. The head of this tribe, who had been accused of encouraging his people to fight the Americans, was arrested along with four of his sons. The result was that the entire tribe became a fighting unit.

Nighttime house-to-house searches by coalition patrols, usually triggered by tip-offs from collaborators in search of members of the resistance, have changed people's lives, especially in very conservative areas in central Iraq. Random road checks and house-to-house searches, often based on inaccurate information, have made a bad situation worse. Culturally inappropriate behavior—male soldiers body-searching women, for example—and collective punishments have further alienated the population and helped entrench popular support for the resistance.

Muthana Harith Al Dari, the spokesperson of the Association of Muslim Scholars in Iraq, told me that these incidents have had serious consequences for women. Worried about strangers breaking into their homes in the middle of the night, arresting their husbands, and forcing them out into the street in their night clothes, they now go to bed fully dressed and in fear. Al Dari stressed that such behavior by American forces has shaken the confidence of the Iraqi people. Many people would argue that this was the main cause behind the spread of the resistance. That, coupled with increased security measures, has created an atmosphere of anger and frustration. The situation has been further inflamed by higher unemployment and crippling price increases; thus, intensifying the strength of the resistance seemed the only way to force the occupiers to leave the country.

I was invited to lunch on a farm just outside Tikrit by a prominent Tikriti on June 20, 2003. My host, Salah Omar Al Ali, had formerly occupied some of the most senior positions in Saddam's Baath Party, including minister of information and Iraqi representative to the United Nations. Due to serious differences with Saddam, he was forced into exile in London, from where he coordinated an opposition group to the regime called the Iraqi National Accord. His family members who remained in Iraq were banned from taking any government jobs to pay the price for his opposition to the regime. Salah Omar returned to Iraq shortly after the regime fell and was organizing the lunch to bring together all the tribal leaders of the area to discuss how they could prevent Tikrit from becoming a battlefield between American forces and pro-Saddam resistance fighters.

When I met Salah Omar Al Ali it was the day after a number of attacks had been launched against American troops, and the atmosphere was characteristically tense. The tribal elders had been horrified by scenes of looting and mass killings in their city and nearby villages. One of them explained to me that they had set up a force of about ten thousand men and distributed them around the surrounding areas to prevent mainly Kurdish fighters and looters from entering their city. Several meetings were set up between heads of tribes, American commanders, and the Kurdish leadership, which at that time was represented by Jalal Talabani.

The elders then approached leaders of Al Baath, and some of Saddam's relatives in Tikrit, to persuade them not to turn the area into a war zone. In return, the elders promised they would control the city, with the proviso that Saddam supporters such as Fedayeen Saddam and units of his army who had moved into Tikrit would disperse to allow American forces to enter the town unprovoked. And that is exactly what happened. The head of the Tikrit tribes issued a statement reminding Iraqis that they had paid a heavy price for Saddam's behavior. Thousands had been executed or taken prisoner, and only Saddam's immediate family had benefited from the power he exerted over Iraq for more than thirty years. Because of this, Tikrit fell without a shot being fired instead of enduring the bloody battle that was anticipated.

Tikrit is usually referred to as the birthplace of Saddam Hussein, but the province was also named after the twelfth-century historical legend Salah Aldin Al Ayubi, known in the west as "Saladin." This Kurdish warrior and Sultan of Egypt captured Jerusalem from the Crusaders, and the Muslim triumph that followed ensured his place in the history books. Saddam Hussein was proud of their shared beginnings and often compared himself to Saladin. He commissioned murals of himself riding a white horse, emulating the great warrior riding his charger into battle.

On the main road leading to his hometown, I stopped to take some shots of yet another of Saddam's palaces, which had been transformed into American military headquarters. A group of twelve or so young Iraqi men had just finished a game of soccer. They surrounded me, asking what I was doing there, and from the way they spoke it was clear they were typical Saddam Hussein supporters. One of them, Walid, whom I guessed was in his late twenties, began by accusing the media of not reporting the large number of attacks they had carried out against American forces in their area, despite the high number of casualties that had occurred. He described an assault a few days previous that had been carried out in broad daylight against a police station, in which at least five American soldiers were killed or injured. When I pressed him for information about the group he was affiliated with, he smiled and said they were supporters of Saddam Hussein. I asked him whether the inhabitants of Tikrit supported his group, to which he replied that recruitment was easy because people were upset by the inappropriate way American soldiers searched people's homes and that they stole money—something I was to hear on many occasions.

Walid's companion, a young man on crutches, joined in: "Why don't you stay here overnight, and then you can see for yourself how we defend ourselves against the Americans when we attack their headquarters or their checkpoints down by the river." I asked Walid for his address in case I needed to interview him again, and he gave me vague instructions to go to a market, not far from the playground, and ask for him. Driving toward the high street along side roads, to avoid the heavy traffic that had built up around a random checkpoint in the middle of the market, we came across another checkpoint manned by U.S. marines. Four Iraqis were sitting on the ground, hands on their heads, with large amounts of confiscated ammunition and RPGs lying around them. The marines demanded our IDs, and then waved us on. I noticed assorted graffiti that had been freshly written on walls, warning parents to keep their kids away from American soldiers. Other scrawlings threatened collaborators who continued to work for the U.S. coalition forces–either as translators or domestic workers in their compounds or bases. Still other graffiti congratulated Saddam Hussein and the resistance, while others threatened shopkeepers who sold goods to the Americans. Indeed, one of the small restaurants we visited had been hit by a hand bomb the night before, because its staff had served sandwiches to American soldiers.

Despite all of this, business was booming in Tikrit. American soldiers went on a spending spree to see themselves through their mission. They were beginning to sense that their presence in Iraq was for the long term. Shopkeepers reported record sales in electrical goods, and the factory that produced ice cubes could barely cope with the demand due to the sweltering temperatures, which soared over 120 degrees Fahrenheit that summer. One ice-cube trader who sold to the U.S. troops was very nervous after he received threats from members of a resistance group. His tactic was to quietly increase the price of his ice cubes in the hope it would discourage his American clients. But they refused to pay the inflated price and insisted on their regular rate. When the ice seller approached their commander to explain the reason, he was arrested together with his son and held for several days.

I decided to remain in Tikrit for the night as Walid's friend had suggested. I looked up a brother of Salah Omar, a professor at Salah Al Din University, who had offered me his home if I needed to stay overnight in the town. Waiting for dinner with my host in his back garden, which had a view of the palace I had filmed earlier, we heard several rounds of mortars coming from the fields on the other side of the Tigris River. My immediate thought was that it was the work of Walid and his comrades. About eight mortars were directed at the U.S. headquarters. The U.S. marines used James Bond–style tactics; sliding down ropes dangling from helicopters, using heavy tanks to smash through fortified gates, and sending foot soldiers to surprise-search houses while snipers kept watch on rooftops. But despite the high level of training undertaken by the U.S. forces, resistance fighters like Walid were undaunted.

Eager to discover if Walid had been involved in the mortar attack, the next morning I headed for the marketplace where he had assured me he could be found. After inquiring and drawing a blank at several shops, a man overheard me and whispered directions to the village where Walid lived. Driving toward the bridge spanning the Tigris—which bore the scars of the recent liberation war in Tikrit—we found ourselves in thick traffic. Long lines of cars were being halted by stringent American security checks, where exaggerated frisking was inducing road rage among drivers, who were complaining noisily.

We eventually reached a small village that was close to the left bank of the Tigris, its roads unpaved and bordered by lime trees. As we approached a small cluster of houses, we spotted a man in his forties running to the other side of the road, armed with an AK-47 assault rifle. When he saw that we were not American forces, he visibly relaxed, and I asked him if he knew a young guy named Walid. He denied knowledge of him, but as we continued along the street we came across another man, who confidently pointed out a simple house surrounded by an orchard of lime trees. The door was open in the heat of the day, and as I called a greeting from the doorway, I found myself face-to-face with a youth in his early teens whom I remembered from the football game the day before. He was one of Walid's brothers. He smiled in recognition and said that his brother hadn't slept at the house that night. He also said there had been a lot of movement by the American army in their village and surrounding fields after mortars were fired on the U.S. headquarters the previous evening. Walid's brother volunteered to help me find him, but just as we were about to leave, American forces surrounded the car of my driver, Abu Hassan, and began asking him questions through their interpreter. They wanted to know what we were doing in the area, and I explained that I had been looking for a friend who lived in the neighborhood, indicating Walid's brother. It was clear they were trying to establish who had been responsible for the previous night's attack against them, which I had observed with my host. Satisfied, they let us leave, and we had no alternative but to retrace our tracks over the bridge. We joined another line of cars going in the opposite direction, which stretched for more than a mile, while thorough searches were being carried out by young American foot soldiers. I never did find Walid or discover whether his militia had been responsible for that mortar bombardment, but as his village was under suspicion and Walid was nowhere to be found, I could only wonder.

However, Walid's brother did introduce me to his cousin who lived on the outskirts of Tikrit. Saddam's hometown was not how I imagined it. Despite its grandiose palaces, the roads were mere dirt tracks, and my impression was of a poor neighborhood with simple, mud-baked houses. Walid's cousin was preoccupied by bulldozer activity that the Americans were engaged in to destroy all the trees along the riverbank. Ancient date palms, pomegranate, and lime trees were being uprooted to prevent the local resistance fighters from using them as cover to direct their attacks. The area had become known locally as "RPG-7 Alley"–named after the rocket-propelled grenades that have become the weapon of choice of the Iraqi resistance.

Walid's cousin was also a staunch supporter of Saddam Hussein, and he explained why the local resistance was so successful against the Americans: "We can melt into the crowds undetected, and we have great support from local people and their tribes. Our cells vary from between groups of five to eight, depending on the target. Small cells ensure the continuation of the resistance in case the American forces arrest them. We know that they can weed out groups, either from intelligence they receive from collaborators, or by torturing captured resistance fighters. So we have to prepare ourselves against any tactics they might use. We employ everything at our disposal; homemade mortar bombs which can be triggered remotely on roads used by U.S. convoys, to SAM-7s–the rocket-propelled land-to-air missiles which we used recently to down a U.S. helicopter."

The following day I went to the main mosque to wait for worshippers coming out of Friday prayers. The Imam's sermon of the day was a call for jihad to defend the honor of men and women who had been humiliated by the behavior of American soldiers. It was the same theme I had heard many times that June. At the mosque, I was told the story of a tribal leader in the city whose son-in-law was shot dead by U.S. forces. His house was directly across from the mosque on the main road. The man was totally blind, and he was shot while reaching out for his walking stick. The soldiers' explanation to the man's family was that they feared he was reaching for a weapon to use against them while they were searching the house. There was no formal apology for his killing. His family complained to the American headquarters not just for the wrongful killing of the blind man, but for the fact that money had been stolen during the search of their home. This was just one incidence among many that turned Tikritis against the Americans.

Although Saddam Hussein's birthplace is formally acknowledged to be Tikrit, he was actually born in the village of Al-Awja, just outside the city. During the summer of 2003 the search for Saddam was gaining momentum. American forces were using the latest technology to trace and monitor his communications and movements. Satellites, spy aircraft, thermal scans, and unmanned drones were just some of the equipment being employed to unearth the former dictator. The area is surrounded by farms with large expanses of fields—an obvious area to conceal someone wishing to hide.

I paid a visit to Sheikh Mahmoud Al Nada, chief of the Al Baijat tribe, to which Saddam Hussein belongs. I first met the sheikh during lunch for the tribal leaders hosted by Salah Omar Al Ali, and I was interested to speak to him further about Saddam and his possible whereabouts. On describing the directions to his house, he told me, "Look for the largest house in the village and you will find me."

"My house is bigger than Saddam Hussein's!" he said as he greeted me. Although welcoming, he wasn't keen to discuss the present situation. He reminded me of his tribal responsibilities by saying that as head of a tribe, he has to protect all of its members, including Saddam Hussein. "I don't think it is wise to criticize him when he has already suffered, but I thought he was much cleverer than to be tricked into the trap laid for him."

Sheikh Al Nada recalled his friendship with Saddam. They swam and went hunting together until just a few years ago. His opinion, whether true or not, is shared by many Iraqis and colors their attitude toward the American presence in Iraq. "Washington's intention was not just to remove Saddam Hussein, but to be in full control of Iraq's wealth, as our country is sleeping on the largest reserves of oil in the world." On that hot day at the beginning of July, I asked Sheikh Al Nada where he thought Saddam might be hiding. He gazed through the large picture window overlooking the baked fields dotted along the Tigris and replied, "I am sure he is hiding somewhere in this area." Five months later, on December 14, Saddam Hussein was arrested exactly where Al Nada was pointing—in a hole in the ground at a farm in nearby Balad.

It was Al Nada, as tribal leader, who was able to exert his influence on the American forces to release the bodies of Saddam Hussein's two sons, Uday and Qusay, for burial in Tikrit. The brothers were killed in Mosul when American forces surrounded the house of Nawaf Al Zaidan on July 22, 2003. The tip-off had come from Al Zaidan himself, who had been lured by the prospect of being awarded fifteen million U.S. dollars cash per brother for information leading to their whereabouts. Al Zaidan is now living in the United States under an assumed identity.

On Friday, April 11, 2003, Mosul fell without a single shot being fired. Americans were surprised to find there was virtually no resistance when they entered the city. Mosul was the headquarters of the Fifth Division of the Iraqi army, an elite force similar to the Republican Guard that was inaugurated in 1963 during the presidency of Abdul Salam Arif. It was later to become known as Saddam's personal presidential force. But as that Friday wore on, this apparent bloodless collapse took a turn for the worse. There were heavy clashes with the U.S. forces inside the governate building. The Americans claimed that locals shot at them; the locals denied it. What ensued horrified and angered citizens.

People went rampaging through the streets, and there was indiscriminate looting. Banks, theaters, and shops were robbed, hospitals were ransacked–even ventilators were removed from babies' cribs. Hospital beds were wheeled out into the streets and carted off by their new owners. The Pentagon promised that thousands of its soldiers would secure Mosul and prevent such a scenario. They arrived, but it was too late. The looters came from surrounding areas and were identified as mainly Kurdish fighters. Their actions were neither approved of nor encouraged by the Kurdish leadership, but they had been enabled to operate because of a lack of coordination between the Kurdish and American forces and the tribal leaders of Mosul. Also, the withdrawal from Mosul of Saddam's troops was unexpectedly swift, and occurred in the middle of the night when the streets were empty and no army was around.

A young Imam from one of the prominent mosques close to the governate building looked around in disbelief and said, "This is not what we've been promised. The people of Mosul will not allow Iraq to become another Palestine."

Later that morning, during the midday Friday prayers–the most important prayer session of the week–I heard the same sheikh asking his worshippers to be patient, their cause would win out. His words provoked appeals from other mosques, requesting help to protect their city by erecting barricades and checkpoints and calling for a 6:00 PM curfew to put a final stop to the looting. Mosul has somewhat romantically been described in guidebooks as the "Pearl of the North" or the "City of Two Springs" because of its mild climate, but it will now be referred to in years to come as the original breeding ground for nationalist freedom fighters.

On Saturday morning, April 13, 2003, just two days after the fall of Mosul, my driver was annoyed to find we were driving behind a large American convoy as we headed into the city. The industrial landscape of oil refineries, cement factories, textile mills, and tanneries grates against the elegant nineteenth-century houses, historical mosques, and the nearby ruins of the ancient Assyrian city of Nineveh. There are many Aramaic-speaking Christian Assyrians in Mosul, which is home to the largest Christian population in Iraq.

The large American convoy was the first of its kind to head toward Mosul. Iraqis watched in disbelief as the American Abrams tanks rumbled through their streets. Young and old waved their hands in a sign of welcome to their liberators. Some kept their feelings to themselves. We followed the convoy as it continued its journey over the bridge that spans the Tigris River. Unknown to us at the time, the city had come under intense fighting just two hours before, leaving fifteen Iraqi civilians dead.

The convoy had been deployed from its base in the Kurdish area to help diffuse the tense situation. We found ourselves in the middle of a terrifying scene of wild shooting and screaming. We saw armed men firing randomly at cars. Fearing we too might get shot, we abandoned the car and made our way back toward them on foot. I tried to reassure them I was from the media and wanted to find out what was happening. "We don't trust the media," one of them yelled.

Then they started firing again—this time at two Kurds, who were driving a pickup truck. I begged them to stop, but they said, "They are looters and deserve to die." A few seconds later they attacked the Kurds and started kicking them before they managed to escape. Trying to convince them that I was an independent journalist, I asked the armed men what group they belonged to. They described themselves as coming from a mixture of ideologies: former army officers, former Baathists, members of Fedayeen Saddam, or affiliated to one of the Islamic organizations. They were united by the single objective of protecting their city against the American occupation. For them, Saddam Hussein was still the president, and they would continue his work. One of them told me, "We are prepared to sacrifice our lives just as Hamas and its military wing in Palestine have done, and this can be repeated not just in Mosul but all over Iraq."

This was the first hint that suicide bombings would become a feature of this war of resistance. The situation had become too frightening, and we left with gunshots firing all around us. By the time we reached the governate building in the center of Mosul, American soldiers were erecting a barbed-wire barrier around the square. Helicopters and F-16 planes were flying low to protect the soldiers and to prevent crowds from gathering. My cameraman, my driver, and I had arrived on the scene unaware of the battle that had occurred earlier.

As an Arab journalist, my appearance protected me somewhat

from public anger and made communication with the locals easier. I was told how they had watched in shock at the events that had ensued following the unexpected withdrawal of Saddam's resistance fighters from their city.

On April 15, 2003, American forces opened fire against an anti-U.S. demonstration. The Americans claimed they had killed five or six civilians and there were others injured. However, witnesses and doctors at Mosul's Al Jomhouri Hospital, the main hospital in the city, confirmed that at least fifteen dead and many more wounded had been taken to various hospitals in the city. A doctor took me to the mortuary, where I was able to count the bodies for myself, and the number was indeed fifteen, with the possibility of more people dying from their injuries. I was also shown the names of those who had died, including one Egyptian.

This event enraged the local people, who vowed to take charge of their city, and a coalition of various resistance fighters brought their weapons onto the streets. By the third day, the Americans pulled in backup support for their forces after more than one hundred people were reported killed. These forces wanted a strong visual presence in the city. The first thing they did was to secure the governate, the focal point of the city. The head of American Special Forces in Mosul, Colonel Robert Waltemeyer, ordered all employees to leave the building. He then gave orders for the Iraqi flag to be replaced by the American flag. This was not the wisest decision.

Mosulites massed once more in fury over this flagrant insult. Mishan Al Jabouri, a tribal political figure and the newly installed governor of Mosul, tried to diffuse the situation by explaining that the Americans were there to help them regain their freedom. The tactic backfired. The Mosulites were not convinced. They angrily attacked Al Jabouri, attempted to burn his car, and forced him to flee.

Later that day I tracked Al Jabouri down to a safe house that I discovered had once belonged to Ali Hasaan Majid, otherwise known as "Chemical Ali" for his role in Iraq's chemical massacre against the Kurds in the north. I had known Al Jabouri in London when he had fled following a dispute with Uday Saddam Hussein. Al Jabouri told me: "Yesterday, I was working in my office, running the affairs of Mosul province when a group of U.S. officers arrived to say that they were going to move the American military governor's office from the airport to the Mosul government building. They wanted to make a full reconnaissance of the building. I wasn't at all happy with this new arrangement. I thought it would inflame things and make people even angrier. However, the Americans did their recce [recon], explained their requirements, including the flag business, and left. I then went to the American governor and told him that the idea of raising the American flag above the governate building in the heart of Mosul was not likely to be popular. The building runs the civic affairs of the people, and for this reason I was determined to keep the Iraqi flag flying. I told him, 'You are the governor, but please consider my advice. The people of the city trust me.'

"The American governor didn't promise anything, so I asked if I could invite my fellow Iraqis in charge of the various departments to lunch so they could air their views. His reply was that I could invite whoever I wanted, but they were determined to have American insignia around the building. The following morning, around 11:00 AM, the American forces arrived in the city center and surrounded the governate building. An equally large number of Iraqis converged and raised the Iraqi flag, shouting, 'With our soul and blood we sacrifice ourselves for Iraq.' I came out of the building to find about two hundred of my supporters. I attempted to pacify them, and I held out for about forty minutes. Shouting above the noise of the crowd, I told them that the Americans are here merely as temporary occupiers. They would leave the country as soon as they can ensure everything is restored and peaceful. Some made requests concerning services, and I promised them we would help.

But after that the crowd started to shout anti-American slogans. I told them we were not the ones who brought the Americans here–it was circumstances, together with the mistakes which Saddam Hussein's regime had made. I then left the crowd and started back to my office. People were beginning to throw stones. Some waved Iraqi flags and others used megaphones to appeal to the crowd not to throw stones.

"The Americans too tried to control the situation. But the closer the crowds got to the building, the tenser the situation became. They burned a car belonging to one of our office workers. Stones were injuring American soldiers, who were not retaliating. They fired in the air and over the heads of the crowd as a warning. After ten to fifteen minutes of this, the demonstrators continued their stone-throwing and challenged the U.S. soldiers to shoot. The clash ended with more than fifteen Iraqis killed and many more wounded. I left the building, refusing to operate from there. I was not going to work under the American governate. They failed the first real test. They failed in Baghdad, and now they've failed in Mosul."

Notes

1. Galabias are the traditional Arab dress for men and women.
2. After the 1958 revolution, the president, Abdul Karim Kassem, changed the name of the province from Al Dalaim to Al Ramadi. In 1968, under Ahmad Hassan Al Baker's presidency, the name was changed again to Al Anbar.
3. The Al Dulaimi tribe is one of the largest and most well-known Sunni tribes living in Al Anbar province.

CHAPTER TWO

FOREIGN FIGHTERS

Eighteen months before the horrifying events of 9/11 in 2001, I stopped off in Beirut to visit family, en route from London to Islamabad. During my stay a friend asked me if I could do a favor on behalf of his cousin Samir once I reached Pakistan. Samir was concerned about his son Ziad, who had disappeared before completing his studies in Hamburg, Germany. He first became alarmed when Ziad's Turkish girlfriend called from Hamburg to tell Samir of his disappearance. She thought he might have gone to Pakistan or Afghanistan to be trained by one of the militant groups who operated from camps on the borders of the two countries, explaining that Ziad had undergone a personality change after becoming involved with some radical Islamic elements living in Germany at the time. He used to enjoy going out dancing with her, drinking beer, and having fun. He was a friendly and easygoing boyfriend, she reported, and religion was never a topic of conversation. But he began to spend his free time with his religious male friends, visiting the mosque and studiously learning the Koran.

Ziad, who was in his early twenties at the time, grew up in a privileged environment in Lebanon's Bekaa Valley. He came from one of the largest families in the Al Marj area, not far from the highway that links Beirut with Damascus. Although he was Muslim, Ziad was sent to a Catholic school, and according to his family, his childhood dream was to fly planes. "But we discouraged him," they said. There had been no history of militancy within his family, who are bankers, entrepreneurs, and farm owners. I asked my friend if he could give me any hints as to which group Ziad might have joined or the city to which he may have traveled. He knew nothing more. My chances of tracking him down were pretty slim, but I promised I would make inquiries.

When I returned to Beirut a few weeks later, having been unsuccessful in my quest for Ziad, I immediately called my friend to discover whether he had heard anything more. The good news was that Ziad had turned up in Germany again. However, the family was not aware of the fact that their rather spoiled son had joined the ranks of Al Qaeda.

A year and a half later, I was back in Beirut on vacation when the World Trade Center and Pentagon attacks occurred. Along with the rest of the world, I watched in disbelief at the magnitude of the terrorism unfolding. The feeling of revulsion I felt intensified as I remained glued to the TV and devoured every newspaper trying to make sense of what had happened. After two or three days of this, Munir and Rima, close friends of mine, suggested we all go to the movies to escape the distressing situation. We chose the lighthearted *Chocolat*, starring Juliette Binoche and Johnny Depp.

Minutes before leaving for the theater, the FBI released the names of some of the hijackers involved in the attacks. One of those listed was Ziad Jarra. He was described as being of Egyptian origin. Trying to enjoy the movie, my mind kept returning to the Ziad, who I was sure was Lebanese, not Egyptian. I excused myself from the theater, explaining to Munir and Rima that I needed to contact my newspaper in Saudi Arabia as I thought I may have an exclusive—that one of the hijackers was from Lebanon.

I filed the story from my Beirut apartment before sitting down once again to watch the continuing TV news updates about the hijacked airliners. There was no mention of a Lebanese connection. The next morning, satisfied that my newspaper had published my story and noting that none of the Lebanese newspapers had discovered the nationality of Ziad Jarrah (the surname in Lebanon is transliterated with an "H" at the end), I called an old friend, Hani Hammoud, who was press adviser to the late Lebanese prime minister Rafic Hariri. His surprise at my early morning call turned to disbelief when he learned that one of the hijackers was a fellow countryman. I read him my *Al Watan* (an Arabic newspaper) story of that morning, about the missing student in Germany.

A series of diplomatic phone calls was set in motion. Hani Hammoud immediately called the prime minister to break the news. This was followed by many more calls to ensure that I stood by my story. Prime Minister Hariri then informed President Emile Lahoud and the American ambassador, who were meeting in Beirut.

Ziad Jarrah's parents were not yet aware of their son's involvement in the attacks. Ziad's father had only just returned home from the hospital after undergoing open-heart surgery. They discovered what must have been shocking news to them through Brent Sadler, the CNN correspondent in Beirut, who appeared live that afternoon to report that one of the hijackers was in fact Lebanese, not Egyptian. When the editorial staff at CNN's headquarters in Atlanta asked for the source of the information, Hani

Hammoud called me once again to ask if I would agree to be interviewed by the network to describe what I knew about Ziad Jarrah and to confirm Brent Sadler's story. I declined for the simple reason that I felt I had hurt the family enough with my newspaper story and didn't want to compound it further by repeating it in front of the world.

The father, still in pain from his surgery, was broken by the realization that his son could have become so radicalized as to participate in such a dreadful act of terrorism. In what was no doubt a state of denial, he showed the media a family wedding video as if to prove that this party-loving young man couldn't possibly have become involved with religious fanatics. In the video, Ziad was dancing with girls and clearly enjoying the spirit of the occasion. Even up to the last moments of his life, he had reassured his family that he was doing well at flight school in Florida, where in June 2000 he began his studies to become a pilot. But throughout his training he had a parallel life. He had become involved in a sophisticated mission to blow up Capitol Hill.

Ziad, it later transpired, was the pilot of the ill-fated United Airlines Flight 93, which took off from Newark Airport on September 11, 2001. He never made his expected target; the plane crashed into a field in Pennsylvania after passengers reportedly stormed the cockpit with cries of "Let's roll."

*   *   *

Shortly before dawn on March 20, 2003, 320 Tomahawk cruise missiles exploded over Baghdad city in an ugly son et lumière announcing the beginning of "Shock and Awe," George W. Bush's opening salvo on his war against the Baath regime and its leader. Saddam Hussein immediately called on the wider Arab world to unite against America in jihad. Hundreds of disaffected young Arabs from every kind of background, whether Islamists or nationalists, from Iraq or countries beyond, wasted no time in volunteering. Those who lived in other Arab countries were offered visas or other diplomatic assistance to facilitate their passage to Iraq. Some of these fighters received in-house weapons training; others were already trained, having fought for their countries in other conflicts or undergoing their country's statutory national service. A number of them were veterans of previous jihads such as Chechnya and Afghanistan. Some went to Iraq with the blessing of their families, while others left it for friends to break the news to their parents after they had departed. These foreign jihadis didn't need to travel as far afield as Afghanistan, or indeed the Western world, to wage their war, as Ziad Jarrah had done. They could challenge U.S. forces right there on their doorsteps.

Within one short month it appeared that their jihad was over before it had really swung into gear. Although these Arab "foreign" volunteers who believed they were battling against "Crusaders" fought fiercely during the coalition forces' final assault on Baghdad, the unexpected and sudden collapse of the Iraqi regime meant that the defeated foreign fighters found themselves with nowhere to go.

These foreign fighters were now stateless. Saddam's regime had confiscated their passports and IDs, leaving them with nothing to prove their identities. These young Arab volunteers who had traveled from Yemen and Saudi Arabia, Syria and Jordan, Lebanon and the Occupied Territories—particularly the Gaza Strip—found themselves unable to return home. So they found refuge among the many insurgency groups at large in the country. One of these was Al Ansar Al Islam.

Al Ansar Al Islam controlled a small enclave in the mountainous Kurdish region that borders Iran. It is believed to have a core number of eight hundred fighters, including Arabs from other countries. Many of the group's members crossed into Kurdish Iraq from Afghanistan through the unpatrolled border that Afghanistan shares with Iran. The organization was styled in the form of the Taliban to fill the vacuum that had been left after the fall of its leader, Mullah Mohammed Omer, and the disappearance of Osama bin Laden into the labyrinth of mountain corridors between Afghanistan and Pakistan. According to Washington, Al Ansar is linked to Al Qaeda and was officially designated a foreign terrorist organization by the U.S. Department of State in 2004.[1] They were accused of training and deploying suicide bombers against the U.S.-led coalition.

Any person going to work outside the Ansar-controlled villages was obliged to pay a Jizyeh, or tax, of fifteen Iraqi dinars per day. This went straight to Al Ansar's "treasury," where the money was used for day-to-day living expenses. They had few other sources of income, as the members did not work. Girls were prevented from going to school or university, and the militia watched for any woman defying the burka dress code by venturing out in public unveiled. This violation could further swell the funds of the treasury with an instant fine of one hundred dinars.

Twenty-four hours after the massive aerial bombardment over Baghdad, U.S. Marines launched up to fifty cruise missiles against Islamic targets in the northern town of Khormal in Iraqi Kurdistan. Two offices belonging to Ansar Al Islam were destroyed, killing at least forty-five people and many others wounded.[2] Some of the badly injured were taken over the border to hospitals in Iran for treatment.

I was in Mosul, in northern Iraq, at the time of this attack and was curious to find out more about the group. I made my way toward Khormal with my Kurdish translator, Ahmed. It was early spring, and the snow was just beginning to melt on the craggy mountain ranges that circle the northern, eastern, and southern borders of the Kurdish-defined area. The majority of people here are farmers or cattle breeders, and most wear distinctive and colorful traditional dress. The narrow country roads were obscured by dust, thrown up by the many four-wheel-drive vehicles that are favored by the Kurdish militias as they sped their way to the front line, weapons protruding from the open vehicle windows, and flags bearing the insignia of the Patriotic Union of Kurdistan (PUK) fluttering from their radio antennas. There were relatively few American forces on the ground at that time, apart from small clusters of American Special Forces.

My journey continued upward into the mountains, about fifty miles southeast of Sulaymaniya, where the PUK has their administrative capital. I had an arrangement to meet the Kurdish leader Jalal Talabani, whom I was told would be visiting the front that day to get a close-up of their war against Ansar Al Islam. Talabani, a veteran Kurdish leader, created the PUK to rival the traditionally dominant Kurdistan Democratic Party. Now in his seventies, he is widely referred to as "Mam Jalal," meaning Uncle Jalal. With a law degree from Baghdad University, he now leads a militia that is thought to number about 150 thousand fighters. Talabani's military commanders had enlisted help on the ground from the small groups of American Special Forces that are active in the area. From the road, we could see Khormal in the distance. Palls of smoke and the sound of heavy gun exchanges could be heard. We were advised by the Peshmerga to drive out of the area.[3] The final battle to smoke out Ansar Al Islam and its allies was going to be fought that day, March 28, 2003.

Kurdish officials informed me that two to three hundred Al Ansar militants had been killed in two weeks of heavy fighting. A final bombardment by U.S. F-16s and the enormous American B-52 bombers forced the remaining Al Ansar fighters to flee over the mountains to the safety of Iran.

We were in a spring-green meadow facing a small farm, with a backdrop of the craggy Hawraman mountain range, which forms the Iranian border. Jalal Talabani, who is renowned for enjoying the pleasures of food, had organized a grand-scale prebattle picnic. I counted two hundred people at this al fresco lunch, including PUK military commanders and fighters, bodyguards, senior American commanders, and members of the American Special Forces. The latter had recently taken part in a battle in the mountain village of Biara to support their Kurdish allies, the Peshmerga, against Al Ansar Al Islam. During a typical Kurdish meal of soup made from strained yogurt, mutton, and rice, Talabani explained to me that the Al Ansar terrorists had fled to Iran after losing their fight but that he was going to establish contact with the Iranian government to insist they hand them over, as they had been responsible for killing hundreds of Kurds.

Throughout lunch, we watched U.S. Humvees pounding along the dusty roads as they transported American Special Forces. Villagers looked on in anticipation while their kids waved excitedly at the convoy. I reflected upon how unthinkable it would have been a few years ago to imagine that the United States would come this close to the Iranian border. A Kurdish politician who had newly arrived among our group reminded us that Iran is now more or less surrounded by American troops. "They are in Afghanistan, Turkey, which is an active member of NATO [North Atlantic Treaty Organization] and now Iraq. Not to mention just across the Persian Gulf, where it has troops in Saudi Arabia and the Gulf States."

An Internet communiqué issued by Ansar Al Islam on March 31, 2003, announced that its members had regrouped in the north of Iraq and that it was preparing to carry out suicide bomb attacks against American and British forces in the country. The group added that they would be adopting new tactics to avoid being attacked from the air as happened a few days before at the start of the Iraq war. The emir of Al Ansar in Kurdistan, a Kurdish Iraqi named Abu Abdullah Al Shafi'i, promised the Muslims of Kurdistan and the world at large, to turn Iraq into a graveyard for American and British forces, described by the statement as "Crusaders." Al Shafi'i claimed that more than three hundred mujahid had enlisted to carry out such attacks.

Biara was my next stop, and once the lunch party started to disperse, my translator, Ahmed, and I followed the precipitous road, which was barely wide enough to allow two cars to pass simultaneously. Spent bullets and mortar shells littered the roadsides; the road itself was pockmarked by large bomb craters. As we drove slowly upward into the mountains, Ahmed explained that he was originally from Kirkuk. During Saddam Hussein's Arabization program to displace Kurds from the oil-rich areas, which began in the 1970s, Saddam had forcibly evicted most of the Kurdish people from that town and other Kurdish villages, replacing them with Sunni and Shia Arabs. Ahmed's family found refuge in Irbil.

As we arrived at the war-damaged mountain village, it wasn't difficult to identify the remains of Al Ansar's administrative offices. Slogans praising Osama bin Laden and his organization littered the ground, while crude drawings and cut-out magazine photographs illustrating the American civilian planes plowing into the twin towers of the World Trade Center were still pinned to the remaining walls. The battle forced most of Biara's residents to flee the area, leaving behind only a few people who had been held hostage by the fighters.

I was surprised to see a young man approaching me, as the village was practically deserted. The man was in his mid-twenties, and because of the way he was dressed and the fact that he was accompanied by bodyguards, I assumed he must be the son of a VIP in the Kurdish movement in the area. He was Westernized and, I soon learned, had studied in London. He introduced himself as Asir and began to tell me a story about his father: "This group [Ansar Al Islam] and their friends moved here just to terrorize our people. We Kurdish people want to live free in our homeland like the people of Lebanon or any other liberated country. These terrorists came here with the help of outsiders to disrupt this process. They've killed many people, destroyed many places, and they have broken many hearts, including my own.

They killed my father, Shawket Shukair [a leader of the PUK, under Jalal Talabani], while he was trying to negotiate with them. He was even holding a white flag in peace. The Peshmerga came and rooted them out and killed many of them. Well done to them."

As night was falling, we left the skeleton of what was once Biara village and wound our way back down the narrow mountain road to Halabja, where we planned to spend the night. Halabja had become the focus of world attention when it suffered a massive chemical weapons attack during the Iran-Iraq War in 1988. Mustard gas and the nerve agents tabun, sarin, and VX were the ingredients of a deadly cocktail that formed the basis of a series of chemical bombs dropped from the aircraft of Saddam Hussein's forces. Five thousand inhabitants of Halabja and its immediate area died from the horrific effects of chemical poisoning and created a generation of children suffering congenital malformations and other serious birth defects.

The next morning, I was to meet Sheikh Ali bin Abdul Aziz, the spiritual leader of the Kurdish Islamic movement, which is well established in Halabja and the surrounding mountain villages. Just a few days before, Al Ansar Al Islam had been forced out of the town, which they had controlled for two years.

In his late eighties, Sheikh Ali rarely speaks to the media, but he agreed to meet me at his office. As I drove through the streets, I noticed large groups of people making their way to the graveyard to pay their respects to those who had recently died. Most members of Al Ansar Al Islam who were killed in the recent fighting were from this town, which accounted for the large numbers of mourners. Women are not usually expected to visit the graveyard to grieve. Instead they go to the homes of the bereaved, wearing their long black dresses or traditional Kurdish costume, to prepare food for the men when they return from burying the dead after midday prayers.

I entered the small compound that served as Sheikh Ali's office to find the spiritual leader and his adviser already waiting for me. His bodyguard kept watch from an adjacent room. I wanted the sheikh's views on the radicalization of Al Ansar Al Islam, a group that had gone to Afghanistan, apparently, as moderates but returned to Iraq as extreme militants. Sheikh Ali adjusted his bottle-glass-thick spectacles before launching into his feelings about their tactics: "Their behavior is not recognized by Islam," he said. "We have advised them so many times that God will not be happy with their actions, but they refuse to listen and rebel against our movement. I have personally met members of the Taliban in the Qatari capital, Doha, and tried to convince them that their methods of law and order were not acceptable, but they weren't interested either."

Sheikh Ali explained to me that Al Ansar was originally part of the mainstream Kurdish movement when it was established in the 1970s, but due to a change in their ideology—particularly when they returned to Iraq after becoming involved with the Taliban in Afghanistan—they split apart from this liberal movement in 1998 and went about their separate and murderous ways. "Our aspirations were to build many generations of good people who would help each other and spread the message of Islam, as God, peace be upon Him, asked us to do. When there was a need to carry weapons, we did so only to defend our message and our families against the aggressors.

"When the bad situation developed and Al Ansar began fighting against other Kurdish organizations, mainly the Patriotic Union Kurdish Party we were asked to mediate. The PUK welcomed our mediation, whereas Al Ansar refused, and as we have the overall responsibility for the welfare of the people in this region, we continued our efforts to convince them to listen to the voice of wisdom. They ignored us. We continued in our efforts, especially as most of their members are either close relatives or from our area. We asked some of the elders involved in our combined movements to talk to them to try and negotiate a solution. Eventually we lost hope of making any progress and decided to cease our mediation. We started having arguments with these rebels who questioned our relationship with Iran and other Kurdish political parties and why we were dealing with the Kurdistan Democratic Party. We responded by telling them that we are following the path of the Prophet Mohammed, who taught us to have a dialogue with our enemies as well as our friends. We have a good relationship with Iran, because they opened their borders for us when we needed them, and we share their heritage. So why shouldn't we deal with them? If you live here and are as isolated as we are, you have no alternative but to be tactful with everyone." To further prove his point Sheikh Ali went on to say: "I was against the idea of accusing other Afghan leaders, such as the late mujahideen leader Ahmed Shah Massoud and President Burahnudin Rabbani, as Kafirs or infidels who have betrayed Islam, because they are good Muslims.

"Later we discovered that Al Ansar had been negotiating directly with the PUK, but just last week I heard that they had killed Shawket Shukair, one of the Kurdish leaders with the PUK, who had gone to their village, Biara, in peace, bearing a white flag."

I was interested to find out whether Sheikh Ali had information about the foreign fighters affiliated with Al Qaeda who were operating in this northern region: "We know for a fact that they have Arab foreigners with them from Jordan, Palestine, and Al Ahwaz. [He was referring to an area in Iran where the people are of Arab descent.] Some of them took part in the war against the Russians in Afghanistan and came back to this part of the world to set up training camps. I wasn't certain if they belonged to Al Qaeda–they kept that fact from us."

The Ansar Al Islam supported Osama bin Laden. After the

defeat of the Taliban, many of the group's members crossed into Iraq from Afghanistan and embarked on a recruitment drive to swell their ranks and open up another frontier from which to operate when they thought the time was right. Arab fighters who found their way to the Kurdish areas of Iraq forged a lifestyle similar to the one they adopted when fighting in Afghanistan. They chose to live in the mountains, with virtually inaccessible routes to their remote villages, and made themselves popular within their chosen communities. Some even married into Kurdish families who admired these fighters for their tough and courageous performance on the battlefield. The mystical Sufi faith and the orthodox Salafi movement were well represented in the region and made it easier for the foreign fighters, with similar religious interests, to assimilate and regroup under different names, such as Al Ansar Al Sunnah, or the Salafi Jihadis, or Al Tawhid Wa Al Jihad, whose leader is the notorious Abu Musab Al Zarqawi. Together, these groups formed the basis of the ruthless organization Al Ansar Al Islam. Abu Musab Al Zarqawi became the leader of the umbrella organization, Al Tawhid Wa Al Jihad, and his organization has claimed responsibility for multiple beheadings, kidnappings, and suicide bombings against foreigners, coalition forces, and the newly established Iraqi police force and army. Such ruthless acts of terror compelled the United States and George W. Bush to name Zarqawi the most wanted terrorist after the emir of Al Qaeda, Osama bin Laden.

What is it that drives these men like the young Lebanese hijacker Ziad to wage their war on foreign soil? Why do they leave their homes and families to wage jihad against America? The answer, I believe, lies in part in the personality and charismatic leadership of people like Zarqawi and Osama bin Laden. Answers can also be found by understanding the antipathy that these young, ideological jihadis hold toward America.

Abu Musab Al Zarqawi comes from Al Masoum, a rough

neighborhood within Al Zarqa, a town about fifteen miles from the Jordanian capital, Amman. Al Masoum is locally referred to as the Chicago of Jordan because of its past history with drugs and gun crime, while Al Zarqa itself is home to Jordan's greatest concentration of followers of the conservative Salafi movement. Most of Zarqawi's Jordanian supporters first met him at an Al Qaeda training camp in the Afghan city of Herat in the early 1990s, during the heyday of the Taliban. Younger ones have read about his exploits in Iraq and were willing to join him in this latest battlefield.

During the drawn-out buildup to the Iraq war, discontent festered among young Arabs who were opposed to America's policies in the region, particularly its support for Israel—the only country that has refused to abide by international law and implement UN resolutions to solve its long-running conflict with the Palestinians.

Zarqawi's supporters meet in the small, simple houses of Al Zarqa or at the nearby Palestinian refugee camp, Al Rasifa. Unlike the other young men in Jordan, who wear the standardized uniform of jeans and T-shirts, these Salafis stand apart with their long, untrimmed beards and tendency to wear *shalwar kameez* (literally, pants-shirt)—the baggy trousers and long shirt that are traditionally worn throughout Pakistan and Afghanistan. They openly speak of jihad, and many of them have served prison sentences in Jordan for expressing their radical views. Apart from discussing the political situation, they read the Koran, argue about matters of Sharia law, and discuss the works of well-known Salafi scholars. Some of Zarqawi's admirers are kept under police scrutiny and are required to report daily to the local police, who are aware of their possible intentions to join Zarqawi in Iraq.

The bedouin Bani Hassan tribe is the most influential tribe in Al Zarqa, with a membership of around 350,000. Zarqawi is a member of one of its branches called Al Khalileh. Tribal loyalty ensures that major losses—either from American forces, its allies, or from Iraqis whom they see as collaborators—are a signal for celebration among his tribe. Even Zarqawi's family has been drawn into his plots. His father-in-law, through his second wife, is Yassin Jarad, a Palestinian by origin who lives in Al Zarqa. It is claimed Jarad was responsible for the assassination of the head of the Supreme Council for the Islamic Revolution in Iraq (SCIRI), Ayatollah Sayed Mohammed Baqir Al Hakim. Al Hakim was killed on August 29, 2003, along with seventy-five others, in a car-bomb blast in Najaf shortly after delivering his Friday sermon at the Imam Ali Mosque, the holiest shrine for Shia Muslims.

Like Osama bin Laden, very few people have been able to get close to Zarqawi. Through interviews with many different people who have known him over the years, both inside and outside prison, in Iraq, Jordan, and other parts of the world, I have tried to gain a better understanding of bin Laden's mentality and mind-set. The following observations also include interviews and meet-ings with Zarqawi conducted in a safe house, close to the Sunni Triangle, in the two years following the fall of Saddam Hussein.

The road leading to the rendezvous with Abu Musab Al Zar-qawi, leader of the Tawheed and jihad movement, was a rutted track through farmland, one hour's drive beyond the boundary of the Sunni Triangle. His minders, all wearing scarves to conceal their identities, were Iraqis—there was not a single foreign Arab among them. Zarqawi sat cross-legged on a thin sponge mattress covering a dirt floor. The room had mud walls and a wooden ceiling, and its doors opened onto farmland. The hi-tech equipment used to search visitors seemed incongruous with the simplicity of his surroundings.

Despite his reputation—a terrorist mastermind who beheads his kidnapped victims and whose deadly bombing cam-paigns have created mayhem countrywide—he is an unthreatening personality in the flesh. He doesn't raise his voice and seems an unlikely leader for such a ruthless organization, which has claimed responsibility for most of the suicide bombings in Baghdad and other parts of the country since the fall of the Iraqi dictator.

Though quietly spoken, his brain is sharp, and he has a street-wise mentality. He is conversant with all kinds of technology, using sophisticated methods of communication to prevent detection, and some liken him to Bill Gates because of his wizardry with computers. He remembers people by their full name, with a gift for recognizing people even when they are disguised. He is organized, energetic, and totally self-reliant, moving around without bodyguards. His visitors are received unarmed, as he relies upon his quick reactions and screening devices for his protection. He is thin, with a preference for simple food such as dates, figs, and strained yogurt. He drinks only water. His spare time is spent reciting verses from the Koran, discussing Islamic issues, listening to video or taped lectures, as well as monitoring news stories to keep abreast of developments in other parts of the country and the world in general.

Zarqawi is assiduous in keeping up-to-date with international affairs, using all manner of technology—even when on the run—and is clued up on the opinions of the principal players on the global political scene. He speaks knowledgably about the American administration's plans and policies toward the Middle East and the Islamic world, and he can recall in detail the political views of the previous U.S. secretary of state, Colin Powell, which were out of step with the policies that the Pentagon and Defense Secretary Donald Rumsfeld were pursuing in the region. He accuses the American administration of establishing a puppet government in Iraq that will serve only Washington's long-term interests; uppermost of these is to get their hands on the largest oil reserves in the world.

Zarqawi, now thirty-nine years old, has been in and out of jail since 1991, after he returned to Jordan from his first trip to Afghanistan. He was first jailed for petty crime, then for possession of rifles and bombs. In 1994 he was jailed for political activities and found himself sharing a cell with a Salafi spiritual leader known as Abu Mohammed Al Maqdasi (his real name was Isam Al Barqawi), who was influential in introducing Zarqawi to a highly politicized Islam. During his three-year sentence, he devoted himself to the Koran and influenced other young prisoners with the leadership qualities he learned from his spiritual mentor. By now, radical, religious, and politicized, upon his release in 1997 he and Al Maqdasi became involved with a Salafi jihadi group called Bayaat Al Imam that planned a terrorist campaign in late 1998 against tourist attractions. The group targeted places of religious and cultural interest that were likely to be thronged by American and other foreigners as well as one of the main tourist hotels, the SAS Radisson Hotel in downtown Amman.[5] The plot was foiled, and along with several others, Zarqawi was arrested once more and sentenced this time to fifteen years. But before serving even one year of that sentence, King Abdullah of Jordan, who came to the throne in January 1999, granted an amnesty that released all sixty-four prisoners being held on charges of extremist-related violence. Zarqawi was freed after serving just months of his sentence. He returned to Afghanistan in 2000 to begin his jihad on foreign soil, where he mastered bomb-making techniques.

Noaman bin Othman is a Libyan national and one of the many Arabs who joined a jihadi group in Afghanistan. He first met Zarqawi in the city of Khost. Zarqawi's emir at that time had been the so-called Abu Al Harith Al Salti (his name suggests that he comes from the city of Al Salt in Jordan), along with a Palestinian named

Abu Mouad Al Khosti, who was later to die while fighting against the Afghani Shia fighters in Kabul. The group Zarqawi associated with in his Afghanistan days were mainly fellow Jordanians, including another brother-in-law (by his first wife), Saleh Al Hami, who wrote articles for the *Al Jihad* magazine, which was published in the Pakistani frontier town of Peshawar. Bin Othman recalls Zarqawi gathering together a group of eighty to one hundred young Jordanian and Palestinian fighters in Logar. They referred to him respectfully as their emir, therefore assuring Zarqawi of his leadership potential. They were not part of Al Qaeda at that time, and some say that Zarqawi preferred not to get involved with bin Laden and his activities in those days. Until 2004, Zarqawi felt that bin Laden did not concentrate enough on the Arab-Israeli conflict but fought his wars elsewhere—in Yemen, Sudan, Afghanistan, Chechnya, and Bosnia. For Zarqawi, a home-grown Jordanian brought up in a Palestinian environment close to the border with Israel, fighting Israel was his first priority. Young Jordanians, especially Islamists like Zarqawi, have always had a chip on their shoulder about the fact that their government has maintained a warm relationship with Israel.

After America bombed Afghanistan in 2001, Zarqawi moved to Iran, where he came under pressure from the Iranian authorities, leading him to border-hop into Iraq. He was not interested in establishing any contact with the Baath regime at that time. Instead, with the help of the established Al Ansar al Islam, Zarqawi and his men found refuge in the Iraqi Kurdish mountains, where they began working together to secure a route for their comrades who were fleeing from Afghanistan. When the Iranian government discovered what they were up to, they were told not to come any closer than three miles from the Iranian border in order to avoid confrontations with the border police. Some of Zarqawi's men arrived in the area as early as 1998, already trained in military techniques and, most specifically, in wiring vehicles for suicide missions.

Islamic militant sources during meetings in Fallujah and Ramadi confirmed to me that Zarqawi's terrorist agenda in Iraq started well before the war. In 2002 a splinter group from Al Ansar Al Islam made an assassination attempt on the prime minister of the Kurdish government in Sulaymaniya, Dr. Burham Saleh. He survived and was later appointed deputy prime minister in the first Iraqi interim government, led by Dr. Iyad Allawi.

Suicide bombings are carried out by many different cells that are active in Iraq, but predominantly by Zarqawi's group, known as Al Tawhid Wa Al Jihad. The most audacious of these attacks, considering the security that surrounds them, targeted prominent international institutions—the UN compound and the Jordanian embassy in Baghdad and the Italian military base in Nassiriyah. As many as five suicide attacks a day occur throughout the country, which inevitably leads to the question of how militant organizations like Zarqawi's manage to indoctrinate and recruit so many fighters who are prepared to blow themselves up.

The kind of support Zarqawi enjoys from Iraq's border countries is best understood through a communiqué issued by Saleh Al Awfi, the leader of Al Qaeda in Saudi Arabia, to the Jordanian terrorist leader on March 27, 2005: "Our group is ready to send fighters and suicide bombers whenever you need them. We have hundreds of jihadis prepared to die for the cause and many tons of explosives. You will find in us the strongest support you will need to force others to come to a better understanding of the word 'terror.' For us it translates as 'victory.'"

I met Mohammed in the PUK jail in Sulaymaniya. He was one of several fighters who had been arrested during a battle against the PUK in the Biara Mountains. A Palestinian from Gaza, he was encouraged to join the ranks of Al Ansar Al Islam after visiting Zarqawi's hometown in Jordan. Al Ansar members facilitated his passage to Baghdad, and from there he made his way north to Kurdish Iraq. He was arrested after most of his comrades had fled to Iran, having been flushed out after battling with the Peshmerga and American Special Forces. I asked Mohammed why he had chosen to travel such a distance to fight U.S. forces in Iraq when he just as easily could have fought the Israelis right there in his hometown in the occupied territories. His response was short and to the point: "They are one and the same enemy, and if we succeed in defeating the U.S. here, it will be the beginning of the end of the Jewish state."

Palestinian and Lebanese fighters from North Lebanon and west of the Bekaa Valley are known to have been killed fighting in Samarra and Fallujah. Two of the dead were Omer Darwish and Fadi Ghaith, who were both from Al Qaroun. Residents of the town, west of the Bekaa Valley, confirm that the two men were followers of the extreme Salafi school of Islam, which believes in a literal interpretation of the Koran. It isn't difficult for Lebanese nationals to travel to Iraq. All they need is an identity card to legally enter the country. Palestinians slip through the unmanned border posts in the mountains running between Syria and Iraq, where they meet up with other sympathetic groups who are willing to accommodate and help these jihadis to reach their final destination.

In Saudi Arabia, when news arrives of the death of a Saudi volunteer killed while taking part in this jihad, it is met with sorrow-tinged pride among their families. One such family lives in Dammam, in eastern Saudi Arabia, well known for its oil fields and gated compounds that house the industry's large number of foreign workers. Jasem Al Sahli, the father of twenty-eight-year-old Suhail, was receiving dozens of friends and relatives who had come to offer condolences and congratulate him on Suhail's *chahada,* or martyrdom. During the customary period of mourning, the father told his visitors that he thanked God his son Suhail had achieved *chahada,* adding that Suhail's dream was to die defending Islam and Arab causes, at which point the father placed his finger on his temple, indicating where his son would willingly take the bullet.

Suhail's older brother, Mohammed, detailed to me his history as a foreign fighter. Suhail was known by his nom de guerre, Yassin Al Baher. After quitting secondary school in 1992 he traveled to Afghanistan, where he underwent training at an Al Qaeda camp. His first assignment was in Tajikistan, where he fought alongside the Chechen rebels, commanded by the hirsute and bearded Saudi-born warlord known by a single moniker—Khattab. From there he made his way to Bosnia, taking part in the Bosnian war against the Serbs. His next stop was Chechnya, where once again he rejoined Khattab and his mujahideen. A few months before the war in Iraq started, Suhail returned to his home in Saudi Arabia and told his family that he wanted to go to Mecca to perform hajj—the pilgrimage that all practicing Muslims are obliged to make at least once in their lifetime. A few days later the family received a call telling them that Suhail was on his way to Iraq to join Al Ansar Al Islam, the group that fugitive terrorist Abu Musab Al Zarqawi was actively involved with at the time.

Mohammed Al Halil died in a suicide mission when he drove a car full of explosives into an American patrol on the road from Baghdad to the international airport in November 2004. Mohammed's father, Saleh Al Halil, was not surprised to receive a telephone call from Iraq informing him that his son had detonated his car as he drove alongside an American Humvee. Mohammed was nineteen years old and studying Sharia law at the Islamic University of Imam Mohammed bin Sa'ud in Riyadh. He had left Saudi Arabia for Iraq on October 23, 2004, after leaving a message for his parents, telling them of his intention to join the jihadi fighters in Iraq. Less than one month later, he was dead.

Open-house mourning for martyrs who have given their lives in Iraq is not just a Saudi custom. It is also being observed in Yemen, where bin Laden's family originated before they moved to Saudi Arabia. In Lebanon, half an hour's drive from the refugee camp where I grew up, in Tyre, you come across the country's largest Palestinian refugee camp, Ein El Hilweh ("the sweet water spring") in the southern city of Sidon. Here, news spreads like wildfire if a "martyr" has given his life for the Iraqi or indeed the Palestinian cause, and celebratory scenes of mourning at the home of the deceased are commonplace. This is not a new phenomenon. I witnessed similar scenes in the Sabra and Shatila Palestinian refugee camps in Beirut, where more than one thousand Palestinians and hundreds of Lebanese were massacred in an Israeli-led operation in 1982.

One of the worst acts of terrorism since the fall of Saddam Hussein occurred on February 28, 2005, in Al Hillah, a predominantly Shiite town sixty miles south of Baghdad. A suicide bomber killed more than 130 people—mainly police and Iraqi National Guard recruits, who were standing in line for their physical checkups at a medical center. A similar number were wounded. Viewers of Iraqi TV were outraged at images broadcast from Jordan showing a ceremony held in honor of Raad Al Banna, the thirty-two-year-old Jordanian who was responsible for the slaughter. The three-day ceremony was held in the town of Al Salt, west of the Jordanian capital, Amman, in celebration of Al Banna's mission and to acknowledge his place in heaven by sacrificing himself for the cause. The cameras closed in on the Al Banna family, offering traditional Jordanian food to guests who had come to pay their respects.

Raad Al Banna had trained as a lawyer, and in 2000 he found a job working for the United Nations in New York until he was deported two years later after immigration authorities refused to extend his visa. Some months after this, his family in Jordan received a telephone call from Iraq saying, "I am calling to congratulate you. Your son has been killed in a 'martyrdom' attack." His father, Mansour, said the caller claimed to belong to a group called Brothers of the Gulf. His family believed that Raad was in Saudi Arabia looking for another job; however, Jordanian officials confirmed to the family that their son had not passed through the southern border from Jordan into Saudi Arabia but had instead traveled northward, crossing the border into Syria from where he entered Iraq.

The television footage caused a public outcry and was equally criticized by leading Shia religious leaders, including Grand Ayatollah Sistani, citing the insensitivity on the part of the Jordanian government for allowing such an event to happen on its territory. They called on the Iraqi interim government to sever diplomatic relations with Jordan and to expel its diplomats from Baghdad. Later, Shia demonstrators stormed the Jordanian embassy and pulled down its flag, replacing it with the Iraqi one. In an attempt to diffuse a possible diplomatic crisis, Raad's famiy tried to convince people that their jihadi son had in fact died in Mosul during a confrontation with the American-led coalition forces. This, however, was contradicted by police officials in Hillah, who claimed to have found documents at the scene, proving that the remains of the body, which was fragmented in the explosion, were those of Raad Al Banna. Al Banna had been a committed follower of fellow Jordanian Abu Musab Al Zarqawi.

The impression gleaned from many of those who know him, targeting police stations is instrumental in Zarqawi's strategy to undermine what he sees as America's self-serving interests in training Iraq's new army and police force:

Abu Musab Al Zarqawi becomes more animated when talking about his bête noire, the American-supported Iraqi police force and army, drawing comparisons with the South Lebanon Army, which Israel installed during its occupation of Lebanon from 1978. This army was more commonly referred to as the Haddad Army after the name of its Lebanese commanding officer, Major Saad Haddad, But the army was controlled by the Israelis, not the Lebanese.

Zarqawi is skeptical that the heavy investment made by the United States to establish and train Iraqis in these two forces will prove worthwhile. He described the recruits as "working for the Americans, and they deserve to be killed. Those who cooperate with the Americans are infidels. They are there purely to serve the enemy's interests." He brushes them off as being merely a front to protect the occupier, and that's why he believes it is legitimate to kill any Iraqi who serves in either of the two forces. "We never kill Muslims without first warning them. We have to first ensure that they are collaborating with coalition forces, particularly the Americans. Many of those who heeded our warnings and stopped working with the occupying forces or left the police force or army have been forgiven and can carry on with their normal life. It's the ones who insist on continuing their association with the occupiers that we get rid of by whatever means."

His dream would be for these combined forces to stand up to the Americans, as Iraq did in what they called Thawrat al Ishreen, "The Twenties Revolution," referring to the 1920s, when they rebelled against the British who then occupied Iraq after World War I. However, he is doubtful that the Iraqi army and police force would have the ability to lead a revolution of this kind, as it lacks the military units and capabilities necessary to carry out such a mission. Drawing a further comparison, he refers to America's experience in Vietnam, where they installed the South Vietnamese army to fight alongside the U.S. forces against the Vietcong. Later, this Vietnamese army rebelled against the [United States], forcing some of its units to collapse.

Zarqawi and his nemesis and leader, bin Laden, are both Sunnis sharing Salafist ideals, and both are highly intolerant of the Shia. The Islamic Party, one of the oldest Sunni political parties in Iraq, is disliked by Zarqawi, and he came close to kidnapping and assassinating its leader, because he believed that "the Party has been got-at and used by the occupier—just like the others." The only positive role Zarqawi believed they played was to act as guardians for the mosques and other religious property belonging to the Iraqi Sunnis, fearing that it might be taken by others—principally the Shia. "If it wasn't for this, we would have treated them [meaning the Islamic Party] the way we treat other infidels and the occupying force." Sunni religious leaders fear that if Zarqawi continues to target Iraq's Shia, population, he will stir up a violent a sectarian war.

Concerning the question of how his organization is financed, his answer was esoteric: "While it was the poor citizens of Iraq who financed this struggle, I have the support of the richest people on earth." His response to how he is armed is more practical: "We get some weapons from the Americans themselves, either by stealing them, paying bribes to the Americans, or penetrating their heavily protected camps by bribing their Iraqi guards. But remember, plenty of weapons in this part of the world were buried underground by Saddam's regime. With a little money we've been able to smuggle large amounts of ammunition and weaponry, and what we have now is enough to enable us to fight the American forces for another four years. He elaborated further by saying they were planning ahead to ensure that they would have enough weapons to outlast the battle, however long that proves to be.

He vows that jihad must continue. "If not, the United States will dominate the Islamic world and put an end to Islam once and for all. America is not interested in listening to the needs of the people in the region." He knows that he is facing an extremely difficult enemy, and that is why he feels there is a great need for a clear vision and coordinated plan to achieve the desired results. He said it is very difficult to infiltrate such a strong force, because "money doesn't buy everyone." "God has given every superpower its weaknesses, and He has given us strength to fight this enemy and overcome it."

On October 17, 2004, a communiqué issued by the Al Tawhid Wa Al Jihad movement in Iraq stated the following: "Announcement of Good Tidings! The Tawheed Wa-Jihad Movement has joined together under the banner of Al-Qaida in a pledge of allegiance between Abu Musab al-Zarqawi, Emir (Commander) of the Mujahideen, and Sheik Osama Bin Laden."

When Zarqawi made his famous statement approving the alliance between his organization and that of Al Qaeda, describing it as, "The pinnacle in the struggle against the Americans," bin Laden returned the compliment by promoting him to "Emir of Al Qaeda in the Country of Two Rivers," meaning Zarqawi was to be Al Qaeda's man in the land of the Euphrates and the Tigris–Iraq.

Pooling the manpower and financial resources of both Al Qaeda and Al Tawhid Wa Al Jihad reinforced the confidence of both organizations to achieve their aims. On the third anniversary of the 9/11 attacks, I visited the tribal areas of Pakistan and Afghanistan, where I met high-placed members of both governments, including President Pervez Musharraf of Pakistan and interim prime minister Hamid Karzai of Afghanistan as well as military commanders on the ground in both countries. The consensus was that this alliance between Al Qaeda and Zarqawi's group had given bin Laden an advantage because of the restrictive circles he now moves in. Even before the fall of Saddam's dictatorship, bin Laden had been looking for another front line from which to continue his fight against America. Zarqawi and the hundreds of young Arabs who had crossed the desert roads to Iraq have made bin Laden's ambitions come true.

In one of Baghdad's many prisons I interviewed several fighters from both Zarqawi's militant group and other organizations. They explained what a difficult task the Iraqi intelligence agencies and those of the American-led coalition had in attempting to trace the leaders of such organizations because of the complex structure of their cells. They described small clusters consisting of just three to five members. They had no knowledge of the whereabouts of their higher command, nor did they know their real names. Some were committed to the cause, and others were just doing it for money. Taking part in an attack can carry a reward of up to two hundred dollars.

During the first week of October 2004, American commanders claimed to have arrested scores of Arab fighters in Samarra following the largest postwar operation in Iraq and the first major push to reclaim rebel-held enclaves before the general election. Those who were arrested were carrying papers identifying them as foreigners with jobs as chicken farmers, tea sellers, or electricians. Captain David Bryant, a U.S. intelligence officer, told me in contradiction to American reports that just twenty-four foreign fighters were arrested, including Sudanese, Egyptians, Saudis, and Tunisians.

The day after Iraq's historic elections held on January 30, 2005, the Iraqi interior minister, Falah Al Naqib, told me, "Zarqawi's people tried to sabotage the country yesterday, but the will of the people was stronger." This was despite threats of sabotage in the run-up to the elections as well as bomb attacks that targeted some polling stations on the day itself. Naqib also disclosed that the bomber who tried to assassinate Dr. Iyad Allawi a few months before the elections was a Sudanese national. "That's why the public must be vigilant and be suspicious of the Sudanese community in Iraq, especially after it has become known through the media that Sudanese nationals have joined the ranks of Zarqawi's organization." The consequence of these reports–and Naqib's statement–has led to the Sudanese community's receiving even harsher treatment from the Iraqi police.

Suicide attacks are well planned, with careful reconnaissance missions carried out ahead of time to ensure success. Videotaped footage of the scene is often posted on the Internet along with the name of the group claiming responsibility. This was the case in the early morning attack on March 9, 2005, at the Hotel Al Sadir and the adjacent Ministry of Agriculture in downtown Baghdad's Al Andalus Square. Hotel Al Sadir is home to many U.S. and other foreign contractors working in Iraq and is consequently well guarded. Zarqawi's group had looked for its weak spot and had identified the entrance that leads to the Ministry of Agriculture building. They calculated that there were fewer guards in this area at 6:45 in the morning than at any other time.

After a light exchange of fire aimed at the guards' checkpoints, two terrorists who were disguised in Iraqi police uniforms ran to the two guards to ask if anyone was wounded. The guards' answer was met with a round of fire that killed them. The bogus policemen ran off to the safety of a waiting car next to Al Firdous Hospital. Then a garbage truck approached the now unmanned checkpoint and sped toward the parking lot of the Ministry of Agriculture, crashing into the wall that separated the hotel from the ministry, detonating a fifteen-hundred-pound bomb. At the same time, other members of the terrorist group who had been providing cover fled the area in anticipation of the explosion, leaving behind their weapons and an enormous smoking crater in the road.

Describing the target as "the hotel of the Jews,"[6] Zarqawi's group claimed responsibility for the explosion by way of a videotape of the attack that was displayed on the Internet. "The mujahideen opened fire on the police and guards protecting the

Jews, and when the entrance was clear, the hero blew up the infidels." There were many foreign workers in the hotel who were preparing for work when the bomb exploded. Zarqawi claimed he did everything he could to avoid harming civilians, particularly by placing a warning out on the Internet. Apart from the two dead police guards and the suicide bomber, forty people were wounded in the blast, including thirty U.S. contractors. The so-called hero was the driver of the garbage truck. His nationality was assumed to be Sudanese from the color of the skin fragments that were later found, which were all that remained of his body. If the bomb had gone off just one hour later, or if a warning had not been posted on the Internet, the civilian casualties could easily have amounted to hundreds. The Ministry of Agriculture employs at least four thousand employees.

Many stories have been circulated by the media about the imminent capture of Zarqawi. The closest the Americans have come was in 2004, when intelligence reports confirmed the presence of a large number of insurgents in the area west of Hit, close to Haditha in Al Anbar province. Zarqawi had been in the area with a group of his fighters when it was besieged by American forces who attempted to arrest the mercurial fugitive. He escaped.

In a meeting at the Baghdad home of Interior Minister Falah Al Naqib, I learned more about Zarqawi's near-capture. Naqib said that one of his units from the Ministry of the Interior, although missing out on the big catch, had arrested one of Zarqawi's entourage. "It wasn't the first time we've closed in on Zarqawi. This time we got there a little late and he managed to slip the net, but we are confident that it won't be long before this terrorist is arrested." Dr. Kasim Dawood, the minister responsible for national security in the interim government, confirmed the story. He also implied that the release of recent photographs of Zarqawi that were found in the pockets of the arrested Zarqawi assistant were indications of "just how close we are getting to trapping him."

During my many visits to Fallujah and Ramadi, I was becoming aware of a change in the atmosphere of jihad against American forces, which by now had spread throughout the whole of Al Anbar province in the Sunni Triangle and upward into Mosul in the north. The traditional Islamic organizations had disappeared, leaving the theater open for hundreds of rapidly flourishing jihadi organizations under an array of names and banners, including the Army of Liberation, the Islamic Army, Al Tawhid Wa Al Jihad, the Sunnah Army, Jaish Mohammed, the Twentieth Revolution brigades, and Al Ansar Al Islam.

The many fighters I came across in Fallujah, Tikrit, Mosul, Samarra, and Ramadi denied that Zarqawi had anything to do with them or had any influence over them. One fighter, his face hidden by a kaffiyeh, told me with emphasis: "*We* were the ones who defended the town of Mosques [meaning Fallujah]." He went on to say, "Out of the many thousands of fighters arrested in the recent attacks, only a handful were Arabs from outside—not more than twenty. The majority of them were living in peace with us." He continued, "When Fallujah came under attack for the second time in less than a year by American forces and the Iraqi army, they accused Al Zarqawi, claiming that he had bases in Fallujah and the surrounding areas." Iraqi government officials, as if to concur with the coalition forces, talked about scores of black-clad fighters walking through the streets of Al Anbar province with the name of Zarqawi's organization written across their headbands.

* * *

Kidnappings have become common in post-Saddam Iraq; one of the most dangerous areas is the eight-hour drive between Baghdad and Damascus. Despite being patrolled by American forces, there is plenty of opportunity for the kidnap gangs and highway robbers to prey on victims who attempt the lengthy journey between the Iraqi capital and Damascus or Amman. They risk not just their money, gold, or other valuables but their lives as well. Occasionally, these highway terrorists are arrested, but many of them, in this long-accepted culture of bribery, offer money earned from their lucrative highway business and are released a day later. I was fortunate not to be flagged down and only had to part with a few dollars as a bribe once I reached the Syrian border. My Iraqi driver explained that there are large areas of the desert running alongside both borders, where Bedouin tribes make daily visits to family living on the other side of the border. When the borders were drawn up during the period of the British mandate, no account was taken of tribal wanderings. But the borderlines surrounding Iraq are clearly not an obstacle for anyone, bedouin or otherwise, if they have a purpose to reach the other side.

In December 2004 Turkish businessman Kahrem Sadek Oglow was seized from Um Qasar, a seaport in the south of Iraq, along with three of his guards. Fortunately for him, he was in a position to buy his way to freedom. Oglow paid half a million U.S. dollars to his kidnappers, former Baath Party officers, who sent one of their people to Jordan in order to collect the ransom.

Ghazi Hayder was another one of the luckier hostages in Iraq who was able to pay for his life. I was seated next to him on the Magic Carpet commuter flight from Baghdad to Beirut shortly after his being released, having spent forty-nine days with his captors. He was still in shock as he described how he was kidnapped from his rented house in the Al Mansour suburb during the night shortly after his arrival in Baghdad. He had gone to Iraq to oversee a business he had set up with Hassan, one of his cousins. No foreigner would rent a house without security guards, but the kidnappers overcame his guards, and Ghazi and Hassan were powerless to defend themselves. The following day, during one of his many interrogation sessions, Ghazi's kidnappers accused him of the usual crime such hostages were accused of–that he was a spy. One minute they suggested he was an Israeli agent, the next they accused him of was working for the Syrian *mukhabarat,* or even that he was working undercover for the CIA. Ghazi pleaded his case, explaining that he was from South Lebanon and that his countrymen were behind the resistance that forced Israel to withdraw from Lebanon. Before long his kidnappers questioned him about his wealth and how much they could demand from his family in ransom for his release. Their opening price was two hundred thousand dollars. Ghazi was staggered by the amount and responded somewhat bravely, "Please kill me with that long sword you have rather than wasting your time waiting for that amount of money, because my parents can't afford it." His interrogator became angry and implied that Ghazi wasn't taking his request seriously. Negotiations continued and Ghazi and Hassan were finally released, but the two former hostages refused to disclose the asking price for their freedom, as they didn't want to compromise their business in Iraq.

Ghazi's worst experience, however, was not his kidnapping. Rather, his worst experience occurred during an afternoon drive with his cousin in the Sunni suburb of Al Adamiyeh. A suicide bomber walked toward a car just a few yards from them and exploded himself, killing the driver and wounding many others. Ghazi lost twenty-two pounds during his trip to Baghdad, but fortunately not his life.

While Ghazi, Hassan, and Kahrem survived their kidnapping ordeals, where money could tip the balance between life or death, others have been at the mercy of cold-blooded killers, where nationality was the principal motivating factor in their capture and eventual death.

On March 31, 2004, four American private security guards who were driving through the wide streets of Fallujah found themselves the targets of a vicious insurgency group. After first coming under a hail of bullet fire, they were dragged from their vehicles, decapitated, and their limp and headless bodies strung up from a bridge and set alight. To the sound of anti-American chanting by the gathered spectators, a fired-up mob then tore down the bodies and tied them to a donkey cart and sent it careering down Fallujah's main street. In a final act of depravity, the crazed crowd tied the badly damaged bodies to the bumper of a car and drove away from the scene. This extraordinary display of barbarity stunned the world, and U.S. officials were adamant that the deaths would not go unpunished.

Witnesses claimed that the attack was planned in advance. Insurgents had given previous notice to businesses along the wide four-lane highway warning them that a confrontation with American forces was imminent and that they didn't want civilians to be hurt. A week after the attacks, on April 6, U.S. marines, backed by two battalions of Iraqi forces, launched Operation Vigilant Resolve. They stormed into the western districts of Fallujah, causing nearly one-third of the city's inhabitants to flee. U.S. Abrams tanks and AC-130 gunships took part in the attacks, which were met by guerrillas armed with Kalashnikovs and rocket-propelled grenades. Guided laser bombs were then fired from U.S. aircrafts at a mosque. The insurgents found themselves undermanned and under-resourced. As the death toll mounted, Iraqi forces refused to support the operation. A cease-fire called five days later, on April 11, was ineffective. As skirmishes continued overnight, more than six hundred civilians lost their lives, according to Dr. Rafe'e Iyad Al Isawi, the director of Fallujah Hospital. Finally, between April 26 and 29, 2004, having taken three days for the situation to diffuse, the all-out assault ran out of firepower.

Frequent air strikes by American military planes targeting Abu Musab Al Zarqawi continued throughout the summer. His group by now had claimed responsibility for the abduction and violent deaths of many Western hostages, including that of the British engineer Kenneth Bigley in October 2004. Fighting in and around Fallujah escalated after news reports suggested that more insurgents had moved into the area for the anticipated battle ahead. Instead, the opposite was the case, but by then requests had already been made for British troops to be redeployed to the southern bases of Latifiya and Iskandarya, freeing up American forces for its attack on Fallujah.

American forces launched their biggest assault on Fallujah on November 8, 2004. Fallujah was considered to be the nerve center for Zarqawi's terrorist activities, and hostage taking, beheadings, and vicious attacks against American patrols and their bases were occurring on a daily basis. More than ten thousand American troops and four Iraqi army brigades took part in the operation. Most of the people who fled Fallujah were angry, not just with American forces, but also with the insurgents for destroying their lovely city and forcing its inhabitants to leave behind their wrecked homes. Others laid the blame firmly on the shoulders of George W. Bush and Iyad Allawi, the interim Iraqi prime minister. Clerics were also drawn into the pool of blame for allowing foreign fighters to use the town as a base from which to recruit the young and unemployed who were seeking martyrdom, where heaven and victory would be their reward. People who remained in the city were incredulous when they heard reports on the news that more than one thousand foreign fighters had been killed. They claimed that most of the fighters had left the city long before the Americans began their assault. I went to the cemetery in Fallujah, and in the section designated for foreign fighters I counted fewer than one hundred graves. I read the headstone for one of them: "Here lies the body of the heroic Tunisian martyr."

Others I spoke to about foreign fighter presence in Fallujah said they had come across people from Saudi Arabia, Kuwait, Yemen, Palestine, and Syria, but that they were relatively few and not in hundreds as the media claim. The majority of the jihadi elements are Iraqis, mainly Fallujans. This was confirmed by many other people I met in the town and its surrounding areas.

The Iraqi interior minister, Falah Al Naqib, who has survived more than one suicide bomb attack, including one against his well-guarded ministry in early 2005, told me that he did not anticipate a speedy solution to the problem of foreign fighters entering the country. He described the nationalities of some of the suicide bombers, naming Sudanese, Saudis, Jordanians, Syrians, and Egyptians, as well as Iraqis. An Iraqi friend of mine had this to say on the subject: "I totally approve of the idea of finding a way to prevent outside Arabs from entering Iraq at the moment. It is hardly a tourist attraction after all, so anyone coming here is doing so for other reasons. We cannot continue with this difficult and frightening life, where every single minute of the day and night we worry about ourselves, our kids, and our families."

NOTES

1. U.S. Department of State, *Background Information on Terrorist Groups,* 2004.
2. Al Jazeera, satellite television, March 22, 2003; AFP, March 22, 2003.
3. The term Peshmerga, which literally translates to "those who face death," refers to Kurdish freedom fighters.
4. Such interviews include Hussein Kamel, undersecretary of the Interior Department for Intelligence in Iraq.
5. *The 9/11 Commission Report,* chapter 6, "Threat to Threat: The Millennium Crisis." U.S. Government publication released July 22, 2004.
6. Associated Press, March 9, 2005. "Security forces find 41 corpses in Iraq; truck bomber kills 3 in Baghdad."

CHAPTER THREE

THE AMERICANS ARE WRONG-FOOTED: 1990–2005

The date was October 28, 1992. Several suites had been reserved under false identities at the low-key Hilton Olympia in West London, including one that was going to be used as a conference room. The undercover guests were high-ranking U.S. officials representing the CIA, the State Department, and the Pentagon, who were occupying most of the reserved rooms. The others were three influential Iraqi opponents to Saddam Hussein: Saad Saleh Jaber, the son of the Iraqi prime minister during the period of Iraq's monarchy and a vociferous opponent of the dictator since the seventies; Sheikh Taleb Al Suhail, an active tribal leader, who has worked continuously to overthrow the regime after being forced to live in exile in Jordan; and Jasem Muklis, a leading Sunni personality from Saddam's hometown of Tikrit with real insider knowledge of Saddam's clan, family, and contacts.

Al Suhail and Muklis, assisted by Jordanian intelligence, were discreetly flown from Amman to London's Heathrow Airport, where British intelligence facilitated their entry, bypassing normal passport formalities. Muklis was planning to go to Baghdad in the near future and was anxious to leave no trace in his passport indicating that he had traveled outside Jordan. He and Al Suhail were close friends and met regularly. The usual topic of discussion between the two was the situation in Iraq and the need to do something about Saddam. They spoke about the importance of coordinating any efforts to overthrow Saddam, and Al Suhail assured Muklis that he would take care of this. The meeting in London was the start of that effort.

After two days of secret discussions in the hotel, Muklis and Al Suhail returned to Jordan, while the American officials flew to Washington to consult their relevant departments. They promised to respond to the three Iraqi opposition figures via a message to Jaber, who lived in London. Nothing was heard from Washington for two weeks. Jaber finally called his contacts and learned that the administration was not interested in toppling Saddam Hussein in the immediate future.

Fast-forward nine months to the summer of 1993, and a date was finally set to assassinate the Iraqi dictator. It was designed to take place during Saddam's military parade for the annual July 17 Revolution celebrations, and General Sufian Saleh Al Ghriri, the commander of the armored vehicle brigade was in charge. In the run-up to the event, the general received a call from the presidential palace with an order to go to Saddam Hussein's official office to discuss the preparations for his parade. Everything had to be perfect—the Republican Guard's march as they passed by and saluted the president, the podium where he would give his traditionally lengthy and bellicose speech, and most important of all, security had to be watertight. The general, like Saddam a native Tikriti, told his fellow officers of his surprise at this unexpected presidential summons. A few hours later, his officers received another call from the palace, and it was their turn to be surprised. They were told that General Al Ghriri would have nothing to do with their brigade from that day on. They didn't see him again.

Throughout the week leading up to the parade, a number of officers were arrested, together with their families, with no reason given. On July 14, Lieutenant Colonel Bashir Taleb, another retired military officer who served with Saddam's elite Republican Guard, was added to the ever-growing list of high-ranking officers arrested.

On the night of July 17, just a few hours after the annual parade had wound down without incident, Jasem Muklis, who was by then a member of Parliament, found his house surrounded by security forces, who arrested him along with his cousin Mawloud. They were both executed. Shortly after that, more than twelve hundred military officers suffered the same fate after Saddam's security services discovered information they deemed to be incriminating. Their intelligence dated back to the London Olympia Hilton meeting where American, British, and Iraqi opposition figures conceived the plot to assassinate Saddam Hussein.

Sheikh Taleb Al Suhail was bitter about the executions, particularly that of his closest friend, Jasem Muklis. I happened to be in the company of the third co-conspirator from the secret hotel meeting, Saad Saleh Jaber, when Al Suhail telephoned him at his flat in Kensington. Despite all the rhetoric delivered by the U.S. administration about their desire to end Saddam's regime once and for all, I understood from Saleh Jaber that the word from Washington was not encouraging. "They have proved they are not serious enough. We didn't ask them for money, we didn't ask them for logistical help; all we asked of them was to support us with air cover to prevent any of Saddam's other units from hindering our movements on the day."

In the wake of these mass executions, Sheikh Taleb Al Suhail, who was living with his family in Jordan, was advised by the late

King Hussein to leave the country immediately for his personal safety. Al Suhail, together with his Lebanese wife, fled to Beirut, where he owned an apartment. He had been a former Iraqi diplomat and was head of the million-member Bani Tamim tribe, whose members are mostly Shia Arabs. He left Iraq in 1968 when Saddam Hussein became leader of the Baath Party and worked tirelessly for almost thirty years in exile for his overthrow. Just a few months later, on April 12, 1994, Al Suhail was assassinated at his apartment in the Ain Al Tinah district of Beirut. Iraqi intelligence agents had hired a supposed family friend, a Lebanese tailor by the name of George Tarkhaynan, and used him as a lure to gain entry to Sheikh Suhail's home under the pretext of returning some clothing repairs. Al Suhail was gunned down by three agents assigned to the Iraqi embassy in Beirut.

Eleven years later, on February 2, 2005, thirty-eight million Americans tuned in to watch George W. Bush deliver his State of the Union address of his second term in office, which customarily takes place in the chamber of the U.S. House of Representatives. He singled out one guest of honor as a female human rights campaigner: "Eleven years ago, Safia's father was assassinated by Saddam's intelligence service. Three days ago in Baghdad, Safia was finally able to vote for the leaders of her country, and we are honored that she is with us tonight." Safia's father was Taleb Al Suhail.

Some of Safia's family, including her sister Nora and other members of their numerous tribe, accused America of having a hand in Al Suhail's assassination: "The U.S. was a virtual accomplice in Sheikh Taleb's death. The Americans didn't want the coup to succeed and tipped off Saddam about the parade and gave him the names of the Iraqi architects involved in the plot." What grounds did the family have to make these allegations? They believe that because the meeting to plot the coup was so discreet and confidential between the three Iraqi opposition members and officials from the Pentagon, CIA, and the U.S. administration, no one else—not even close relatives of the three men—were aware of this plot. In other words, they believed the tip-off came from somewhere within the American administration.

In 1995 another plot to overthrow the dictator's regime was foiled by Saddam's intelligence. According to one of the Iraqi opposition groups in exile, the Iraqi National Council (INC): "When we informed the CIA of the plot's exposure, we were told that George Tenet, the deputy director of the CIA at the time, ignored it and insisted that the plan was still on. Mohammed Madloum Al Dilaimi, the Baath Party National Guard officer who had been groomed by the CIA to mastermind the coup, was inevitably executed by Saddam's henchmen."

An INC spokesman reflected on how the organization had felt particularly betrayed by Anthony Lake, Clinton's national security adviser, at the time: "When we planned an all-out offensive against Saddam's forces in the Kurdish area in northern Iraq in March 1995, we were promised the support of top-ranking Iraqi officers, who assured us that their forces would back us up. Twenty-four hours before the offensive was due to begin, Lake sent a telegram informing us that the United States had changed their minds about supporting us. This caused a crack within our coalition. Massoud Al Barzani, the leader of the Kundistan Democratic Party, decided against becoming involved with us, and other groups followed suit. We were left with just our forces led by Ahmed Chalabi together with the forces of the other Kurdish leader, Jalal Talabani, to carry on with their plans."

Despite attempts to overthrow Saddam's regime, the wily dictator continued to dodge bullets. Saddam's intelligence team was always one step ahead, and the officers involved in plotting his potential demise were systematically executed. Still, the CIA was sure that the only way to defeat the dictator was to organize a coup from within his regime.

* * *

The brutal invasion of Kuwait by Iraqi forces on August 2, 1990, was the starting point of a full review and reversal of U.S. policy toward Iraq, which over the previous decade had been indulgent toward Saddam's dictatorship, taking Iraq's side in its war against Iran. When Kuwait City was finally liberated by U.S. coalition forces on February 27, 1991, George Bush Senior cautioned against the overt or immediate overthrow of the Iraqi regime, fearing the centrifugal forces it could unleash within Iraq and the region. Because of this, many Iraqi opposition leaders accused George Bush of being responsible for the deaths of thousands of Iraqis after he encouraged them to overthrow the regime in 1991. He allowed Saddam Hussein to crush them despite the proximity of American-led coalition tanks that were close to the Iraqi capital following Saddam's defeat of Kuwait.

Bush Senior gave the CIA the green light to begin courting Iraqi opposition groups, who were, naturally, highly motivated to get involved in the process. One of those groups was the Iraqi National Council, an umbrella organization that was established in Vienna in 1992 for opponents of Saddam's Baathist regime, both inside and outside the country. Two hundred delegates from dozens of opposition groups attended the Viennese meeting. The two principal Kurdish militias, the KDP and PUK, were the main participants. By October 1992 the major Shiite groups were also embraced by the coalition, and the INC held a pivotal meeting in Kurdish-controlled northern Iraq, choosing a three-man leadership council and a twenty-six-member executive council. Its controversial leader, Dr. Ahmed Chalabi, is credited within most Iraqi circles for having invested decades of time and effort lobbying U.S. politicians to support their cause.

Chalabi prides himself on being the man responsible for forcing the CIA to change its tactics when dealing with the Arab world:

"Iraq's relationship with the U.S. should be built on mutual respect together with true friendship," he said.[1] "[But] when you work with the CIA and receive brown paper bags in return, you can't argue if people interpret that as working officially for the agency." Born into a wealthy, Shia Muslim family, Chalabi fled Iraq in 1958 at the age of thirteen and has been based in the United States, Jordan, or London ever since.

The CIA was prepared to overthrow Saddam Hussein's regime at any price, no matter which party—Baathists, Saddam's family, or opposition groups—was in a position to do so. The agency believed it was important to cultivate senior members of the Baath Party in Iraq, as they might prove to be an asset in forming a future government.

As Dr. Ahmed Chalabi became, for a brief period in the early 1990s, the darling of the Pentagon and the CIA, he was tasked with spearheading Saddam's overthrow and was responsible for providing the United States with detailed information and intelligence about the Baathists. In return, his organization received millions of dollars from the CIA by way of a monthly "salary" of $340,000. After the overthrow of Saddam and the consequent failure to find weapons of mass destruction, Chalabi's organization was accused of providing false or misleading information concerning Iraq to the Bush administration.

Entifadh Qanbar, of INC's Washington office, told me: "We were frequently quizzed by the CIA. Their under-the-counter way of channeling money ensured that whoever receives it does so in return for implementing American policies, but it is a recipe for corruption." The Iraq Liberation Act approved by Congress specified that all payments made to any Iraqi party had to be made transparent. In the nineties, Chalabi, along with other senior figures in the Iraqi opposition, was accused of mishandling the American payments. On four occasions the CIA were obliged to send their accountants to London, where the INC had its headquarters, to verify documents detailing how these millions of dollars were being spent.[2] The INC operatives were outraged by this. "How could they expect to get a receipt from an Iraqi official they had bribed to smuggle a defector onto their 'underground railway' to the West? The expense sheets they provided involved very detailed accounting and this just wasn't practical to carry out."

An independent report conducted by the independent commission in Washington for the intelligence committee in Congress concluded that the INC's information did not influence America's decision to go to war. However, an earlier report published in October 2002 found that the intelligence committee had relied on assumptions provided by two members of Chalabi's organization that Saddam was using mobile chemical and biological laboratories to enable him to spirit away his production of banned weapons. UN inspectors found these mobile bio-labs but were unable to discover a sinister use for them. Hans Blix, the chief UN weapons inspector, reported to the UN Security Council on March 7, 2003, saying: "Several inspections have taken place at declared and undeclared sites in relation to mobile production facilities. Food-testing mobile laboratories and mobile workshops have been seen, as well as large containers with seed-processing equipment. No evidence of proscribed activities has so far been found."

In recent years much has been written about Chalabi and his backing by an exclusive group of pro-Israel hawks in the Pentagon. This so-called cabal of neoconservatives has as its principal ringleaders Undersecretary of Defense Paul Wolfowitz and Defense Policy Board Chairman Richard Perle. They enjoy strong backing from Defense Secretary Donald Rumsfeld and Vice President Dick Cheney as well. Those who have followed developments in the Middle East for many years have watched the formation of this so-called cabal with great interest, long before the word "neo-con" became synonymous with American foreign policy. I remember reading a document prepared by Richard Perle in 1996 in which he outlined his vision. Titled "A Clean Break: A New Strategy for Securing the Realm," it was prepared for an Israeli think-tank to advise the then–Israeli prime minister, Benjamin Netanyahu.[3] The plan called on Israel to work with Turkey and Jordan "to contain, destabilize, and roll back various states in the region, overthrow Saddam Hussein in Iraq, press Jordan to restore a scion of its Hashemite dynasty to the Iraqi throne and, above all, launch military assaults against Lebanon and Syria as a prelude to a redrawing of the map of the Middle East, to threaten Syria's territorial integrity." Perle's idea was shared by Douglas Feith, national security adviser, and David Wurmser, adviser to Dick Cheney on the Middle East. Perle and Paul Wolfowitz naively declared that this grandiose plan would solve the Israeli-Palestinian conflict because it would open the door for Israel to become part of "a New Middle East."

The American government's strategy of developing a friendly dialogue with the Arab world goes back decades and is often described as an "intelligence partnership," that is, one in which each partner has something to gain from their relationship with the other. The CIA is renowned for vetting Arab politicians and giving support to various Arab political groups whose interests serve the United States. Within the American administration it is the CIA, not the State Department or the Pentagon, who has the upper hand in deciding what kind of diplomacy the United States should enjoy with a particular Arab government.

The neocons' philosophy is the antithesis of this. It is premised on the idea that the United States should have unmatched scale and influence internationally and that it should indulge or cosset dictators. The neocons believe that the United States should use, in their words, "preemptive" military force as well as political and economic power to overthrow regimes they consider a threat to America or its interests. Until 9/11 the neocons were mostly ignored as a minority sect. But after 9/11 their ideology suddenly seemed to fit the sentiment of the time.

Largely as a result of the neocons' influence, the United States' policy is simple but controversial: we do not hesitate to use military force and political and economic power to overthrow rogue regimes. This runs in stark contrast to what the State Department thinks. Traditionally American diplomats have believed that the best way to deal with dictatorships and other undesirable governments is to open a channel of diplomatic dialogue to convince them to make changes. During the cold war the United States tended to ally with any anticommunist, dictatorial regime, without giving any credence to their records on human rights and pursuit of democratic values.

To the neocons, the CIA and the State Department's policies in the Middle East have been deeply flawed and often shortsighted. Essentially, their policy was to ignore bad behavior as long as the government remained on good terms with the Americans and facilitated American actions abroad by providing the use of an air base or sending a few troops as a fig leaf to give an American operation the appearance of Arab support, even if this support involves overlooking the often authoritarian domestic policies of these regimes. This, the neocons point out rightly, has led to enormous resentment of America.

For the majority of neocon members, their interest in Iraq is fairly straightforward. Many of them are Jewish and strong supporters of Israel, such as Pentagon official Harold Rhode, an Orthodox Jew and a neocon strategist who was studying at Tehran University when Ayatollah Khomeini's revolution forced him to flee. The neocons are criticized both in the Arab world and at home for their views, and they are sensitive to the charges that because they are Jewish their first loyalty is to Israel. In fact, because they are often immersed in oriental culture and languages, they are far more idealistic about the possibility of democracies in the Arab world. So despite their reputation as being pro-Israeli, the neocons are often the first in Washington circles to argue that Arabs both deserve and are capable of democracy

Chalabi was criticized for having a relationship with the powerful Israel lobby in America. In fact, as he happily says, paraphrasing Winston Churchill with a mischievous smile, he would have "made an alliance with the devil if it led to Saddam's overthrow!" What did Chalabi really think about the lobby? "They were shortsighted and focused on securing Israel for the short term rather than seeking a solution with Israel's Palestinian population and Arab neighbors that would give them a better chance of guaranteeing Israel's permanent existence. That's why the neocons never bothered about what kind of regime they were dealing with, as the most important thing was signing peace agreements or treaties with those regimes." Chalabi denies that he tried to court this lobby by telling them that a new Iraq would favor having diplomatic relations with Israel. In fact, Chalabi seems disillusioned about any Israeli role in Iraq. When he visited Israel before Saddam's overthrow, he was not offered a meeting with senior political officials as he expected, but was asked to meet the head of Israeli International Intelligence (Mossad). He refused and left Israel. Later, he described in a private conversation with an American journalist how wrong the Israelis' view of the Middle East was: "Who do they think I am? A spy? Do they think my role is all about giving them information? I am a politician who is interested in talking to Israel about the future relationships between our two countries. I thought it was possible for Israel and Iraq to have a dialogue, but when they told me to meet the head of Mossad, I realized they had a different idea."

The relationship between Ahmed Chalabi and Richard Perle, a leading supporter of the war in Iraq, goes back more than twenty years. They have many friends in common, particularly in the Pentagon. Chalabi is well versed in U.S. politics and shares the neoconservatives' desire to create more democracies, convinced that such an approach would be in the overall interests of the United States and U.S. national security. Among a few of the senior neoconservative members, getting rid of the Iranian regime was at the top of their agenda, but not necessarily at the top of Iraq's. But the INC lobbying machinery went into overdrive to convince these neocons that Iraq and the Arab world, rather than Iran, should be their top priority

Ahmed Chalabi has long been associated with Iran. He has family connections in the country and in terms of politics knows all the different factions, of which there are many, whether they are Islamists, moderates, conservatives, or revolutionaries. He tried to explain to his American neocon allies that if they could pacify the Iranians, the job of toppling Saddam's regime would be made easier, especially if Washington convinced Tehran that a regime change in Iraq would not affect them.

To know Iraq, one has to understand that its population has known little else but war for more than twenty years. The Iran-Iraq War began on September 20, 1980, and after one of the longest and bloodiest conflicts of the last century, a cease-fire was finally reached, eight years later, on August 20, 1988. As far back as the 1980s, Chalabi tried hard to discourage America from supporting Saddam in his war against Iran. He also pressured other Arab governments to do the same—in particular, Jordan, which, with the tacit approval of the U.S. government, was secretly supplying Iraq with heavy weaponry.

While this must have irritated the Jordanians, Chalabi charts the beginning of his troubles with Jordan from the so-called Petra Bank affair in 1989. The Jordanian military seized the Amman offices of the Petra Bank, which Chalabi founded in the 1970s. He was accused of embezzling millions of dollars from the bank, which he denied, claiming that the charges were trumped up and politically motivated. Chalabi fled Jordan after being tipped off by a friendly Jordanian intelligence source that the late King Hussein planned to turn him over to Saddam's regime. But it was Prince Hassan, the king's brother and heir to the throne, who smuggled Chalabi in the trunk of his personal car and drove him across the border to Lebanon via Syria. A military court in Jordan, which met in secret and whose testimony has never been revealed, tried Chalabi in absentia and in April 1992 sentenced him to serve twenty-two years of hard labor and to reimburse 230 million dollars in embezzled funds. Chalabi never returned to Jordan and continued his fight from abroad. Privately, the late King Hussein twice offered Chalabi a royal pardon, but Chalabi refused, against the advice of his inner circle, saying he wanted a trial in open court or to have a statement published saying he was innocent of all charges. He continues to insist on his innocence today.

The honeymoon between Chalabi's group and the CIA didn't last more than two years (1992–1994). Chalabi had established a militia with training camps in the Kurdish areas of Iraq, where he formed a close alliance with the forces of Jalal Talabani. The CIA was unhappy about this allegiance and the INC's use of their substantial funds; thus, disagreements arose. The CIA favored a coup from within the military in Baghdad, rather than the formation of a "liberation army," as Chalabi liked to call it.

In April 1993 an INC delegation visited the United States for discussions with U.S. Secretary of State Warren Christopher and Anthony Lake, the National Security Council adviser. These were the first high-profile meetings between the INC and the American administration after President Bill Clinton was elected. Subsequently, the INC established offices in London and Salahaddin in northern Iraq, from where they conducted a fierce public relations campaign. More importantly, a plan of action was conceived, which they named the "Three Cities Plan." Ahmed Chalabi was hoping to forge an alliance between the two Kurdish militias and his own forces in order to capture two northern cities–Mosul and Kirkuk. While in the south, the INC, together with the Shia militia led by Sayed Mohammed Baqir Al Hakim, would attack Basra. The Americans expressed no interest in the Three Cities Plan, and via messages sent by Anthony Lake to the Kurdish leadership, they emphasized they would not support such an action. This was the first clear indication that the Clinton administration had a different agenda and signaled the end of the honeymoon between the CIA and Chalabi's organization.

Later, the INC said they felt that the CIA had used them as pawns in its propaganda war against the Iraqi dictatorship. An INC official told me, "Some people within the CIA began to take the view that they should stand against us. We couldn't stand against them, as they have greater powers and capabilities." The CIA, so it seemed, appeared to be more interested in fighting Chalabi and his group than it was in fighting Saddam Hussein.

The INC was in Iraqi Kurdistan when Saddam Hussein sent in his tanks in September 1996 to bolster the defenses of Massoud Al Barzani and his KDP militia. Al Barzani was waging war against Jalal Talabani's PUK fighters, whom he accused of receiving support from the Iranians. This was yet another Byzantine development in the Middle East that the CIA was incapable of predicting. The CIA officials in the Kurdish area who had been working with the INC packed their bags and fled overnight, leaving behind their computers, which contained lists of all the Iraqis, Arabs, and Kurds–mostly members of the INC–who had been working with them. The Iraqi *mukhabarat* used these CIA lists to track down and shoot anyone who had not managed to escape. Because of this, Saddam Hussein got wind that Washington was not now in favor of removing him, and he launched an offensive into Irbil, where thirty thousand of his soldiers and three hundred tanks overcame the opposition forces. Promises given to the INC by the United States that they would provide them with air cover to prevent Saddam's forces from bombing them didn't materialize, and

Saddam carried on with his offensive. Even though American fighters were flying at low altitude, it didn't deter the Iraqi regular forces from entering Irbil and executing at least 129 members of the INC alone. This was a defining day in the INC-CIA relationship. From then on the INC decided to no longer sustain a secret relationship with the CIA, and instead preferred to deal through official channels. So they began lobbying Congress directly, and a few years later the Iraq Liberation Act became law. Chalabi never forgave them. It was the beginning of a deep rift between Chalabi and the CIA that continues to this day.

The first mistake the occupying power made was to prevent Jay Garner, a retired general appointed as director of the Office of Reconstruction and Humanitarian Assistance to Iraq, from assisting Iraqis in forming a government that was supposed to prepare the way for an elected government. Instead they came up with UN resolution 1483, which redefined Iraq from being a "liberated" country to an "occupied" one. It was Colin Powell's idea to set up an authority named the CPA (Coalition Provisional Authority) to manage the affairs of the country for one year after first naming an American-appointed Governing Council. Power would then be transferred to an interim government, which would prepare the ground for an election to appoint a parliament, whose main duty would be to write a constitution and pave the way for a second election within the year after it was established.

The head of INC's Washington office, Entifadh Qanbar, who was in Kuwait, working side by side with Garner, described the group's frustration with the American administration at that time: "The State Department in Washington ignored our ideas and tried to assemble their own plan for the future of Iraq. Then other ideas floated into the pot. One of these was to train Iraqi volunteers in Hungary, which would involve less cost, training facilities were available, it was close enough to the Middle East, and [it offered] the potential supply of Saddam's former soldiers and officers who had fled the country and sought asylum in Europe. The CIA, the State Department, and its Near Eastern Affairs Bureau all laid out their individual conditions. The State Department in particular said that while they would be prepared to train these fifteen thousand Iraqis, they would not be willing to pay their salaries. Their justification for this was that they didn't want to be accused of trying to 'buy' their help as if they were mercenaries. The State Department was not consistent here. While denying these men money, they offered Iraqi professionals–whether doctors, lawyers, or judges, et cetera–who lived in the United States but are familiar with the language and culture of Iraq, contracts to go to the country, and paid a staggering twelve to fifteen thousand U.S. dollars a month."

Entifadh went on to explain that according to the INC blueprint, the role of these trained Iraqis was to accompany American forces when they entered Iraq and immediately take charge of the cities and the towns once they were liberated from the Baath regime. The American forces should then withdraw and not become directly involved with the Iraqi population. The INC's proposals were drawn up with the expert assistance of military advisers, including retired general Wayne Downing, an unabashed hawk, who was in charge of Special Forces during the first Gulf War in 1991. Also included in the INC plan was the proviso that lawyers, judges, and prosecutors should be an intrinsic part of the immediate postwar recovery operation so that an effective justice system could be promptly instigated.

The campaign for war got under way at the beginning of October 2002. It was coordinated by the triumvirate of the State Department, the Justice Department, and the Pentagon following a chain of command going down from retired lieutenant general Jay Garner, the first American administrator to oversee the interim administration and reconstruction of Iraq. The war strategy was made available to him a few months later. It was January 2003 when Doug Feith, right-hand man to Secretary of State Rumsfeld and number three at the Pentagon, telephoned Garner at his office in Manhattan. Feith explained that Rumsfeld would like him to put together a team to prepare for postwar Iraq. The State Department referred to the project as "The Future of Iraq." Feith, a balding civilian in the Pentagon and a dyed-in-the-wool neocon, was resented by the generals, because they felt he interfered in a political way with their military plans.

During the third week of February 2003, more than seventy officials and experts gathered at the National Defense University at Fort McNair for two days to discuss and vet the war plans. Topics such as creating a police force and establishing prisons and courts were thrashed out, and these discussions were continued in Kuwait before the teams deployed to Baghdad. Garner held once-a-week meetings to brief the national security adviser at the time, Condoleezza Rice. He also held regular meetings with Rumsfeld and Colin Powell.

Jay Garner was the man tasked with overseeing the formation of a functioning civil administration in Iraq, such as providing basic utilities and restoring law and order. He is an easygoing man, who listens carefully and asks a lot of questions. He retired as a three-star general in 1997 to become president of SY Coleman, a provider of communications and targeting systems for Patriot missiles. In October 2000, after the beginning of the Second Intifada in the West Bank and Gaza, Garner was one of twenty-six American military leaders to sign a staunchly pro-Israeli statement condemning the escalation of violence. The statement was titled "Friends Don't Leave Friends in the Battlefield."

Garner briefed President Bush in the second week of March 2003, not long before he departed for Iraq. "One of the first questions the president asked me was about my background, and this was answered by Secretary Rumsfeld. Then he asked about the reconstruction plans, and I told him that we were going to use the

Iraqi army in the main for the reconstruction. We intended to hire them and form battalions and use them to rebuild their country. All was expected to go well, except that the Iraqi army evaporated after it had collapsed."[4] Garner recalled that when he raised his fears earlier in a meeting with National Security and other departments that the Iraqi army would collapse, "They asked me where I got that idea from and corrected me by saying 'What you mean is they will surrender!'"

"Jay," as General Garner prefers to be known, and others discussed the contents of the State Department's Future of Iraq project, which began in October 2001 under the direction of Tom Warrick. The assumption was that Saddam's exit would be violent and that there would be a period of transition. The State Department, as early as April 2002, formed seventeen Iraqi working groups, the vast majority of which were either exiles or ex-Baathists, especially those from the military. Their work was to cover transitional justice, public finance, public outreach, democratic principles, water, agriculture and the environment, defense, local government, economy and infrastructure, civil society, transparency and anticorruption, education, refugees, free media, foreign policy, oil and energy, and cultural heritage.[5] The program was not well received by many in the Pentagon and National Security circles, and Tom Warrick didn't last long in the job. In an interview by the Associated Press with Jay Garner about the early sacking of Warrick, Garner recalled a conversation with Donald Rumsfeld: "Tom was just beginning to get started with us when one day I was in the office with the secretary of defense, and he said, 'Jay, have you got a guy named Warrick on your team?' I said, 'Yes, I do.' He said, 'Well, I've got to ask you to remove him.' I said, 'I don't want to remove him; he's too valuable.' But he said, 'This came to me from such a high level that I can't overturn it, and I've just got to ask you to remove Mr. Warrick.'" The people who are higher placed than Donald Rumsfeld in Washington's hierarchy are few, and the deduction is that Vice President Dick Cheney issued the order. Warrick was an outspoken critic of the Iraqi democracy movement, and the State Department had appointed him as its chief "vetter" of Iraqi officials. Another event that displayed his unpopularity was recounted in *The New Republic* on March 17, 2003, by the INC's Washington chief, Entifadh Qanbar. The incident took place at a gathering of Iraqi democrats the previous December. Warrick, along with the CIA's Ben Miller, stood in the doorway of the meeting and literally tried to block Entifadh's entry, saying, "You can't get in, and I'll have guards to help you out."

There were, therefore, interagency conflicts concerning the Future of Iraq program—one of which was whether to support the INC or not. Garner was asked whether Chalabi had been close to starting up a government in Iraq after the demise of Saddam. "Chalabi has his own circle of friends in the Pentagon, but Rumsfeld is not one of them," he replied. Garner backed this up by saying that while he was based in Kuwait City before heading for Baghdad, he read an article in which Rumsfeld was quoted as saying, "Chalabi is a candidate, but he is not one of my candidates," meaning that he didn't back the INC.

Doug Feith, on the other hand, spoke highly of Chalabi when he met with Garner prior to his departure for the Arab world. He described him as being cooperative toward the United States and knowledgeable of democracy. Feith was worried about the future leadership in Iraq but said he would trust the INC candidates, as they were well educated and experienced in democracy and would have the necessary ability to create a decent government.

Saddam continued to ignore UN resolutions, and the neocons continued to underscore how dangerous the Iraqi dictator was to America. Saddam stepped into their trap when he refused to recognize the seriousness of the situation and continued to block the UN weapons inspectors sent in by Hans Blix, head of the

UN Monitoring, Verification, and Inspection Commission (UNMOVIC). The door was wide open for George W. Bush to do what he has longed for since 9/11–to force a regime change in Iraq.

American tanks rolled in and seized Iraq sooner than even the generals could have predicted. The larger-than-life statues of Saddam that dominated Iraq's towns and cities were toppled like ninepins as excited Iraqis and overexcited coalition troops tore down these graven images of the now emasculated dictator. In less than three weeks after the air assault of Baghdad first began, Saddam's twenty-four-year rule was declared over on April 9, 2003. As events evolved, Washington's billion-dollar Iraq war strategy, named Operation Iraqi Freedom, appeared to have no postwar recovery plan despite marshaling together the mightiest political and military brains of the world's one and only superpower.

After Saddam's army melted away in the face of the American onslaught, looting was rampant and caused devastation beyond imagination across Iraq. Not anticipating or preventing this scenario was one of America's major mistakes in this war. A fervor of lawlessness erupted, made more extreme because it came after years of suppression. The Americans looked weak and unable to control the situation. Baghdad's National Museum of Iraq was ransacked of much of its priceless artifacts; buildings were burned or their structures became so unsafe they had to be torn down; hospitals, schools, factories, and homes were pillaged. Seventeen out of twenty-three ministries in Baghdad were razed to the ground. There were no communications, and electricity supplies were cut. On April 17 Garner met General Tommy Franks in Qatar and asked him if he could travel to Baghdad to meet up with military commanders on the ground in Baghdad to help with the emergency mopping-up operation and restore law and order.

Insurgents were quick to take advantage of the lack of troops and the security problem. American patrols became easy targets on deserted roads, especially as the insurgents knew that these patrols consist of just a few soldiers—perhaps two unarmored Humvees with five soldiers apiece. This makes the U.S. and coalition forces virtual sitting ducks for insurgents to attack them and then melt away into their familiar territory without trace. Also, it is impossible to sweep every road in Iraq. There is not much the patrols can do to avoid roadside bombs and Soviet-made RPG-7 rocket launchers, which the insurgents have discovered are very successful in exploding Humvees and U.S. support trucks.

Garner was clearly in over his head. "Can the military do a better job than the one already started?" he questioned. The whole country would always be better off with more troops, even though some thought the number was sufficient with just a division, part of an armored cavalry regiment, and segments of the Eighty-second Airborne, plus the marine forces who were still there at the time.

On the day Garner arrived in Baghdad, Rumsfeld called him with the news that the president had appointed Paul Bremer as his special envoy to Baghdad. "So I met Bremer on March 10 and briefed him on all the plans we had for starting up a new political process. One of those was to form a leadership group, which consisted of Talabani and Al Barzani [the leaders of the main Kurdish parties], Chalabi and Dr. Iyad Allawi [Saddam opposition leaders], Mohammed Baqir Al Hakim [leader of the Supreme Council of Islamic Revolution in Iraq], and Adnan Pachachi.[6] Then also bring in a Christian, a Sunni, and a moderate Shia into the mix. We also considered arranging a meeting of three to four hundred Iraqis from which we would appoint a working party and then begin drafting out a constitution with them and select what kind of government model they would want. These ideas were discussed with both Colin Powell and Rumsfeld."

Immediately after Garner arrived in Baghdad, on April 21, 2003, obviously there were no communications with the Iraqi government side, as they had all disappeared together with its police force. Communications in general were disrupted, along with the electricity and water supplies. Police and other civil service advisers from the United States finally began arriving in Iraq during the last week of May 2003, several weeks too late. They came with neither addresses nor contacts for the Iraqis with whom they would need to liaise in the relevant ministries. So it was left for one of the American advisers to go out into the street to ask whether anyone could identify the faces pictured on their fliers and where they could be located. The situation was not organized—instead it was chaotic.

Garner had actually predicted this scenario and suggested that the money assigned for postwar efforts should be put into policing and justice contracts. The State Department and Justice Department could hire police and judicial advisers and have them ready, prepared, and on standby to go immediately to Iraq as soon as the Americans arrived. Unfortunately money was not allocated on time, contracts were not signed, and that is why some had to wait until mid-May 2003 before they could head for Baghdad. Included were U.S. Aid and State Department contracts relating to education, agriculture, infrastructure, and reconstruction specialists.

One other problem Garner faced was that there were not enough military forces allocated to escort both the ministerial and government teams around the offices of different ministries. They could move people around Baghdad only if there was an armed Humvee both in front and in back of each civilian vehicle. As there were between sixty and one hundred advisers to be ferried around each day, this was a huge security requirement, but it was necessary in order to get the government back on its feet in the immediate aftermath.

While it was true that the Pentagon was in charge of the Iraqi affairs, many of those supervising the program were from the

State Department, and some were staunch opponents of the INC-influenced Iraq Liberation Act. Among them was Tom Warrick, who, having been sacked from the Future of Iraq project, had succeeded in securing a position in the Coalition Provisional Authority. Warrick was responsible for changing the U.S. status in Iraq from a liberation force to an occupying force.

Chalabi's advisers claim that the CIA spent two hundred million dollars to prepare the ground for occupying the south of Iraq a few months before the war started. Many well-known Iraqi personalities were flown to the holy city of Najaf in anticipation of the uprising against the regime. Once American forces arrived on Iraqi soil, however, none of this happened. The satellite telephones and bags full of American dollars that were distributed among the heads of tribes as encouragement to do America's bidding failed to achieve the desired outcome.

One of those personalities to arrive in Najaf in early April was Abdul Majid Al Khoei, a moderate, forty-year-old Shia cleric who lived in North London. He traveled to Najaf on a British military flight, and after twelve years in exile, one of his first impressions on arrival was how shocked he was by the poverty he now witnessed—the result of long years of repression, sanctions, and now the war. Soon after his arrival, Al Khoei visited the golden-domed Grand Imam Ali Mosque, where he became worried about what appeared to be a mob heading his way. He was in the process of using his CIA-supplied Thurraya satellite phone to plead for help as the angry mob surrounded him. He was murdered in a frenzied knife and sword attack before he could help rebuild Iraq. The man America relied upon to influence the Shia in southern Iraq was now dead, and their reputation as a country that would protect its people was in ruins.

Paul Bremer made his entrance on May 12, 2003. It was rumored that Garner was fired because of a dispute between the State Department and the Pentagon. On his return to Washington, however, he denied this, saying that he was always under the impression that his job in Iraq would be for only a few months and that his mission had been, as he put it, "to put a team together, take it over there and hand it over to a presidential appointee, and that's what happened." It was a face-saving statement. All the months he and his team had spent preparing for the postwar situation had been overtaken in a matter of days with violence and anarchy that should have been predicted.

Paul Bremer's game plan was to restrict the power of the interim government and impose American legislation on the country. One of the laws he signed was to give the seven voting commission members of the Independent Electoral Commission of Iraq the authority to disqualify any political party or candidate from contesting in future elections.

Dr. Iyad Allawi, the first interim prime minister, found it difficult to overrule some of Bremer's decisions. When he tried to appoint a member of his close circle, Dr. Kasim Dawood, as national security adviser, he found that Bremer had already appointed Dr. Muaffac Al Rubai in the post for a five-year term and named Dawood as the minister responsible for security. Bremer installed inspector generals for five-year terms in every ministry. He regulated communications, public broadcasting, and securities markets. At a conference in Madrid, Spain, on the role of the private sector in the development of the new Iraq, the Coalition Provisional Authority described Iraq as "a uniquely attractive place to do business in the Middle East." After outlining the advantages, he described the oil-rich country as "rapidly recovering from the effects of the war and decades of under-investment" and promised, "When the recovery is over, the potential will be unleashed in the country's newly free markets." In September 2003 new foreign direct investment laws were signed, permitting foreign investors to own up to 100 percent of enterprises in all sectors apart from natural resources. "Profits, dividends, interest, and royalties may be fully remitted, land may not be bought but may be leased for up to forty years."[7] Defending his own policies, Bremer said that such decisions were necessary to jump-start democratic reforms before handing over complete sovereignty to an Iraqi government. The many decisions he has taken were defined by the Coalition Provisional Authority as "binding instructions or directives to the Iraqi people."

Many bureaucrats in both the State Department and the CIA feel they have won the battle against the neoconservatives. In fact, however, the neocons were chastened, not defeated. The unpredicted insurgency in Iraq has left them retreating to rethink some of the practical implications of their idealistic philosophy, but they have not given up their drive to deliver democracy to the Middle East, even if they have to resort to force, because they still believe this is the best long-term strategy to secure the future of America.

Corruption and mismanagement of Iraqi affairs in this interim period between April 2003 and June 2004 was rife. Billions of dollars that had been allocated for the purpose of putting Iraq on the road to recovery disappeared. There was an international outcry at the way lucrative reconstruction contracts seemed to favor those whose businesses helped bankroll George Bush's 2000 election campaign. One of those businesses was Halliburton Energy Services, the Texas-based U.S. oil services conglomerate that was awarded a two-billion-dollar government contract together with its subsidiary Kellogg, Brown and Root (KBR). Halliburton has given substantial amounts of money to the Republican Party, and the company's former chief executive was none other than Dick Cheney.

The FBI conducted an investigation into whether the Pentagon had behaved improperly by awarding no-bid contracts to U.S. companies such as Halliburton, which was additionally accused of overcharging taxpayers by sixty million dollars for fuel in Iraq. They also questioned whether the Bush administration showed favoritism toward Dick Cheney, the former vice president of the company, which could constitute a criminal act. During the last week of October 2004, FBI agents interviewed Mrs. Bunnatine ("Bunny") Greenhouse, the chief contracting officer for the Army Corps of Engineers, who had gone public the weekend before with an admission that her agency had unfairly awarded KBR a no-bid contract worth almost a billion dollars as part of the reconstruction effort in Iraq. Greenhouse's lawyer, Stephen Kohn, said that such investigations by the FBI should restore public confidence, and he called on the Pentagon to protect his client. FBI agents collected documents from army offices in Texas and elsewhere to examine how and why Halliburton got the contract. Although the Army Corps of Engineers was authorized to spend up to seven billion U.S. dollars for the oil restoration work, the actual money spent was only one-third of that.

The FBI investigations concluded that corruption was on a wide scale and that there were suggestions of commissions being paid into foreign and offshore bank accounts. Such corruption became a way of life in the fledgling stage of the new Iraq. Eight billion dollars was spent without proper accounting documentation, with contracts to rebuild infrastructure being agreed to at a hundred times more than the actual cost. Eight thousand names were registered to look after security in different ministries in Baghdad, but only 602 of them were bona fide salaried staff. The other names on the list were "ghost" employees. Another pointed example of financial mismanagement was the apparent cost of training police in neighboring countries. It was estimated that the cost of training each policeman in Jordan was forty thousand U.S. dollars. This is significantly higher than it would have cost to send a student for a full year of advanced studies at a prestigious Ivy League college. This suggests that commissions were involved that hiked up the official training costs.

Parking lots around the Green Zone in central Baghdad–which

houses the headquarters of the American forces and the American embassy—have become a well-known labor exchange, where individuals or small traders mingle with contractors to find a job or win a contract for cash. According to Franklin Willis, a former official of the Coalition Provisional Authority, huge cash payments were made to Iraqi contractors out of the back of pickup trucks in scenes reminiscent of the Wild West. Speaking at a Senate hearing on February 14, 2005, which was called by Senate Democrats, Willis showed photographs of himself and other U.S. officials holding plastic-wrapped bundles of one-hundred-dollar bills, totaling two million dollars, which he used to pay security contractor Custer Battles. "We told them to come in and bring a bag," Willis said, adding that "a combination of inexperienced officials, fear of decision-making, lack of communications, minimal security, no banks and lots of money to spend led to chaos." Former CPA head Paul Bremer, in Willis's defense, said it was wrong to assume that "Western-style budgeting and accounting procedures could be immediately and fully implemented in the midst of war.

According to the Custer Battles Web site: "Custer Battles wants its customers to understand the risks of doing business in difficult environments. The company provides security services, risk management consulting, and other services . . . [and] it has provided security services to companies and government agencies involved in reconstruction efforts in Iraq."[8] It appears that the CPA was taking financial risks by employing the Virginia-based company, as it has been charged in a lawsuit with defrauding the Coalition Provisional Authority of tens of millions of dollars during its work in Iraq. Frank Willis, once again giving evidence regarding charges of corruption, showed photographs of military contractors being handed two million dollars in shrink-wrapped hundred-dollar bills. Pratap Chatterjee, the director of the corporate accountability watchdog known as CorpWatch, gave some examples of Custer Battles's alleged fraud: "Charging $95,000 for a helicopter pad that they were supposed to build in Mosul, they billed $157,000 for it. And Mike Battles himself actually absent-mindedly left a piece of paper detailing how $3.74 million spent, had been billed as $9.8 million." The company was founded in 2001 by two former U.S. Army Rangers—Scott Custer, who tried to recruit mercenaries for work in Afghanistan, and Michael Battles, who was unsuccessful in his bid to run for Congress against Pat Kennedy in 2002.

On June 28, 2003, nearly eleven months before the start of Pentagon investigations on charges that coalition soldiers were looting homes and abusing their powers when they searched Iraqi homes or frisked civilians at checkpoints, I met the commander of the American-led forces in Iraq, General Ricardo Sanchez. I told him that civilians were accusing soldiers of robbing them of their valuables, both cash and jewelry. General Sanchez, surrounded by his bodyguards, shook his head in disbelief. But in a statement issued by the army's Criminal Investigation Command in Washington on May 30, 2004, they acknowledged they were investigating at least two dozen cases—eighteen thefts and six cases of assault against Iraqi civilians during raids, patrols, and house-to-house searches over the previous fifteen months. This low-level petty theft was fuel to fire the anger of the Iraqis.

If America had any serious intentions of pulling out in the near future, one would ask why they have occupied one of Saddam's most opulent palaces—the presidential palace—and expanded its territory far beyond the walls of the dictator's original architecture. Such symbolically expansionist behavior has stirred up local anger. Just as important to vehicle-dependent Baghdadis is their frustration at the huge traffic jams that snake around what has become the largest American embassy in the world, with a CIA post employing five hundred agents (also the largest of its kind in the world).

George W. Bush was apparently quietly impressed when he heard about the scale of the American embassy in Baghdad, and no doubt the irony of it being housed in one of Saddam's most magnificent palaces was not lost on him. With splendid views over the Tigris River, and stretching over five hundred acres, it must be the most prized piece of real estate the American government has ever possessed on foreign soil. It was and is a bizarre scene. Americans in camouflage uniforms and dusty boots can be seen treading over the imported marble floors, wandering through high-ceilinged rooms, and gazing up at endless crystal chandeliers. They tried to parse the Arabic phrases embroidered in gold on the marbled walls—in fact, these were lines from Saddam's poetry. They set up their barrack beds in Saddam's ornate, Italian-style VIP rooms and shaved in marble hand-basins with golden taps.

Iraq's infrastructure has almost collapsed since Saddam was overthrown. A friend of mine from Al Sadr City, a popular and well-known Shia-dominated suburb of Baghdad, told me that he and his neighbors frequently get together to discuss their deteriorating living conditions. They lived in crumbling tenements where the electricity would go out for hours a day, leaving them suffocating in the heat of 140 degrees. Water supplies came and went with no reliability. Employment too has suffered. The latest figures released on March 28, 2005, by the combined Ministries of Planning and Labor and Social Affairs indicate that unemployment for those over fifteen years old has risen to 28.1 percent for both sexes, amounting to 30.2 percent for men and 16 percent for women. Statistics compiled by the International Labor Organization put the figure at between one-quarter and one-third of the working-age population. Although there were no employment statistics taken during Saddam's time, nearly everyone capable of working had a job, albeit one that was poorly paid.

The United States deserves recognition for overthrowing the

Iraqi regime, and President George W. Bush should be given credit for insisting on holding the first elections in the new era on time as scheduled, but millions of people in the country are now living under a climate of terror and fear that is becoming dangerously out of control. The daily terrorist attacks taking place in Iraq are well orchestrated, and the contribution made by Baathists and previous regime officers in these attacks is considerable.

However vicious and murderous Saddam's regime was, under his iron rule there was virtually no crime—no burglaries, no rapes, no murders. Yet the lawless place that Baghdad has become has disconcerted the Iraqi population and undermined America's efforts to prove that life is better under democracy. "Under Saddam—and I'm not saying I support him here—but my wife could walk home any hour of day or night and I would know she was safe. Now I must accompany her even to the market to buy food, because I worry she might be kidnapped or worse. This has happened to women and girls in our neighborhood on many occasions." This was said by Ali Ribat, a thirty-year-old Baghdadi from an old Sunni family. While the Americans have been dealing with high politics, what they have neglected, partly because they live in isolation in the Green Zone, is that the daily life of many Iraqis had become much more difficult under their administration.

Bremer described the plan for the postwar period as having "erred in projecting what would happen after Hussein's demise, and focused on preparing for humanitarian relief and widespread refugee problems rather than the bloody insurgency war now being waged by at least four well-armed factions." Bremer's comments encouraged retired generals to speak out to express their concerns about troop strength. Prior to the war, the army chief of staff, General Eric K. Shinseki, advised that he thought the invasion plan lacked sufficient manpower, for which he was criticized by Pentagon officials.

After handing over political power from the CPA to the interim Governing Council on June 28, 2004, Bremer didn't take long to confess the frustrations he had faced in Iraq. In a speech at DePauw University, Indiana, on September 16, 2004, he said he had frequently raised with the administration the issue of insufficient troops and the difficulty of containing violence in the immediate aftermath of the liberation from Saddam, and felt that if he had been more insistent when his advice was spurned, the situation in Iraq might be different today. Elaborating on that theme at an insurance conference in White Sulphur Springs, West Virginia, on October 4, 2004, he said that "horrid looting" was occurring when he arrived to head the U.S.-led Coalition Provisional Authority and that "We paid a big price for not stopping it, because it established an atmosphere of lawlessness. We never had enough troops on the ground."

Bremer was recalled to Washington before many of his plans had been realized. It became clear that it would take at least three years to reach the stage of ratifying a constitution, and under the American vision the candidates who would write the constitution would be selected by the CPA. Grand Ayatollah Ali Sistani, the Shia religious leader, expressed anger about the length of time it would take to reach this stage and said that it was unacceptable for a constitution to be prepared by unelected actors. His outburst necessitated the intervention of Lakhdar Al Ibrahimi, the UN secretary general's special envoy to Iraq, and sent Washington into spin control to calm the troubled waters. Sistani finally accepted that elections should be held after a reasonable preparation period, while insisting that the unelected government that preceded it should not exert control over the future of the Iraqi state.

Before he served in Baghdad, one of the main concerns of Sir Jeremy Greenstock, who was Britain's special representative to Iraq from 2003 to 2004, was how to convince the Sunnis in Iraq that they too have a role to play in the Iraq of the future. After consultations with Bremer in Baghdad prior to his departure, a further meeting was held in Washington, where Sir Jeremy was joined by Colin Powell and British Foreign Secretary Jack Straw on November 19, 2003, to discuss what steps needed to be taken to ease the escalating violence, to pacify the Sunnis, and to encourage them to get involved in the political process.

I had the opportunity to chat with Sir Jeremy Greenstock at the Foreign and Commonwealth Office in London about his forthcoming mission to Baghdad a few days before he traveled to Baghdad on the inauspicious date of September 11, 2003. He was going as Britain's special representative to help, as he diplomatically put it, "the Americans through the rough weather and to offer independent advice." He talked about the importance of developing a political process that would end the occupation as soon as possible and leave Iraqis in charge of their own affairs. Greenstock, who is knowledgeable about both the region's complexities and its language and culture, realized that a different approach was needed to tackle the problem.

Unlike former Ambassador Bremer, Sir Jeremy Greenstock was well equipped to deal with problems arising from having an occupying force in the country. In an article in *The Economist* on May 6, 2004, he outlined his vision of change: "The return of power into Iraqi hands as soon as made sense; no Saddam or Saddam clones in government; no irresolvable inter-communal tensions; established individual and minority rights; minimum corruption and incompetence; and restored services." He continued: "The principles on which Paul Bremer worked, as chief administrator in Iraq, were entirely compatible with the outline I have described. We had clear ideas on the next stages. They had to be adjusted as snags arose, but this was skillfully done; and they were underpinned with a whole range of practical improvements to the Iraqi infrastructure. After a shaky start and some semi-admitted mistakes, we felt we were going somewhere."

Greenstock was faintly amused when I said that the media under the CPA was run in a similar way to how Saddam Hussein and his revolutionary command used to run the *Al Thawra* newspaper, the mouthpiece of his regime. *Al Sabah,* the CPA-funded newspaper, used to have Bremer's picture on its front page, just as Saddam used to. They would also make a fanfare out of reporting that they had fixed a light in one of the suburbs. This became farcical at a time when the whole country was in darkness because of the CPA's failure to restore even basic services such as the electricity supply.

Bremer's final departure from Iraq was without pomp and ceremony. The American administrator chose to avoid any unpleasant surprises, which the insurgents had promised during his official handing over ceremony, and quietly departed two days earlier than the planned date of May 30, 2003. Very few members of the Governing Council attended his leaving, because they hadn't been told about the change in the schedule. Just prior to leaving Iraq, Bremer met with the council and asked what future plans they envisaged for their country. I was later told by one of those present that a fellow council member replied with a hint of mischief, "After your de-Baathification policy, we will work hard on our de-Bremerization policy!"

Sir Jeremy decided that the best solution would be to negotiate with all the tribal leaders in the main center of unrest and violence in Iraq, the Sunni Triangle, and try to convince them to put their weapons aside and to take part in the political process. Equally important was to persuade them to allow the coalition into their areas to carry out vital infrastructure reconstruction work to restore electricity, sanitation, and water supplies. The reconstruction would have the added benefit of requiring a workforce, thus creating more jobs for the tens of thousands who became unemployed when the army and the police force were dissolved. Sir Jeremy began a series of meetings with tribal elders, which he attended personally or mediated through his deputies. Some of the meetings were held in neighboring countries such as Jordan, Syria, and as far as Saudi Arabia in order to communicate with sheikhs in the extended branches of their tribes.

Lakhdar Al Ibrahimi, Kofi Annan's special envoy to Baghdad, who found himself working alongside Bremer, arrived in Iraq in February 2004 to investigate the logistics for arranging a general election. He didn't mince words when he described Paul Bremer as a dictator in response to the U.S.-appointed Governing Council's announcement that it had selected Dr. Iyad Allawi as the new prime minister. When asked by reporters what role the Americans played in forming the new government and selecting the president, Al Ibrahimi's reply was crisp and clear: "Ambassador Bremer runs things in Iraq. Bremer is the dictator of Iraq. He has the money. He has the signature."

The mother of all catastrophes in Iraq's postwar history has to be Paul Bremer's de-Baathification policy. There were more than a million members of the Baath Party in the country when Saddam Hussein lost his grip of power to the American coalition forces. In May 2003 Bremer issued a directive banning the party, and all high-ranking members from the top four levels of its structure, from occupying any government or state post. The havoc this caused countrywide has been blamed for much of the growing anarchy that is now destabilizing the country. The number of Baathists subsequently killed on the streets of Baghdad was beyond imagination. During the two years after the end of the war, not a day passed without dozens of Saddam's party faithful being found murdered and their bodies disposed of as if they were rubbish. Much of this was the result of old scores being settled. However, Bremer and his CPA turned a blind eye to what was happening, which has culminated in the creation of a new terrorist army, for which everyone in the country is now paying the price. One of my confidantes told me about a meeting she attended with Bremer. Her father had been assassinated at the hands of the Baathists, and she told Bremer, "I know who killed my father, so why don't you do something about them or bring them to justice?" She said that Bremer answered her in such a way that she understood he was encouraging her to go and get rid of them herself. When she asked why, he responded by saying, "Do you want me to go and kill them for you myself?"

If the history of the Iraqi Baath Party is inextricably linked to and tarnished by Saddam, it is also vital to remember it as a political movement. Despite calls from Shia political leaders, including Ahmed Chalabi, to prevent the former Baath Party from regaining power, its story may not be over. While countless top-level Baathists were killed or captured in 2003, many high-ranking, efficient, and extremely organized members have reemerged whose military prowess has proved pivotal. They have emerged from their beleaguered position, drawing strength from the antioccupation sentiment, especially within the Sunni population. They have joined ranks with Islamist militants, including Zarqawi's Al Qaeda affiliates, carrying out ferocious attacks against both the America-led coalition forces and Iraqi security forces and police. They remain politically unscathed, in the shadows, and a force to be reckoned with.

NOTES

1. As recalled by Marie Colvin, *Sunday Times* (London), in an interview with the author, June 6, 2005.

2. Richard Perle, et al., "A Clean Break: A New Strategy for Securing the Realm," Institute for Advanced Strategic and Political Studies' "Study Group on a New Israeli Strategy toward 2000," Washington, DC, 1996.

3. Entifadh Qanbar to author during a series of interviews held in London in the first half of 2005.

4. Jay Garner, interview on *Frontline,* July 17, 2003.

5. "Preparing for Post-Saddam Iraq: Plans and Actions," Security Studies Program Seminar Paper given by Charles Patterson, retired colonel from office, October 27, 2004.

6. Pachachi served as Iraqi foreign minister and ambassador to the United Nations before the Baathists seized power in 1968.

7. "Why Invest in Iraq," released by the Coalition Provisional Authority, U.S. State Department, at the "Conference on the Role of the Private Sector in the Development of the New Iraq," Madrid, Spain, October 23, 2003.

8. See www.custerbattles.com.

CHAPTER FOUR

THE MORAL LOW GROUND

The small farming hamlet of Abu Ghraib lies twenty miles west of Baghdad. Its name derives from the willow trees that thrived in its marshy landscape during the Ottoman Empire. This graceful tree, symbolizing grief, is still planted in the burial grounds. However, since 2003 the name Abu Ghraib has become synonymous with a different type of grief and sorrow. One of the world's most malevolent prisons—a 3.5 million-square-meter compound overlooked by twenty-four castellated watchtowers—now casts its shadow over the surrounding fields, palm, and willow trees.

It was from this prison that an Iraqi woman cut a small lock of hair and sent it to the head of her tribe, accompanied by a letter appealing for help: "Save us! Our bellies are swollen with child. We are pleading with you to burn down and destroy this prison because of the torture that is happening to us here. This abuse has damaged our pride as women and as Iraqis."[1]

It takes great courage for a woman who has been raped and is pregnant to appeal for help from a male tribal leader in Iraq's conservative society. The penalty of bringing "dishonor" to your family and tribe is likely to result in death.

This appeal for help was not sent from Abu Ghraib during Saddam Hussein's era, however. It was sent in early 2004, when Abu Ghraib was being run by the American Coalition Provisional Authority. Salah Al Nasrawi, an Iraqi writer who had been a visitor to the prison during Saddam Hussein's regime, told me: "It was the hope of every Iraqi after the fall of the regime that the symbol of dictatorship and torture would be totally demolished, and the shocking memories it evokes would vanish with it." Far from vanishing, this symbol of inhumanity has morphed into another grotesque form. Under American control, Abu Ghraib has come to symbolize a new era of humiliation and abuse.

No one would have believed what occurred were it not for a series of graphic and degrading photographs that were shown around the world. They revealed both the nature and scale of the abuse–not just at Abu Ghraib, but in many of the American- and British-run prisons in Iraq. Once the horrifying pictures had been shown by the world's press, American officials were forced to admit that they were just the tip of the iceberg. There were over two thousand more disturbing photographs, some of which showed women being raped or forced to undress. These images, which were suppressed by the Defense Department, were finally shown to members of the Senate in a confidential session held on May 12, 2004. One hundred senators were invited to crowd into Room S-407 in the U.S. Capitol to view the pictures that Pentagon officials delivered to the Senate. The lawmakers viewed them in a wood-panelled, windowless room on the fourth floor, where electronic equipment is barred, a combination lock secures the door, and a Capitol police officer performs sentry duty outside.

Trying to get an accurate figure for the numbers of Iraqi men and women imprisoned behind the solid concrete walls of Abu Ghraib prison during Saddam's brutal rule is almost impossible. Estimates suggest that as many as fifteen thousand prisoners at a time were crushed into a space originally built to contain forty-six hundred inmates. Prisoners were subjected to sadistic torture and execution by Saddam's *mukhabarat* and the elite Republican Guard.

A prison guard who worked at Abu Ghraib during Saddam's time recalled that executions were scheduled every Wednesday, and the president himself signed the execution orders. Other gruesome punishments, such as cutting off ears, were meted out to soldiers and officers who had been caught trying to escape military service. Likewise, tongues were removed from political prisoners who had dared to speak out against the regime. According to a 2001 Amnesty International report, "Victims of torture in Iraq are subjected to a wide range of forms of torture, including gouging out of eyes, severe beatings and electric shocks . . . some victims have died as a result and many have been left with permanent physical and psychological damage."

British and Dutch contractors built the penitentiary to replace the former principal prison—Baab Al Mouadam in Baghdad. The decision to build a new and larger prison was made by the Iraqi Economic Planning Council in March 1964. Although it wasn't officially opened until 1970, according to Hamid Faraj, the head of the Committee for Political Prisoners—who referred to Abu Ghraib as "the Bastille of Iraq"—the first political prisoners were taken there after the coup that brought the Baath Party to power in 1968.

The prison was divided into five separate compounds, including one to house prisoners serving less than a five-year sentence, one for long-term sentences, and one for political prisoners who were communists, nationalists, or Baath dissidents. Shiites who belonged to the ultraconservative Al Da'awa Party or who were accused of sympathizing with its ideologies were summarily executed. Of the remaining two compounds, one had specially designed cells for those in solitary confinement, and the final one was for those being held on bail. Farmers from the Abu Ghraib hamlet recall the long lines of mothers and fathers, brothers and sisters who would stand perspiring under the intense summer sun, or shiver in the harsh cold winters while waiting for clearance to visit their loved ones behind bars.

Saddam released most of Abu Ghraib's prisoners in a general amnesty during the buildup to the war. Only political opponents to his regime remained under lock and key. The moment the regime was toppled, the prison was subjected to the same spontaneous frenzied looting that erupted throughout the rest of the country, and grim stories soon emerged. The local mosque organized a team of volunteers to uncover the mounds of dirt piled up against the former political wing of the prison. Inside the dark, concrete-walled rooms they found the ashes of prison documents that had been burned by guards who were trying to eliminate incriminating evidence before they fled. Outside, under the shadow of those cold buildings, the voluntary digging crew uncovered the hastily buried bodies of prisoner after prisoner after prisoner. A witness to the scene claimed he saw the bodies of ten people unearthed, all of whom had been shot in the back of the head, their bodies still in prison uniform. A few of the dead had handwritten notes stuffed into their prison shirt pockets that revealed their scribbled names. Others had no documents to suggest their identity. In one bizarre case, a man's dentures, which presumably had been carefully removed before he was shot, were found in his top pocket. When one of the diggers attempted to throw them away, assuming they were worthless, he was told to replace them in case the man could be identified by his false teeth.

Abu Ghraib would see more horrors in the future, but on that day, when Iraqis came to witness the exhumed cells, many broke down in tears when they caught sight of the large ropes fashioned with a hangman's noose suspended from the high ceilings. On the floor below each rope were the trapdoors. Former prisoners among the watching crowd recalled that hangings were scheduled around the clock on Tuesdays and Thursdays.

Previous detainees asked the coalition and the interim government to convert the prison into a memorial to the Iraqis who had suffered at Abu Ghraib, a symbol of a dictatorship that had executed hundreds and locked up tens of thousands more. But the Americans decided that this was not the time for memorializing. A team of U.S. prison experts was dispatched to convert Saddam's former torture chamber into a modern, American-style prison. This was done virtually from scratch. Lane McCotter, a controversial executive of an American private prison company, was contracted to construct the new Abu Ghraib.[2] Comparing it with other prisons in Iraq, he described it as "the only place we agreed as a team was truly closest to an American prison." McCotter set about rebuilding the prison—everything from walls and toilets to handcuffs and soap. He employed one hundred Iraqis who had previously worked there under Saddam Hussein, and paid for everything with wads of cash, up to three million dollars that he carried with him.

Formally known as the Baghdad Central Confinement Facility, the new Abu Ghraib was visited by a delegation of Iraqi female lawyers in March 2004. They met a small number of imprisoned women, who recounted appalling stories of rape and humiliation at the hands of their American guards. Some of the women said they were so traumatized by what they had been through, they would rather die than return to their families dishonored. One woman, the wife of a Baathist, told the female delegates that when soldiers asked her to undress, the Iraqi translator who was with them closed his eyes in shame. Many women were raped in their cells at night. Most of them were either married to, or were sisters of, insurgency members or ex-Baathists. Their incarceration was intended to force husbands out of hiding, or pressure wives or sisters to disclose information that would lead to their arrest.

The number of women raped by American forces in Abu Ghraib jail has for the most part gone unreported. Iman Khamas, director of the nongovernmental organization (NGO) known as the International Observatory Center for the Occupation, confirmed stories of so-called honor killings of three former women prisoners from the Al Anbar province. Members of their own families murdered the women after they were discovered to be pregnant as a result of their treatment in prison. Khamas also described the case of an ex-prisoner whom she simply calls "B," who was returned to her cell after being raped seventeen times in one day by Iraqi police in the presence of American soldiers.

Huda Al Naemie, a human rights activist and professor in the Department of Political Science at Baghdad University, repeated similar stories.[3] She told of an educated young man she had come across who told her how tortured he was feeling about his sister, who had just been released from Abu Ghraib prison and was pregnant. She came to him in tears of shame, explaining that American soldiers had raped her in front of a male Iraqi prisoner, and she asked her brother to kill her. He was so troubled, he sought advice from a religious sheikh, who advised against honor killing. Huda was unable to track down the young man again to follow up on what eventually happened to his sister. She alerted various human rights organizations as information about similar cases started filtering in on a regular basis. She described another incident where she was confided in by one of her own colleagues at the university—an economics professor who had been raped by U.S. soldiers in Abu Ghraib prison in front of other prisoners. The professor told Huda how thankful she was to have had the support of her family after they sought advice from a religious family friend, who had advised that she should be allowed to live.

There is no such concept in Islam that is called "honor killing." Islam holds every person in high esteem and does not permit people to take the law into their own hands. According to the Holy Koran, Islam maintains the protection of life and does not sanction any violation against it: "Whoso slayeth a believer of set purpose, his reward is hell for ever. Allah is wroth against him and He hath cursed him and prepared for him an awful doom" (An-Nisa: 93).

A social worker at the Iraqi Ministry of Justice, Rafida Shalal Al Jobouri, described two further dehumanizing acts at the jail.[4] Huda, the wife of an Iraqi judge, and her sister, who lived in Al Adamiyeh, a Sunni suburb of Baghdad, left their home to look for Huda's son, who had been taking part in a peaceful demonstration against American forces in a nearby street. American soldiers, who didn't believe their story, arrested and raped both women. In another incident, an eighteen-year-old woman from Fallujah was arrested on the night of her wedding and taken to Abu Ghraib. She, too, was violated, and upon her release she pleaded with male members of her family to kill her. They did so two days later. All of these incidents add up to more than a few isolated cases of rape at Abu Ghraib. Dr. Muthana Harith Al Dari, spokesman for the Committee of Islamic Scholars in Iraq, stated that the committee had received many letters from female prisoners confirming that women were committing suicide after being raped. Dari confirmed that the committee is compiling information about the mistreatment of prisoners in Abu Ghraib to be used in a war crimes tribunal at a later stage.

An elderly Iraqi woman in her seventies was arrested in July 2003 and accused of having links to a former member of Saddam Hussein's regime—a charge that the woman, who wished to remain anonymous, denied. She claimed she was mistreated in a Baghdad detention center next to Baghdad Airport that is under the same command center as Abu Ghraib. Anne Clwyd, Tony

Blair's human rights envoy to Iraq, has been pursuing her case. In an interview, Clwyd related how the Iraqi woman described having a donkey harness placed on her and being forced to the floor on all fours, where an American prison guard then "rode" her like a donkey. Clwyd immediately informed U.S. generals, who were "shocked" when she gave them the details.[5]

* * *

The graphic and sexually explicit photographs that focused the world's attention on the sadistic and brutal behavior that was taking place in the American-run prison came to light when they were aired by CBS television on their *60 Minutes II* program on April 28, 2004, and published alongside an article by Seymour Hersh in *The New Yorker*. The photographs revealed that sexual torture was being directed toward both male and female inmates. I have spoken to some of the victims who appear in the now infamous photographs, and the experience has left them with a deep and collective feeling of degradation and humiliation. The sexual nature of the torture is more shocking and insulting to Muslims than the physical torture such as electric shock treatment or beatings. Homosexual acts are against Islamic law, and it is *haram* for men to be seen naked in front of other men.[6] Many of the prisoners I tried to talk to were too ashamed to tell me what happened to them. Such feelings of fear and shame will no doubt remain with them for the rest of their lives.

There are broader implications, too. The photographs of the abuse enforce the Arab perception of the nature of contemporary culture that America and its allies wish to impose upon them. It is not just Islamic fundamentalists who find such displays of sexuality and lack of moral values abhorrent. Iraqi society in general is conservative, and its citizens are truly shocked by what they interpret as lewd and decadent behavior of Western society.

An Iraqi cameraman working for Al Jazeera television was arrested while filming in Samarra, about seventy-five miles north of Baghdad. Early one October morning in 2003, Sohaib Badr El Din Al Baz was on his way to film at Samarra Hospital. American soldiers, recognizing that he worked for the controversial Arab satellite station, arrested him, covered his head with a plastic bag, tied his hands behind his back, and led him to the American base nearby. At ten o'clock the same morning, an American officer who had come to interrogate him said, "Some military personnel respect the media, but I hold no respect for any of you." During questioning the officer accused the twenty-six-year-old of assisting the insurgents. He was then beaten, as the officer accused him and his TV channel of knowing in advance when an insurgency attack was going to happen. Sohaib went on to describe his experience: "It was the Holy month of Ramadan, and I asked if they would allow me to pray. The officer's reply was to put two fingers in my eyes and pushed my head towards the wall, warning me that I would never be set free again and I would be taken to Guantanamo Bay. He told me to forget all about Al Jazeera and my future.

"This went on for two days, during which I was constantly beaten and subjected to different kinds of torture. I was then taken to the military base near Baghdad International Airport, where I stayed for two days with my head covered by a plastic hood. Often soldiers would put their guns to my head and threatened to shoot me. I was in constant pain from the frequent blows I received to my body and from having my head knocked against the walls. Finally I ended up in Abu Ghraib, where I was subjected to similar experiences, which have now been seen by the world. I was asked many times to strip. When I stopped half-naked, they would kick me. There were so many soldiers that I had no option but to undress fully. It was winter and I could not sleep at night it was so very cold, and for thirty-five days I wasn't allowed to take a shower. I could hear other prisoners crying in pain. I saw an old man and his young son being tortured together and forced to undress in front of one another while they were beaten by the soldiers. I felt humiliated for the son when he was ordered to put on female underwear. I was then moved to another tent, in which there were more than forty prisoners. One of them was about to die. He was in real pain, but when we informed the guard about the seriousness of his situation, they told us to wait until the morning. Not long after his cry for help, the man was dead."[7]

The tent he was referring to was part of a tented camp on the grounds of Abu Ghraib that was known as Camp Ganci. In May 2004 its name was changed to Camp Redemption at the request of the Iraqi Governing Council.[8]

Nabil Shaker, who was arrested in July 2003 and sentenced to seven months in jail after being caught robbing a bank, claimed to have witnessed an American male soldier sleeping with an Iraqi female prisoner on a regular basis. In a subsequent report ordered by the U.S. military in Iraq to investigate abuse and torture at the jail, the chief investigator listed "A male MP [Military Police] guard having sex with a female detainee" as one of the "intentional abuses of detainees by military police personnel."[9] These violations against men and women prisoners led to demonstrations and pickets in front of the prison organized by the Islamic Party, who called on the authorities responsible to release all the women for the sexual abuse they had undergone.

The infamous photograph of a line of naked men, plastic hoods over their heads in the presence of a mocking, female U.S. soldier was among the hundreds of sickening images to emerge from Abu Ghraib. Haider Saber Al Abbadi was one of the six men photographed. Haider, who was thirty-six years old, had been a corporal in the Iraqi army before it was dissolved. Ironically, he was tortured and imprisoned many times because of his family's opposition to Saddam's regime and his own absence from his military unit. His arrest by American soldiers occurred during a trip to Baghdad to pick up some official military documents. His driver, a local man, had the misfortune of owning a make of car similar to those that were favored by insurgents in suicide attacks. His car was pulled over by soldiers at an American checkpoint in July 2003. Both men were arrested, because the driver had neither documents to prove ownership of his car nor his personal identity card. Haider spent three months in a jail called Camp Bucca, in the south of the country, before being transferred to the notorious Abu Ghraib.

While at Abu Ghraib, Haider endured sexual torture and humiliation at the hands of his American guards. "I was standing towards the left in that photograph where the female American soldier [cigarette dangling from her mouth and grinning] was pointing at our naked bodies with her finger." Haider said he recognized her from the brief time he was allowed to remove the hood from his head. The soldier to whom he referred was Private First Class Lynndie England from Fort Ashby, West Virginia, who became the face that scandalized the American army. "That awful day we were dragged to a bigger space, where we were beaten by the soldiers when we refused to perform sexual acts. Cold water was poured over us, and we were threatened with a knife. They made us form a kind of human pyramid. I was made to sit on the shoulder of one of the prisoners. The female soldier—we used to call her Miss Maya—tried to make me masturbate while she was pressing on her breast." When Haider refused, he was beaten again and forced to follow the soldiers' instructions. "The soldiers were laughing, but I was shaking. They were dragging us around like animals."

Haider was still traumatized when I spoke to him after his release in June 2004 in Baghdad. When he wasn't chain-smoking, he was nervously wringing his hands, and the embarrassment he felt just talking about his ordeal was painful to watch. On several occasions he was ordered by U.S. soldiers guarding the prison to undress. His hands were then tied to the door handles of his cell while an enforced sexual act took place. After these episodes, Haider and the six other men who were photographed with him were taken to a solitary confinement cell for twenty-five days before they were allowed to return to the main prison. In January 2004, U.S. investigators came to the prison to show him sixty photographs that the guards had taken, to confirm that he was one of the victims. Haider was finally released on April 15, 2004, after enduring six months in Abu Ghraib.

Intelligence officers and an Egyptian translator were present during some of these incidents. Haider also said that he was conscious of being photographed, as he could sense the camera flash through his hood. "I was so ashamed of the footage, which was broadcast worldwide. I felt everyone knew me. For weeks I didn't leave my house. In the end, I had to move from Al Nassiriyah, where I grew up, to somewhere where no-one would recognise me. . . . Whatever happens to these soldiers, it will not give me back my dignity. Who will return this respect to me? My honour has been crushed underfoot."

"Miss Maya," otherwise known as PFC Lynndie England, was charged by a military court in May 2004.[10] She was accused of "assaulting Iraqi detainees on multiple occasions; conspiring with another soldier, CPS Charles Graner, to mistreat prisoners, committing an indecent act and committing acts that were prejudicial to good order and discipline and were of a nature to bring discredit upon the armed forces through her mistreatment of Iraqi detainees." England was reassigned from Iraq to a military police unit at Fort Bragg, California.

The whistle-blower who finally brought the disgraceful behavior to light was Army Specialist Joseph Darby, a twenty-four-year-old from Pennsylvania who was a reserve soldier from Unit 372 Military

Police Company. Darby was chatting to his friend Charles Graner, one of the much-photographed, alleged ringleaders of the abuses, shortly after Thanksgiving leave in early December 2003. Graner gave Darby three computer disks containing the graphic images the world has now seen. According to Special Agent Bobeck of the Army's Criminal Investigation Division at a court hearing, Darby claimed after viewing the sexually explicit photographs, "Initially, I was kind of shocked and bewildered, and I didn't know what to do." In January 2004 he wrote an anonymous letter describing what he had seen and passed it under his unit commander's door. "He felt very bad about it and thought it was very wrong," Bobeck recalls. Darby, testifying via a speakerphone said, "It's a hard call to make a decision to put your friends in prison." He claimed that Graner had told him, "The Christian in me knows it was wrong, but the corrections officer in me can't help but want to make a grown man piss himself." Darby has since been promoted to sergeant. Charles Graner was sentenced to ten years in a military prison. Donald Rumsfeld, in his testimony before Congress, congratulated Darby for his "honorable actions," saying, "There are many who did their duty professionally. Specialist Joseph Darby alerted the authorities that abuse was occurring."[11]

The scandal reached fever pitch on January 19, 2004, when Lieutenant General Ricardo S. Sanchez, commander of the Combined Joint Task Force Seven, ordered an investigation into the detention and internment operations at the prison. The investigation was carried out by Major General Antonio M. Taguba, and his fifty-three-page report, marked "Secret/No Foreign Dissemination," disclosed numerous "sadistic, blatant and wanton criminal abuses" that have proved to be a gross embarrassment for the Pentagon and the White House. Taguba is the second-highest-ranking Filipino-American officer in the U.S. Army, and is the son of Thomas Taguba, an army sergeant who was taken prisoner by the Japanese during the Battle of Bataan in World War II.

Taguba's report itemized a litany of torture methods used in the prison: "breaking chemical lights and pouring the phosphoric liquid on detainees, pouring cold water on naked detainees, beating detainees with a broom handle and chair, threatening male detainees with rape, allowing a military police guard to stitch the wound of a detainee who was injured after being slammed against the wall in his cell, sodomizing a detainee with a chemical light and perhaps a broom stick, and using military working dogs to frighten and intimidate detainees with threats of attack, and in one instance actually biting a detainee." The detailed investigation led Taguba to conclude: "This systemic and illegal abuse of detainees was intentionally perpetrated by several members of the military police guard force."[12]

America's chief jailer in Iraq was Brigadier General Janis Karpinski, who took over command of the sixteen military prisons and correctional facilities throughout Iraq–including Abu Ghraib–on June 30, 2003. Karpinski had cherished a life-long ambition to be a soldier, and after serving in the Gulf War in 1991, she remained in the Arab Emirates as an adviser for developing women's military training programmes. She had no previous experience with running a jail. General Taguba's report recommended that Karpinski should be "Relieved from Command and given a General Officer Memorandum of Reprimand." Taguba then cites eleven failings on her part, including: "Failing to ensure that MP [Military Police] soldiers in the 800th MP Brigade knew, understood, and adhered to the protections afforded to detainees in the Geneva Convention Relative to the Treatment of Prisoners of War."[13] Karpinski, addressing the Commonwealth Public Affairs Forum in San Francisco on April 8, 2005, said in defense of her soldiers: "I don't think any of them had a fair opportunity. I will never change my position on that. . . . I guarantee you that none of those soldiers knew enough about the Arab culture to be able to say this is the right thing that we should do. Somebody who was very familiar with what would work told them how to do those things."[14] General Karpinski has been suspended from her command and is writing a book on Abu Ghraib.

Although Brigadier General Karpinski has taken the rap for the catalogue of abuses at the U.S. prison facilities in Iraq, there were others, equally culpable, who were flagged by General Taguba's report. Taguba refers to a private company called CACI International, Inc., that was contracted by the Pentagon to carry out interrogation and what military commentators call "torture-lite." Taguba identifies Steven Staphanovic and John Israel, both from CACI, as being involved in the abuses. CACI–pronounced "khaki" in military parlance–is thought to have military links with Israel, and one of Staphonovic's coworkers, Joe Ryan, who was not named in the Taguba report, now says that he underwent an "Israeli interrogation course" before going to Iraq.[15] General Karpinski alluded to this in an interview she gave after she was suspended: "I saw an individual there that I hadn't had the opportunity to meet before and I asked him what did he do there, was he an interpreter–he was clearly from the Middle East. He said, 'Well, I do some of the interrogation here, I speak Arabic but I'm not an Arab, I'm from Israel.'"[16]

The Israeli Defense Force has sent urban warfare specialists to Fort Bragg in North Carolina, the home of U.S. Special Forces, and according to two sources, "Israeli military consultants" have also visited Iraq.[17] Brigadier General Michael Vane mentioned the cooperation with Israel in a letter to an army magazine in July 2003 about the Iraqi counter-insurgency campaign.[18] "We recently travelled to Israel to glean lessons learned from their counter-terrorist operations in urban areas."

It appears that Washington had been given several clues that all was not well in America's prisons in Iraq. A spokesperson for the International Committee for the Red Cross in Geneva announced in a TV interview broadcast in Germany that the president of its organization, Jakob Kellenberger, had gone to Washington in January 2004 to alert the U.S. government about the mistreatment of prisoners held by the Americans.[19] He met with key members of the U.S. administration: Foreign Secretary Colin Powell; his deputy, Donald Rumsfeld; Deputy Secretary of Defense Paul Wolfowitz; and Condoleezza Rice, the national security adviser. The same German TV station disclosed sections of the ICRC report that were shown to the high-powered foursome indicating that "prisoners were being badly treated and tortured."

The report was leaked to the public via the *Wall Street Journal* on May 6, 2004, without the consent of the ICRC. The organization defended criticisms from the media about its failure to disclose earlier the information it had about torture in Iraqi prisons, saying: "The preparation and submission of such (confidential) reports is part of the ICRC's standard procedures in the field of its visits to prisoners worldwide. . . . This notion of confidentiality is an element vital to obtaining access to prisoners worldwide, and that access is in turn essential for us to carry out meaningful work for the persons detained."[20] The report itself was handed over to the coalition forces in February of 2004.

Coalition forces military intelligence officers cited in the Red Cross report claimed: "Between 70% and 90% of the persons deprived of their liberty in Iraq had been arrested by mistake."[21] Very few of the prisoners had committed serious crimes. They were there either because of a tip-off by someone trying to settle old scores, for crimes related to driving offenses, or for failing to carry identification papers. Others were held because they were a relative of someone suspected of having connections with insurgents or a leading Baathist, or they just happened to be in the wrong place at the wrong time. The report attributed the brutality of some arrests to the lack of proper supervision of battle group units. It also highlighted the dismal conditions in the jail. U.S.

officers mistreated inmates by keeping them naked in totally dark, empty cells, and abuse of Iraqi prisoners was "widespread and routine," contrary to President Bush's contention that the mistreatment "was the wrongdoing of a few." The twenty-four-page document describes "serious violations of international humanitarian law" and cites abuses, some "tantamount to torture," including hooding, brutality, humiliation, and threats of "execution." "These methods of physical and psychological coercion were used by military intelligence in a systematic way to gain confessions and extract information and other forms of cooperation from persons who had been arrested in connection with suspected security offences or deemed to have an 'intelligence value.'"

In other parts of the Arab world–including Syria, Egypt, and Algeria–such methods to extract intelligence information have long been denounced by human rights organizations. The disclosures have put the United States on a par with those regimes, and the U.S. State Department has been accused of not complying with Geneva Conventions and its rules on human rights. The damage this has done to American policy was described by Monah Al Solh, a Lebanese intellectual, as "extremely serious because it is totally out of line with the type of freedom and democracy which the United States is trying to promote in this part of the world." The director of the Arab Institute for Human Rights in the Qatari capital, Doha, Abdul Baset Hassan, said he hoped what went on in Abu Ghraib "would serve as a lesson for these soldiers, and I hope that American soldiers will now be educated on how to respect human rights." The Grand Mufti of Egypt, Sheikh Ali Gumaa, was also quick to voice his outrage. He condemned the treatment of Iraqi prisoners by American soldiers as "the work of a powerful occupier and superpower who has no respect for either international law or the rules governing humanity."[22]

The psychological effects of the abuse and torture on prisoners are a concern of many human rights organizations. Douglas A.

Johnson, executive director of the Center for Victims of Torture, testified to the Congressional Human Rights Caucus on June 23, 2004: "What happened in Iraq was most definitely torture. To label the acts as mistreatment, abuse or a prison scandal seriously misrepresents the gravity of crimes committed." He went on to say: "The common misperception is that torture is only a physical act. But throughout history, as torture has used the body as a weapon against the mind, the actual objective of the pain, humiliation and fear has been to produce long-term damage to the victim's personality. . . . We must work together to remove this black stain from our flag and from our souls. Torture is the most effective weapon against democracy."

The Abu Ghraib scandal permanently tarnished the image and reputation of the United States. President Bush, in what has been described as a damage-limitation exercise, addressed an Arab audience in two separate interviews given on May 5, 2004. One was broadcast by the Saudi-financed Al Arabiya satellite TV station, and the other to Al Hurra, which is based in Washington: "First I want to tell the people of the Middle East that the practices that took place in that prison are abhorrent and they don't represent America. They represent the actions of a few people. . . . Our citizens in America are appalled by what they saw, just like people in the Middle East are appalled. We share the same deep concerns. And we will find the truth, we will fully investigate. The world will see the investigation and justice will be served."[23]

Commenting on the broadcast, an Iraqi from Tikrit complained to me that there had been no clear apology from President Bush for the "abhorrent practices." But what Iraqis found more surprising was that while Arab human rights organizations were quick to condemn, there was no comment from at least fifty of Iraq's political parties. Other Arab governments were silent, too. These governments are guilty of routine acts of torture themselves, but this does not excuse their reticence in speaking out.

What is more likely is they didn't want to anger their American supporters. A Baghdadi summarized his feelings to me as one of "deep humiliation and disrespect. You can witness this for yourself when you are stopped at the checkpoints to be searched. They [the Americans] have no respect for old or young, male or female. This is not the freedom and democracy we were promised in the days and months before the fall of the regime. Saddam was a brutal dictator, and his *mukhabarat* used worse practices than this, but even they were ashamed to talk about it. They at least kept it secret and did not film or photograph it."

Arab public opinion seems united in its prediction that the behavior displayed by the Americans in Abu Ghraib prison and elsewhere will swell the ranks of the resistance groups. These scenes of torture will be imprinted on the Arab psyche for decades, and the enemies of the United States will continue to use it against Washington and its policies.

* * *

While the ICRC claimed it had alerted the U.S. government to the misdeeds of its soldiers in January 2004, Amnesty International added to the controversy by saying it too had given warnings about Iraqi deaths and torture occurring in the custody of coalition forces, both to the Pentagon and the British Ministry of Defense. This was before another set of photographs were released, this time taken at a British-run facility called Camp Bread Basket in Basra. One of the photographs showed an Iraqi man suspended in the air by a rope attached to a forklift truck. Another showed a trussed-up prisoner cowering as a soldier appeared to be in the process of landing him a punch. Others showed two naked prisoners appearing to simulate sex. These photos were discovered after Gary Bartlam, a private in First Battalion Regiment of Fusiliers, handed in some film for processing at a local photo-developing shop in Tamworth,

Staffordshire, after returning from duty in Iraq. The photographic staff alerted the police, and as a result, Bartlam, one of the youngest soldiers to serve in Iraq, was arrested together with four other soldiers from his unit. He was eventually sentenced to eighteen months in a youth detention center and dishonorably discharged from the army.

In the face of a growing outcry by the British public, British Prime Minister Tony Blair issued a qualified apology to Iraqi prisoners who had been mistreated by British forces. Blair expressed regret at claims that soldiers beat and humiliated Iraqi prisoners in a breach of the Geneva Conventions. His statement reflected that his government has been unsettled by the outcry over revelations that British soldiers are now being investigated for abuse against prisoners. Choosing not to preempt the Ministry of Defense investigation, Blair said: "We apologize deeply to anyone who has been mistreated by any of our soldiers. That is absolutely and totally unacceptable. Those who are responsible for this, if they behaved in this appalling way, they will be punished according to Army discipline and rules."[24]

From the point of view of the Arab world, torture and sexual abuse are a systematic policy of both American and British governments. Irene Khan, general secretary of Amnesty International, told me that her organization had approached both the British and U.S. governments to voice concerns that they had evidence of the tortures described as far back as May 2003.[25] Meetings were held with the Ministry of Defense and the Foreign and Commonwealth Office in Whitehall. Further letters were sent to the secretary of state for Defense, Geoff Hoon, in July and October 2003 in which these concerns were emphasized. Amnesty International received no response, and the government did not act upon the information. The U.S. administration tried to convince the world that these abuses were isolated cases by their soldiers and not representative of the behavior of the majority. As events unfolded, witness statements from soldiers confirmed that they were under orders to carry out torture and sexual humiliation to force confessions from Iraqi prisoners. The original source of those orders is still to be identified, but the mind-set in which these orders took place could be explained by the following two memoranda. As far back as January 25, 2002, Alberto Gonzales, the new U.S. attorney general, was the White House legal consultant before the invasion of Iraq. In a memorandum, Gonzales advised the Bush administration that the Geneva Conventions do not cover prisoners of war and detainees of America's "war on terror," or the "new paradigm," as Gonzales called it. In "my judgement," he writes, "this new paradigm renders obsolete Geneva's strict limitations on questioning of enemy prisoners and renders quaint some of its provisions."[26]

Similarly, a secret memo by the Pentagon concluded that President George W. Bush is not obliged by any rules that prevent the use of torture, and the Justice Department will not charge any American officers who torture prisoners to retrieve information.[27] The report was prepared by civilian and military lawyers after they had briefed Defense Secretary Donald Rumsfeld in response to complaints by Guantanamo Bay prison administrators about their inability to retrieve information from prisoners through normal means of questioning. The memo, which was prepared on March 6, 2003–two weeks before the invasion of Iraq started–affirmed the importance of extracting information from prisoners in order to protect the lives of thousands of Americans. In this case, the normal rules will not be applied to officers carrying out their duties. The president, who is the commander in chief of the American forces, has the right to approve what kind of interrogation is required to retrieve information.

Arab commentator Abdul Wahab Badrakhan reminded his Arab readers of the many investigations that have been carried out on similar cases but whose files were closed without effective punishments being meted out.[28] He was referring to those conducted by the Israeli Defense Force investigating deaths or injury to Palestinian civilians by Israeli army fire. More often than not, the soldier concerned is given a light sentence or freed, which does little to deter other soldiers from repeating the same behavior. "Many Iraqis, on seeing the pictures in their local newspapers after the CBS footage was broadcast, thought that the intention of the degrading behavior was to humiliate them. What it did was to damage the reputation of the coalition." Badrakhan called for President Bush "to thank the media for drawing his attention to what has been going on. As the American president has repeated many times—Iraq should set an example for other countries in the Middle East to follow." But as many investigations carried out by American officials at the Pentagon have taken place without the knowledge of the president, if it were not for the media, Bush would presumably still be blissfully unaware.

"A year ago, I did give the speech from the carrier, saying that we had achieved an important objective, that we had accomplished a mission, which was the removal of Saddam Hussein. And as a result, there are no longer torture chambers or rape rooms or mass graves in Iraq. As a result, a friend of terror has been removed and now sits in a jail. I also said on that carrier that day, that there was still difficult work ahead." George W. Bush was speaking in the Rose Garden at the White House during a press conference for Canadian Prime Minister Paul Martin on April 30, 2004. He was referring to his premature speech the previous May declaring the end of major combat in Iraq, while standing on the deck of aircraft carrier USS *Abraham Lincoln,* beneath a banner reading "Mission Accomplished." Those two words have come back to haunt the American president, just as the image of a hooded Iraqi prisoner, balancing on a small box with electric wires attached to his body, will haunt the memories of the people of Iraq. These images are likely to become emblematic of this

American war against Iraq. The people of Iraq now have a new ugly stereotype—an American who is brutal, sadistic, and practicing double standards. The damage to American credibility must be judged as irreparable. President George W. Bush promised to liberate Iraqis from brutality and dictatorship. Now the "liberated ones" see the messenger of Western values and democracy in a completely different light.

NOTES

1. *Al Hayat,* June 26, 2004.
2. *New York Times,* May 21, 2004.
3. *Azzaman,* May 29, 2004.
4. *Al Hayat,* May 11, 2004.
5. Interviews with Anne Clwyd, Associated Press, May 5, 2004, and BBC Radio 4, September 4, 2004.
6. *Haram* is an Arabic word meaning "forbidden" or "against Islamic law."
7. Agence France-Presse, May 4, 2004.
8. www.globalsecurity.org/intell/world/Iraq.
9. Article 15-6, "Investigation of the 800th Military Police Brigade," February 2004, authored by Major General Antonio M. Taguba.
10. CBS; Associated Press, May 8, 2004.
11. *New Yorker,* May 10, 2004; CNN, August 6, 2004; ABC News, December 28, 2004.
12. Report of Investigation of the 800th Military Police Brigade, first published by Seymour Hersh in *New Yorker,* May 2004.
13. Reuters, San Francisco, April 9, 2005.
14. Telephone interview with Janis Karpinski, June 29, 2004, for *The Signal,* Santa Clarita, California.
15. Robert Fisk, "Iraqi Abuses: The Things Bush Didn't Mention in His Speech," *The Independent,* May 26, 2004.
16. Interview with General Janis Karpinski, BBC Radio 4, July 3, 2004.

17. *The Guardian,* December 9, 2003.

18. Vane is the deputy chief of staff at the U.S. Army's training and doctrine command.

19. Spiegel TV, May 10, 2004.

20. Press Conference, ICRC Headquarters, Geneva, May 7, 2004.

21. "Report of the International Committee of the Red Cross (ICRC) on the Treatment by the Coalition Forces of Prisoners of War and Other Protected Persons by the Geneva Conventions in Iraq During Arrest, Internment and Interrogation," Paragraph 7, February 2004.

22. Mena News Agency, May 4, 2004.

23. Al Arabiya TV, May 5, 2004.

24. *Europe Day* broadcast, French TV, May 10, 2004.

25. Interview of Irene Kahn by author on May 10, 2004.

26. Ghali Hassan, "The Resort to Torture," Online Journal Special Report, March 15, 2005.

27. *Wall Street Journal,* June 7, 2004.

28. Al Hayat, May 3, 2004.

CHAPTER FIVE

THE OCCUPATION THROUGH IRAQI EYES

In March 1991 Saddam Hussein's regime was confronted by the most serious internal challenge it had ever faced. One hundred thousand Shia from southern Iraq were killed or buried alive in mass graves after their Iranian-supported insurrection against the Sunni-dominated Baathist regime was crushed by Saddam's forces. When in 2003 they were finally liberated from Saddam's rule, these same villagers from the Shia city of Al Amarah hired diggers to unearth their sons, brothers, and daughters from the unmarked massed graves where they had been so cruelly buried twelve years earlier.

The soldiers of the First Battalion of the British Parachute Regiment had no idea of this history. They were on a routine patrol of Al Amarah on June 21, 2003, when they were told to raid a house belonging to Ali Al Hassan. They broke down the doors and forced their way in, holding their guns, cocked and ready to shoot anybody in front of them. Umm Basem, Ali's mother, whose husband had been executed by Saddam Hussein, was horrified by this intrusion of unknown gun-carrying men in uniforms. The family froze in fear as these British soldiers ordered them not to move while they were searched. Umm Basem later said she had never experienced anything like it, not even when Saddam was in power. Ali's family, all practicing Muslims, were deeply upset by the sight of dogs running loose in their bedrooms, sniffing through clothes and wardrobes, and through the room specially reserved for prayers, in search of hidden weapons. By the time the British soldiers pulled away from the area in their camouflaged vehicles, rumors had already begun circulating around the town about their use of sniffer dogs and the fact that they had violated tribal honor by body-searching the women. Locals seethed with anger. They tracked down the soldiers and confronted them with rocket-propelled grenades, killing the six soldiers.

In the West dogs are often treasured members of the family. They are a familiar sight in both European and American airports, where they play an important role in antiterrorist activities—seeking out explosives by sniffing along lines of passengers at check-in desks or rooting through luggage. This is considered routine and reassuring. But the cultural implications for dogs performing a similar job in Iraq should have been considered. According to Islam, dogs are permitted only for hunting or to guard the home. In a hadith from the Holy Koran,[1] the Prophet said: "Whoever keeps a dog except for hunting or for guarding crops or cattle will lose one large measure [qirat][2] of his reward each day."[3]

British forces denied any wrongdoing by their soldiers while carrying out their mission, saying, "They have been in the area long enough to understand the sensitivity of the people."[4] But the violence spilled over, and later that day six more Royal Military Police were killed.

This is perhaps one of the most poignant examples of escalating anger resulting from the action of foreign troops. None of the attackers were involved with any of the insurgency groups or were in any way organized. Such incidents reflected pure and simple outrage at how the British forces behaved. After that day, similar incidents have continued to take place in the south of Iraq, where attacks by unnamed groups have claimed many lives of the American-led coalition forces.

There are hundreds if not thousands of true stories recounting tragic mistakes committed by British and American forces. Yet the level of cultural insensitivity and arrogance displayed by the Anglo-American troops has only added to the toxic mix. The military acknowledge that "mistakes" happen, but coalition commanders appear to do very little to register or document these incidents. When they are confronted with them by the media, their answers are almost pat: "We are not aware of any such incident happening recently."

When it became clear that house-to-house raids were alienating the Iraqi population from the U.S. Army, those in charge finally agreed to scale down their "iron-fisted" approach in July 2003. However, this new edict did not seem to apply in the case of Dr. Al Sayed, a British-trained physician who on the evening of July 31, 2003, was enjoying the company of eleven of his relatives at his home. U.S. troops surrounded his house in a wealthy Baghdadi suburb, then stormed the gate and fired hundreds of bullets that peppered the outside walls. Dr. Sayed's screams, pleading with the soldiers that he would open the doors for them if they would only stop shooting, went unheeded. The sixty-two-year-old physician told me that at least three dozen soldiers then burst in and turned his house upside-down. After almost an hour of ransacking his home, the commanding officer apologized to Dr. Al Sayed, saying there had been a mistake. They had raided the wrong house. By then the doctor had been hit with the butt of a rifle and knocked down by a soldier before being kicked in the ribs. Doctors who later X-rayed him confirmed he had broken ribs. His wife, who was cowering with their young nieces in the next room, witnessed her husband being bound with plastic cuffs. Although they apologized to Dr. Sayed, the soldiers nevertheless arrested his three sons and took them to Camp Bucca military jail in southern Iraq for questioning. According to their mother, who visited them in the prison, her sons had not been accused of any crime nor had anyone even questioned them as to why they were there. They were finally released three months later.

Perhaps one of the most striking examples of the occupying forces' iron-fisted approach to ordinary Iraqi civilians was the case of Fattah Al Sheik. This neat-looking man in his forties, with a carefully trimmed beard, is a member of the first elected assembly in Iraq. He belongs to Muqtada Al Sadr's Shiite political wing, which, despite boycotting the 2005 election, is trying to break into politics with around two dozen sympathizers in the Iraqi National Assembly. One morning he was making his way to the convention center inside the protected Green Zone, where a meeting of the recently elected assembly members was due to take place.[5] Fattah arrived at the designated checkpoint, where a young American soldier stopped him, dragged him by the neck from his car, tied his hands behind him, and forced him to the ground. Fattah's pleas to be released, identifying himself with his Member of Parliament card entitling him to enter the Green Zone, were ignored. He asked if he could speak to one of the Iraqi translators who normally accompany coalition forces at checkpoints, as he didn't speak any English. In reply the American soldier grabbed Fattah's pass and threw it away, saying, "To hell with your assembly."

Six other members of the assembly who, like Fattah, had legitimate reasons to enter the highly sensitive Green Zone witnessed the episode. This incident produced great anger among the assembled politicians, who immediately postponed their meeting for an hour in protest against the harsh and unnecessary treatment of their colleague. Fattah was finally allowed through security to the convention center after the intervention of several Members of Parliament who had seen his distress. He was given the floor to explain his ordeal. Some members broke down in tears as they listened to Fattah's story. He, too, was unable to stop crying, constantly dabbing his eyes with tissues as he relived the humiliation. The politicians called for a full apology from the American forces and the American embassy in Baghdad. There were also cries for U.S. forces to vacate the Green Zone altogether so that Iraqi officials and the peoples' representatives would not have to undergo a similar ordeal.

The following morning, the incident was reported as front-page news in every Arab newspaper: "Deputy Cries in the Iraqi Parliament! American soldier strangled me and pushed me to the ground, my hands tied behind my back," screamed the headlines.[6] This incident went unmentioned in the Western media.

Mader Chawket, the Iraqi National Council's deputy member of the assembly, called for a full apology for the humiliation Fattah had undergone and asked for a withdrawal of American forces from all cities, and from the Green Zone in Baghdad as a starting point.[7] A female doctor and assembly member by the name of Amera Muhammed Al Baldawi was one of those who witnessed the treatment of Fattah. "I was shocked when I saw my colleague being dragged from his car, his hands being tied behind his back, and being beaten by the soldiers," she said. Member of Parliament Hana Al Tae'e corroborated her story and described how Fattah was "beaten by several American soldiers more than once." She called for Iraqi security forces to be put in charge of the entrance leading to the assembly "so that we can avoid being humiliated like this on a daily basis."[8]

General William Webster, whose division has been responsible for security in Baghdad since January 1, 2005, made a personal visit to the convention center to apologize to all 275 elected members of the assembly for what had happened to Fattah Al Sheik, and to reassure them that not only would he begin immediate investigations, but that the American embassy would also look into the incident.

Such incidents have added to the pressure on both the American-led coalition and the newly elected government in Baghdad as they struggle to convince all parties that a new era is about to commence, that Iraq is well on the road to recovery and able to take care of its own affairs.

*   *   *

The Kurds, Shia, and Sunnis, together with the other groups that make up the diverse cultural and religious tapestry of Iraqi society, have all reacted in distinct ways to the arrival of the Americans and their continued presence. In order to understand the dynamics of post-Saddam Iraq and the differing reception that the U.S. troops received from each group, it is important to understand their historical experience before the invasion, particularly under Baathist rule.

Within a few hours of U.S. Special Forces arriving in Irbil and the surrounding Kurdish areas after the start of the war, a sense of relief spread among the Kurds. There were worries that Turkish forces might take advantage of the unstable situation and extend their security zone inside Iraq to secure its borders against any separate militant Kurdish fighters who were willing to infiltrate its territory. Nonetheless, when American marines patrolled the streets and souks of Irbil and Sulaymaniya, they were greeted with smiles of gratitude in the hope that this time the administration in Washington would not abandon them.

That sunny spring day of April 9, 2003, was a day to remember. I was in the northern Kurdish region that the Kurds prefer to call "Kurdistan" when news of Saddam's final fall from grace and power filtered through. In each of the towns of Irbil,

Sulaymaniya, and Salahaddin, I watched circles of *dabkah,* the traditional Kurdish street dance, where even in this conservative society, men openly danced alongside women, as they expressed their joy at the fall of a regime that had expelled the Kurds from their original villages, forcing them to take refuge in the safety of the mountain areas.[9] Some of the men handed out sweets to passers-by, and car horns blared in an extraordinary display of exuberance.

The Americans began establishing air bases in Harir and Sulaymaniya that soon became the focus for sightseeing trips by Kurdish families who were impressed by the way the marines, newly landed under cover of darkness in these remote areas in their AC-130 transport planes, immediately began securing their bases and preparing the ground for the arrival of back-up troops. In just a few days, several thousand American soldiers had arrived in the area. By now Saddam's forces had massed together to form a front not far from the cities of Mosul and Kirkuk. Kurdish fighters supported the small groups of marines who were orchestrating the air strikes by pinpointing potential targets on the ground. At one stage, a group of other journalists and I saw them defending their positions with light weapons against attacks from those positions held by Iraqi forces, who were attempting to push the Kurdish Peshmerga back from its front line.

Although it was a serious confrontation, I could not help note how bizarre this scene appeared: simple Kurdish fighters with their baggy trousers, turbans, and well-used Kalashnikovs working side by side with American marines wearing their crisp camouflage uniforms and bristling with the wires of the latest military technology. These hundreds of Peshmerga milled around, protecting the Americans, waiting for a chance to move forward. Once in a while an American marine would call in a location, and on cue, depending on the size of the target, either an F-16 Fighting Falcon or the long-range B-52 Stratofortress, referred to by its crew as BUFF (Big Ugly Fat Fellow), would deliver its salvo of bombs according to the marine's instructions. It was like watching two armies converging toward the same battle from two different centuries.

A few days later, along the roads leading to Kirkuk, thousands of cars, vans, and trucks were crammed to bursting point with eager passengers who had procured whatever means were available to them to get to their former towns. This was to be their first visit since the Baath regime's brutal Arabization policy. We were following this bumper-to-bumper tail into Kirkuk, less than a few hours after the withdrawal of the regular Iraqi army, when I saw an old Iraqi military truck being fired upon. The driver appeared to have lost his way and had run into a group of Peshmerga fighters. The man fled for his life, and we narrowly avoided being caught in the hail of bullets that followed him. It was a very tense moment, as we had passed many blood-covered bodies of Iraqi soldiers on the side or even in the middle of the roads who must have come from the nearby military air base. That soldier was lucky. I will never forget the bullet-riddled body of a high-ranking Iraqi officer I saw in the middle of the road. From his epaulets, I could tell he was a general. The gold embroidery had been torn from his shoulders and neatly placed on his chest.

At the traffic island that marked the entrance to Kirkuk's city center, there used to be a dominating statue of Saddam, much the same as the one in Baghdad's Al Firdous Square, which was pulled to the ground in front of the world's TV screens. Similar scenes were now being played out in Kirkuk. Crowds were dancing and singing around Saddam's statue, now toppled from its pedestal, celebrating the liberation of their town and people from decades of mistreatment and marginalization. Not far from the town square, I noticed a Kurdish woman who was watching the celebrating crowds with her husband and children but didn't seem to be participating in the excitement. When I approached her to ask about the thoughts that were going through her mind, her response was heartfelt: "I am so worried that the world might forget about us, and Saddam Hussein will make a comeback and kill us all, as he tried to do before."

Since then, Iraqi Kurds have made a major contribution to the political process through their roles in both the Governing Council and subsequent governments led by Dr. Iyad Allawi and Dr. Ibrahim Al Jaafari. The appointment of Kurdish politician Hoshyar Zebari as the Iraqi foreign minister in the first interim government received an astonished reaction within Iraq, and the Arab world in general, as it was the first time a Kurd had won a place as Iraq's top diplomat. The surrounding Arab countries were not convinced that the regime change was for the better and regarded the interim government as America's puppet. The U.S. administration was forced to intervene and use its influence to convince the various Arab capitals to welcome Zebari and allow him into their diplomatic club.

As Zebari proved successful and became more familiar with Arab political occasions, the subsequent election of another Kurd as president was a further benchmark of the Arab political scene. Jalal Talabani, who was head of one of the two main Kurdish organizations in northern Iraq, the KUP, became the first Kurd to occupy the presidential post since the creation of the Iraqi state. Like Zebari, his appointment was met with surprise by people both inside and outside the country.

During negotiations within the Shia-led coalition that took place after the January 2005 elections, eyebrows were raised when the Kurds insisted on bringing to the table their long-term demands; that is, to have Kirkuk as their capital, to maintain their Peshmerga militias, and to resist at all costs Sharia law becoming the only source of legislation in the new constitution.

Although the Kurds were beginning to enjoy the freedom and independence they dreamed of, they were not sanguine enough to prevent rivalry erupting between the two main Kurdish organizations led by Massoud Al Barzani and Jalal Talabani. They failed to reach an agreement to establish one government in the past, and each declared two separate governments—one in Sulaymaniya, and the other in Irbil. On many occasions they resorted to violence, and fierce battles were waged in the mid-1990s. It was only in January 2005 that they finally agreed that one government was the solution, and Masoud Al Barzani was appointed as the head of Iraqi Kurdistan. The Kurds' acquiescence was driven by fear that if they failed to bury their differences and unite, they may well be stripped of the achievements they had attained since the defeat of Saddam Hussein in Kuwait when the United Nations established a safe haven for them in northern Iraq in 1991.

* * *

The experience of the Sunnis is in stark contrast to that of the Kurds. In general, Sunnis greeted the occupation of their country with trepidation, sadness, and fear about the future. They were concerned that they would end up paying the price for Saddam's Sunni-minority stranglehold on the country and their longer history of being the preponderant power in Iraq since the seventeenth century. A poll conducted in April 2004 by the Iraqi Center for Research and Strategic Studies concluded that two-thirds of the Shia population believed that the American-led coalition was there to liberate them, while the same poll showed that two-thirds of Sunnis believed that this war had come to shame them. This was reflected on the ground, with Shia areas largely quiet in comparison to the volatile Sunni-populated areas in the center and the north of the country, widely described as the Sunni Triangle. With the American victory, the Sunnis felt tarred for having been Saddam supporters, even though thousands had suffered under his regime.

Many of the Sunni intellectuals I have spoken to agree that Saddam ruled the country under the Sunni banner, but this didn't mean that Sunnis were automatically spared his wrath or torturous behavior. The fate of many high-ranking officers from the Sunni-dominated cities of Tikrit, Ramadi, Fallujah, and even Mosul, is well known. Many of them were executed in the throes of planning to eliminate his dictatorial regime. But it was Samarra's Sunni population who suffered the most. Samarra was a more prominent town than Tikrit, and Saddam attached great importance to its status. Lieutenant General Falah Hassan Al Naqib, the Iraqi army's chief of staff, had worked his way up the military ladder as a career soldier since the 1940s. Having attended military school, he was well disciplined and had a long military career behind him. He was not, therefore, a Saddam appointee. Saddam could afford only the most loyal of soldiers in his army, and since taking power had preferred to handpick his officers. Al Naqib was sidelined and posted to Spain and then Sweden as an Iraqi ambassador in the late 1970s. General Wafiq Jasim Al Samarrai, also from Samarra as his name implies, faced the same fate but chose to defect and seek refuge in the United Kingdom in the early 1990s. He had been the head of military intelligence in the Iraqi army. Despite being head of intelligence, when Saddam planned his war against Kuwait, Samarrai had no knowledge of the intended invasion. He learned that Iraq had invaded Kuwait from a news broadcast.

My driver, Ahmed, and I tailed the first American convoy to enter Mosul the day after the city was liberated. I prefer to keep a safe distance from military convoys because of their target value to the insurgents, but also because soldiers in these convoys fire their machine guns at almost everything that moves around them. Hundreds of Iraqis have been accidentally killed in this manner.

Mosul is home to most of Iraq's main ethnic groups, but Sunnis are the majority. Their anger could be felt rippling through the crowds lining the roadsides to watch the late arrival of their so-called liberators, twenty-four hours after the fall of Mosul. They were counting on the American forces to intervene and put an end to the out-of-control looting that had broken out. Everything possible had been stolen—from a useless broken chair to items of value such as new cars, furniture, or money from the government banks. In three decades of covering war zones, I had never witnessed such scenes. The greed of the looters and the scale on which they operated, unchecked by any form of law and order, was a pattern being replicated in all the fallen cities, and led Mosulites into confusion about what could be in store for them. They had watched in disbelief as the withdrawal of the Iraqi army opened the way for the disorganized Peshmerga occupation of their town. The Americans hadn't even arrived, but the beleaguered Iraqi army had fled in anticipation. Left behind was a huge vacuum with no security. That day, one of the city's elders appealed to me: "Where are the Americans? Is this the freedom and liberation they promised us when they removed the regime?"

Three months later, just a few miles from the "spider-hole" in Salah El Din province where a disheveled and disorientated Saddam Hussein was to emerge without resistance,[10] I was invited to the farm of Sheikh Bader Al Rifai, one of Tikrit's tribal elders. It was late June, when the temperature regularly soars over 120 degrees Fahrenheit. Al Rifai ushered me to a wooden bench under the eaves of his farmhouse, the coolest corner he could find in the unrelenting heat. He attempted to make himself comfortable on the hardwood bench, but his tall and slender frame fidgeted in the oppressive heat. After offering me mint tea, Sheikh Bader recalled the meeting when his fellow tribal leaders put together a strategy to convince the parties concerned as to how to avoid a potential battle in Tikrit and its surrounding areas between Saddam's loyal forces and those of the Americans. Everyone had predicted that the liberation of Tikrit, Saddam's hometown, would most certainly be bloody. "Well, it was difficult times then," he recounted, "but thanks to the wisdom of the elders in the area, and the understanding and cooperation between American commanders and the Kurdish leadership, a peaceful end was arrived at after the fall of Tikrit."

Tikritis were understandably reserved in welcoming their new "occupier." During the first few days they watched what was happening around them from behind the safety of the typical high walls and iron gates that surround their houses. "But as the days went by," Sheikh Bader added, "myself and the other elders who consulted with the occupying force received every assistance possible to restore basic services such as water and electricity, and to control law and order" in the wake of the free-for-all looting that gutted hospitals, museums, and schools. So a symbiotic relationship emerged between Tikriti locals and the American soldiers.

However, this arrangement did not last long. In less than a few weeks an altogether different attitude emerged. Tribal elders, who are used to a significant measure of respect, were ordered to step out of their cars and subjected to full body searches by young American marines, with no respect given to their status. In those early days, male soldiers would also body-search women—a cultural taboo. They also stole from homes during cowboy-style raids made at night. Many innocent people were subjected to these infringements on their personal freedom.

The Sunni Muslims are the second largest majority after the Shiite Arabs, and they represent an estimated 30 to 40 percent of Iraq's twenty-five million people. The U.S.-led coalition has generally overlooked them. Excluding the Sunni Arabs and leaving them with no hope of playing a future role in Iraq after decades of governing the country has complicated this post-Hussein era. Many Sunnis have resorted to violence and are chiefly responsible for the bloodiest of attacks. The majority of these attacks have been concentrated within the so-called Sunni Triangle. As we have seen, many residents of the Sunni heartland believe there is no choice but to fight, provide shelter, or offer logistical help to the guerrillas who mastermind these operations–a reflection of the loyalty that is inherent in the tribal system operating in Iraq. Although their attacks on American forces may seem to the outside world as a hopeless case, some really do believe that if the Americans were defeated in Vietnam, they can be defeated in Iraq as well. The ranks of true believers are swollen by those who feel they have lost everything anyway, so why not fight when they know their chances of defeating the only superpower are almost nonexistent.

The Sunnis' sense of bitterness of being overlooked seems partially justified. The Sunnis charge that the majority membership of Shiites and Kurds in the former Governing Council and their influence is a direct result of their close cooperation with the Americans during the Hussein period. Conversely, if asked, the Shiite Governing Council members say that the Sunnis did not form a strong organizational structure, because that wasn't required of them during the Sunni-dominated Hussein regime.

The choice of representatives who were more pro-American was confirmed when a policy described as "de-Baathification" was introduced. This policy, combined with the dissolution of the Sunni-dominated army by Ambassador Paul Bremer and his Coalition Provisional Authority, left more than half a million Sunnis out of work with no savings to rely on to make a fresh start. Feeling abandoned, many were left with no option but to vigorously oppose the occupation. Some of them went further and joined the resistance, either by becoming directly involved in the attacks or by offering financial and moral support to the myriad resistance movements.

* * *

When America requested that the United Nations recognize Washington as an "occupying" force in Iraq, it was after months of public relations exercise to impress on the Iraqi people that the forces were there to "liberate" them. In Iraq, this renaming was a disaster. Even the most pro-American Iraqis were ashamed to defend the U.S. policy. Iraqis are a very patriotic people, and occupation is simply unacceptable to people who are proud of their rich heritage. Before this, Iraqis were already cynical about the purpose of the American mission, believing that the primary purpose of the United States' coming was to control the country's substantial oil reserves. I heard countless Iraqis express their belief that the real reason for American forces to have landed on Iraqi soil was to monopolize the lucrative oil fields in the south and north of the country and to get their hands on the ultimate prize—the Iraqi Ministry of Petroleum. Their request was granted in the form of UN Security Council Resolution 1483, which was adopted on May 22, 2003.

It was hardly surprising to hear an Iraqi intellectual like Fakhri Karim describe 1483 as "The Mother of All Resolutions." It was the first of its kind to be adopted by the United Nations to legalize the occupation of a country, and as a result, Iraqis felt beyond doubt that they were being governed by the emotive word of "occupier" rather than "liberator." Resolution 1483 also called for an interim Iraqi administration, but did not elaborate on how this administration should be formed. Many Iraqis were therefore left with the impression that it would take many years for them to restore their country, achieve sovereignty, and escape from under the thumb of the U.S.-led occupation. Nevertheless, in an apparent face-saving exercise, they attempted to convince neighboring countries that they were not going to allow themselves to be considered a country under occupation. At a postwar forum in Jordan during the second week of April 2005, Iraqi journalists complained to their Jordanian colleagues, "Why do you always write 'occupied Iraq' when you mention our country?" It was clear that the phrase has cut deeply into their pride.

* * *

The Shia rejoiced when Saddam's statues came crashing to the ground. For them it heralded the end of decades of successive Sunni-dominated regimes, and despite ongoing instability in their areas they were optimistic about the future. Expectations were high. The Americans promised democracy and liberty. Short-term inconveniences and struggle could be tolerated with the prospect of a new Iraq in the making. The Shia were determined that their era as the underdogs should not be repeated. They formed the majority in Dr. Iyad Allawi's government and were also significantly represented in the first Governing Council that led post-invasion Iraq. After the Kurdish parties, the Shia political parties are the most organized, but there were fears that the Shia majority would impose their ideas on others—in particular, Sunni Arabs and Kurds—which might fuel unrest and lead to a civil war that could spread to neighboring countries too.

Muqtada Al Sadr, an aspiring ayatollah wearing the black turban and flowing dark beard of that rank, is the young leader of a militia called the "Al Mahdi army." Although he has none of the religious credentials necessary as a leader of the Shia, he has a powerful base among the poor Shia population of Iraq—particularly in the vast Baghdad ghetto, with a population of two million people, named Sadr City. Formerly called Saddam City, after Saddam's fall it was renamed in honor of Muqtada Al Sadr's late father, Grand Ayatollah Mohammed Sadiq Al Sadr, a powerful Shiite cleric, who was murdered by Saddam's agents in 1999 in Najaf. Muqtada Al Sadr, whose status comes from his illustrious ancestry, has a warrant issued in his name, and U.S. military commanders have threatened to "kill or capture" him in connection with the assassination of Majid Al Khoei, the Shia religious leader who was stabbed to death close to the Imam Ali Mosque in Najaf on April 5, 2004, during the first days of his return to Iraq after years of exile to participate in the elections (see chapter 3). Al Sadr was a prime suspect because of his known rivalry toward the returning religious leader. Subsequently, U.S. helicopter gun ships bombarded Al Sadr's offices in the Al Shuaala neighborhood of the capital, where his supporters had barricaded themselves. This resulted in the deaths of at least five people and the wounding of several others.

After months of ignoring Al Sadr, U.S. officials accused him of inciting violence and shut down *Al Hawza,* his newspaper. Clashes with Al Sadr's forces in Baghdad and the southern cities continued, while U.S. troops intensified their street-to-street battles against groups of insurgents in both Ramadi and Fallujah. These clashes with U.S.-led forces appeared to have an incendiary effect, raising the possibility of an alliance being forged between radical Sunnis, including Baathists, and the Mahdi army, Al Sadr's fundamentalist Shiite militia. The streets of Baghdad and other major cities were becoming more explosive than ever, and the American-led forces were accused of intentionally targeting civilians.

The main objective of the Americans was to corner Al Sadr and weaken him in order to strengthen other moderate Shia who were opposed to Saddam's regime while in exile. These people are well known for their long association with the American administration, but their absence from the country for so many years left them out of touch with the people. The confrontation with Al Sadr was miscalculated, and it triggered an intensification of the uprising and strengthened calls to end the occupation.

Some Iraqi intellectuals have commented to me that both the American forces and Iraqi security agencies have found the vague political and security atmosphere the country is experiencing to their advantage, as it has enabled them to carry out mass arrests without worrying about violating any legal framework. Dr. Kamel Qassem, the director of an NGO called the Center for Developments in Baghdad, echoed this when he told me that the occupying forces, together with the local police and army, have capitalized on this environment and the lack of a defined legal code in order to make arrests without due respect to human rights law.

Qassem talked of prisons full of women and children who had no reason to be arrested, let alone imprisoned. The absence of an adequate legal system to bring the occupiers to trial, even if they killed Iraqi civilians unintentionally or otherwise, has given the different forces a "license to kill" without fear of the consequences. This atmosphere is heightened by the fact that in the month after the invasion of the occupying troops, Iraqi police became one of the principal targets for the insurgents. Scores of them were executed, kidnapped, or blown up by suicide bombers.

* * *

American forces will be in Iraq for decades to come, whatever the political outcome. Despite heavy losses suffered during the daily attacks against them, the U.S. government is determined to hold on to the ground it has occupied since the fall of Saddam and make Iraq an example to other countries in the region. The U.S. administration is very aware that the failure of U.S. policy in Iraq will be seen by some as a very sturdy nail in the coffin of the United States as a superpower.

To Iraqis the struggle in their country is about their personal futures. To America it is about the future of a new Middle East they envision from afar. But if the Americans are to succeed, they must gain a better understanding of the basic dynamics of Iraqi society.

Notes

1. Hadiths are the sayings or deeds of the Prophet Mohammed as recorded by his followers.

2. *Qirat* is an Arabic word from which the term "carat" is derived and refers to a bean originally used as a measure for the weight of gold.

3. Yusuf al-Qaradawi, *The Lawful and the Prohibited in Islam* (Indianapolis, IN: American Trust Publications, 1980).

4. *Sunday Times,* June 29, 2003.

5. The first democratically held elections took place in Iraq on January 30, 2005.

6. April 20, 2005 *in Al Quds, Al Kayat,* and Asharq Al Awsat.

7. Telephone interview with Mader Chawket, Al Arabiyah TV, April 19, 2005.

8. Hana Al Tae'e, speaking in the Iraqi Parliament, April 19, 2005, as quoted by several Arab newspapers, including *Al Kayat, Azzaman,* and *Al Quds.*

9. The Baath regime's Arabization policy of 1991 involved the expulsion of Kurds from the Kirkuk region in order to populate it with only Shia Arabs or Sunni Arabs.

10. Saddam's capture occurred on December 14, 2003, after troops from the U.S. Fourth Infantry Division were led to his hideaway after a tip-off.

CHAPTER SIX

SHIAS, SUNNIS, AND KURDS AND THE ROLE OF THE RELIGIOUS LEADERSHIP

T wo years since the beginning of the American-led occupation, the only flourishing business in Iraq is the death trade. Ali Hussein Mohammed owns a workshop in Shuhada Market, a narrow alleyway branching off busy Haifa Street in the center of Baghdad. He can barely cope with the demand for his coffins. His business was inherited from his father, whose own father established it in the days when Iraq was a monarchy, back in the 1950s. Prior to the American-led war in Iraq, Ali was lucky to sell one thirty-dollar coffin a day. Now his business has multiplied fourfold. Iraq's coffin makers are making a killing.[1]

The specter of death and the prospect of sectarian war looms ominously over contemporary Iraq. On April 17, 2005, news broke that Sunni militants had kidnapped around seventy-five Shiites from the town of Al Madain and threatened to kill them unless the remaining Shia residents were evacuated. This kidnapping en masse had all the hallmarks of a sectarian assault. It was the first of its kind in Iraq since the collapse of the regime of Saddam Hussein, who, in his heyday, was a seasoned practitioner of large-scale ethnic cleansing.

But there was a time, even during Saddam's autocratic rule, when Sunnis and Shia were free to marry one another. In the 1970s Iraq was a progressive, technologically advanced nation and had as much in common with Western countries as either Lebanon or Israel had at that time. Literacy was close to 100 percent. But as a result of subsequent wars and the United Nations trade embargo on Iraq, the situation deteriorated, literacy rates fell dramatically, and society rolled backward. Tribalism and religion took the place of modernization and educational development, and tribal identity and the importance of the village a person was born into started to play an increasing role in the heart of political life in Iraq.

The town of Al Madain is built above the ruins of the ancient Mesopotamian city of Ctesiphon, which translates from Persian as "The Arch of Khosrow," a reference to the palace that graced the city when it came to prominence in the first century B.C. Located about eighteen miles southeast of Baghdad, and fringed by orchards of date palms and orange groves, the town lies on a fertile peninsula formed by a broad eastward bend of the Tigris River. The area was favored by the Persian king Khosrow I (Kesra in Arabic) and was the winter capital of the Sasanian Empire. Today all that remains of its former glory is the two-thousand-year-old towering arch that spanned the audience hall of the city's grand palace. It is the largest single-span brick archway in the world. Far from celebrating the existence of this engineering masterpiece in Iraq, Saddam Hussein resented its presence. Saddam hated the Iranians, and during the Iran-Iraq War this Persian archway was like grit to his eye. He asked his advisers to have it destroyed, but an influential architect, embellishing the truth slightly, explained that rather than having a Persian identity, the arch was in fact Iraqi-style architecture. Unconvinced by the architect, Saddam ordered that the structure should be barricaded off with barbed wire, and as a final insult to Persian history, he devised a son et lumiere that re-created the Al Qadisiyah battle of A.D. 636, when the Arabs were victorious over the Persians, in an allegorical reference to his "victory" in the Iran-Iraq War of the 1980s.

Al Madain has an alter ego. It is synonymously referred to as Salman Pak, named after a companion of the Prophet Muhammed and the first Persian to convert to Islam. A verse from a famous Iraqi song warns: "If you don't visit Salman Pak during your lifetime, then life is not worth living." In a lawsuit filed by the families of two people killed on 9/11, Salman Pak was identified as an alleged terrorist training ground by former CIA director James Woolsey in an expert testimony in a Manhattan federal court. This served to bolster George Bush's claim that Iraq was in cahoots with Al Qaeda. According to Woolsey, Saddam's *mukhabarat* intelligence service ran a secret school alongside the legitimate college that instructed Saddam's "freedom" fighters, the fedayeen. Woolsey claimed that this undercover school was teaching foreign fighters the art of passenger airline hijacking.

During the April 2005 Sunni assault, seventy-two-year-old Shia resident Kodhair Abbas fled the town with his family and large numbers of his Shia neighbors, and went to Kut, a town 125 miles from the Iraqi capital. Abbas told reporters how militants had surrounded Salman Pak and destroyed the Al Rasool Mosque, where Shi'ites in the town worshipped. In response, Thaer Al Naqib, the spokesperson for the Iraqi government, confirmed that ethnic cleansing appeared to be taking place. He said that an insurgency group from Al Souira, a predominantly Sunni town thirty-seven miles south of Baghdad, was suspected of playing a role and was led by former members of the Baathist regime. Several families in Al Souira are related to Izzat Ibrahim Al Duri, Saddam Hussein's fugitive deputy, who is represented as number six, the "King of

Clubs," in America's infamous deck of "Iraq's Most Wanted" playing cards.

The insurgents from Al Souira attacked fifteen houses owned by Shiites before warning others through loudspeakers that they should leave the area or die. Abdul, a forty-one-year-old farmer, "said that insurgents had abducted and released his son for ransom and threatened to return and punish those who talked. 'They said they would cut it out,' he said, sticking out his tongue and making a slicing motion."[2] They fled, escaping on boats that took them across the Tigris.[3]

A police source in Salman Pak confirmed to journalists visiting the area that a dispute had taken place between Shia and Sunni residents, which escalated when a Sunni vigilante group kidnapped four Shia males on their way from Baghdad to Al Amarah in the first week of April 2005. They were forced out of their car in Salman Pak, where the armed men instructed the woman accompanying the kidnapped men to inform the Shia of Al Amarah what was coming to them. Al Amarah citizens reacted by kidnapping twenty members of the Sunni Al Delaim tribe, who, in a tit-for-tat, responded by attacking Shia houses in Salman Pak.

Through statements made by their political and religious parties, the Shia claimed that large-scale kidnappings and mass killings against them had occurred. Sheikh Walid Al A'adami, a leading Sunni and cleric of the Abi Hanifah Mosque in Baghdad, claimed the whole story was fabricated and accused Iranian intelligence of plotting against the Sunnis to alienate them further from the Iraqi political scene.

Another elder from Salman Pak, Sheikh Ghani Al Jabouri, described a different version of events. "Since the fall of Baghdad in April 2003," he explained, "many strangers have arrived in Salman Pak and settled here. They confiscated land and built houses in a rapid and disorganized way. The Shia political and religious parties have changed the area's demographics by bringing people from Iran to settle here. Their excuse is that the previous regime forced them to leave Iraq, but now [that] Saddam has gone, the Shias want to return with the added blessing of living close to the grave of Salman Pak, one of Prophet Mohammed's followers."

Sheikh Jabouri said those behind the latest events were "young foreigners," who were causing sectarian tension by attacking locals, stealing, and other criminal activities—a claim that was denied by Abdul Al Zahrah Alami, one of the "strangers" who had built his home in the area. Alami retorted, "Salman Pak has been beyond government control for several months. Both Baathists and Salafist armed groups arrived in the area, fresh from their battles in Fallujah and Latifiya in November 2004 after the American assault against Fallujah to flush out insurgents in the town, and began taking the law into their own hands. They enforced curfews at night to move around freely." He confirmed that around sixty bodies were found in the Tigris River close to nearby Al Souira, but there was no forensic evidence to identify these bodies as belonging to any of the Shia inhabitants who were said to have been kidnapped. Many of the bodies were men, but there were also women and children among the dead, and some of the corpses were bound, headless, or without limbs. Pathologist Dr. Naji Al Azzawi said the bodies had decomposed, indicating they had been in the water for some time—not just the few days since the alleged kidnappings.

The conflicting reports about whether people were kidnapped or not, or whether the bodies found floating in the river were the result of mass killings that occurred in Salman Pak or from elsewhere, are puzzling. Also puzzling is why some people in the town were too scared to talk about what happened. But it is undeniable that whether the events were substantive or merely an excuse to trump up sectarian hatred, there remains a very real and ongoing security issue.

Since the fall of the Baathist regime, Salman Pak and its surrounding area have been under the control of various armed groups. The governor of Baghdad, Hussein Al Thahan, said that leaders among the insurgents have threatened to tighten their stranglehold around Baghdad and are working hand in hand with groups led by the wanted Jordanian terrorist Abu Musab Al Zarqawi. Iraqi forces have to drive through these areas in large, heavily protected military convoys, as do the American soldiers, because of the overwhelming presence of these insurgents.

The significance of this belt of insurgents is compounded by the fact that many of Baghdad's surrounding towns and villages are predominantly Sunni. They will likely play a major role in determining the identity of Baghdad if security deteriorates any further. Frightened Shiites are fleeing the capital and nearby towns of Al Doura, Al Hawsa, and Latifiya, moving to the largely Shia cities of Najaf, Karbala, and Babylon. Yassim Al Kofaji, a Shia from Al Doura, said, "I was forced to leave Baghdad, where I was born and worked as an English language teacher and translator, to go to Najaf in spite of the difficulty in finding another job. I had to leave, as I was receiving death threats."

The events at Salman Pak took a dramatic new turn on April 8, 2005, according to the Iraqi Ministry of Defense, when armed men from a radical Sunni Wahhabi Islamic sect roared into this lawless hotspot in their trucks and rounded up large numbers of Shiites. Three months before, soon after the January 30, 2005, elections, rebels launched a daring attack on the main police station, using rifles, rockets, and mortars. The hour-long battle killed ten policemen and wounded more than seventy-five others. Twenty rebel fighters were also killed. According to locals from Salman Pak, rebels began monitoring the flow of traffic leaving Baghdad and radioed their accomplices farther down the road with the description of any car or convey that was considered a valuable target.[4] This attack came after the rebels' success in weakening the Iraqi police presence in the area.

I happened to be at the residence of the Iraqi interior minister,

Falah Al Naqib, when his office called to say that insurgents were stopping traffic in Salman Pak to inspect people's fingers for the indelible blue ink that was a sign that they had voted in the general election three days earlier. It was the morning of February 2, 2005. Those who were caught with blue-stained fingers had their digits removed as a punishment for voting in what the insurgents considered was an American-fixed election. Over coffee, Al Naqib told me that at least forty Iraqis had required hospital treatment for the wounds caused by these brutal amputations.

The fall of the regime revealed that Saddam Hussein had succeeded in destroying the structure of all political parties in the country, including the old established ones such as the Communist Party and the Al Da'awa Party (otherwise known as the Islamic Call Party), the religious party of the Shiites. Iraqis found themselves without political organizations to fill the power vacuum. Only the Kurds had an established leadership in place, helped by the creation of a safe haven in the north of the country by the United Nations in 1991. Thus, confessional identity took on a greater importance for Iraqis.

The Shia city of Karbala made headline news on March 2, 2004, when approximately 150 people were killed in a series of multiple explosions during the festival of Ashura. A simultaneous attack in Kazimiya killed 80 people. This religious festival is celebrated annually by Shia all over the Muslim world, but this was the first time in thirty-five years that Iraqi Shia were free to celebrate their Holy festival due to Saddam Hussein's animosity toward the Shia branch of Islam. The prime suspect for the bombings was the ubiquitous Abu Musab Al Zarqawi, an associate of Osama bin Laden. But the Shia religious leaders also blamed the Americans for gross security failures during an event that was bound to provoke tension between opposing factions and for raising fears that the Shias would revenge the bombings and bring the country to the brink of a religious civil war.

For Shiites the city of Karbala is considered the gateway to Paradise, and it has become a place of potent symbolism for Shi'ite Muslims since the very foundation of Islam, thirteen centuries ago. It is the dream of thousands of Iraqi Shia to be taken to Karbala to be buried, therefore ensuring their passage to paradise.

The predominantly Shia town became a battleground once more just two months later, the violence spilling into its neighboring holy city, Najaf. This time the fight was between U.S. forces and the army of the Iraqi Shia cleric, Muqtada Al Sadr. The U.S.-led occupation had issued a warrant for the young firebrand's arrest in connection with the stabbing death of another Shia cleric, Abdul Majid Al Khoei, on April 10, 2003 (the day after the fall of Baghdad), after Al Khoei was suspected of being an ally of the Anglo-American coalition. These concurrent events caused an outcry among the Shia community. They called for revenge against the Americans, fuelled even further after U.S. forces blasted some of the holiest shrines in both Karbala and Najaf.

Soon after these attacks, in an interview with Tony Blair on May 25, 2004, I challenged the British prime minister to explain the coalition attacks on sacred sites. Blair replied: "The Americans are not attacking religious sites. What is happening is that people in and around the religious sites are attacking American and coalition troops, and they are having to respond to that attack . . . it is not the coalition trying to attack a holy site of Islam, it is actually people who are trying to disrupt the progress of Iraq, and in doing so, trying to make propaganda against the coalition forces." This is partially true, but the broader implication is that this religious city is packed with mosques, and any heavy engagement would inevitably involve the destruction of many religious sites, so contingency plans should surely have been put in place to prevent this.

The Shia leadership increasingly appeared to be listening less to U.S. plans and taking events into their own hands. The Shiites' fractious response to the American invasion is revealed by the actions of two of its most influential leaders–Iranian-born Grand Ayatollah Sistani, and the young firebrand cleric Muqtada Al Sadr.

Sistani, the Shiites' most senior religious leader in Iraq, was initially very vocal in his opposition to any plans that might affect the Shia representation in Iraq. Sistani called on his followers to demonstrate their opposition to the American plan for a post-occupation Iraqi government, in which the United States wanted to install an unelected government as early as July 1, 2004. Sistani insisted on having a free election whereby the people of Iraq would have the opportunity to choose their own representatives to the National Assembly to prepare the new constitution instead of having a government foisted on them by the Americans. His political strength was evident when, on January 22, 2004, with just one announcement from his mosque, tens of thousands of people flooded the streets of Shia areas. One pronouncement later, he was able to withdraw his supporters, having forced George W. Bush and the U.S. administration to change their initial plan toward Iraq.

Sistani is now able to boast that he changed the mind of a superpower. In an interview conducted by *Al Hayat* on April 18, 2003, Sistani's son Mohammed Rida Sistani said of his father: "He rejected any foreign power that would rule Iraq, and he called for unity amongst all Muslims, Sunni and Shia, and among all Iraqis. Iraq is for the Iraqis. They must administer Iraq, and it is not for them to do so under any foreign power."

According to those who know him from his hometown of Najaf, Sistani has reaffirmed that he will not favor one political party in Iraq but will instead offer himself as a representative for all Iraqis. When some parties became doubtful that the elections could be run as scheduled in January 2005 and pressed for a few months delay, Sistani's position was crystal clear. The election should be held on time, with no delay, he said. When the January date was finally confirmed, Sistani issued a fatwa saying that voting in the January election was an Islamic and legal duty. This fatwa was difficult for Sistani's religious and loyal followers to disobey and was instrumental in mobilizing 8.5 million out of 14 million registered voters to the polls—a considerable turnout despite threats from the insurgents, who in many parts of the country blew themselves up in an attempt to frighten Iraqi voters and deter them from electing their government representatives.

Sistani is considered a moderate, but the emergence of his rival, the young Shia radical Muqtada Al Sadr, is causing the United States and its allies greater concern. At one stage, in May 2004 the Americans were close to proposing to Muqtada Al Sadr that he join the interim Governing Council, but he ruled out the idea on two counts. First, he thought that *he* should be the one to decide who will join the Governing Council or have the majority of the members. Second, he did not trust those members of the council who came from abroad, that is, those Iraqis who had been in exile and were returning to the country at the behest of the Americans. Tensions between Al Sadr and the coalition forces escalated rapidly. In the wake of the assassination of Palestinian Hamas leader Sheikh Yassin, Al Sadr stirred up anti-Israel and anti-U.S. sentiment in his radical weekly newspaper, *Al Hawza.* The United States closed down his publication in March 2004 for a sixty-day period and issued arrest warrants for twenty-eight of his associates. Al Sadr, fearing that the Americans were coming for him, launched an insurrection in many Iraqi cities, including Basra, Najaf, and East Baghdad. His followers formed militias that created serious confrontations with the British and American forces.

Muqtada Al Sadr has benefited from the inheritance of support from his father, Sayed Mohammed Sadiq Al Sadr, even though he lacks his father's religious authority and political experience. However, the element of youth and energy in his faction has given it advantage over the other Shia factions, whose supporters, like those of Sistani, are much older. Al Sadr belongs to a prominent Iraqi family, and his father was a former Iraqi prime minister, whose short term in office lasted from January 29 to June 25, 1948, during the period of Iraq's monarchy. The elder Al Sadr was also one of the founders of the Al Da'awa Party in 1957, which is the most important and the oldest Shia political party in the last century and was originally set up to resist growing communism in Iraq.

While groups like Ansar Al Islam, composed of Sunni militants and associated with Al Qaeda and its leader, Osama bin Laden, believe in confrontation with the Americans as a matter of principle, for Al Sadr and his followers confrontation was used to remind the Americans of his influential role as a Shia leader. Al Sadr also wanted to weaken the standing of the Shia members of the then-interim Governing Council. Al Sadr's announcement in August 2004 that his forces would be placed under the orders of the Shia religious leadership known as Marjaeyeh, led by Ayatollah Sistani, was described by some observers as a tool by which Al Sadr wished to assert his military and political prowess.

* * *

Salah Omar Al Ali, a former member of the Baath Central Command and member of the Sunni Association of Muslim Scholars, summarized how he interpreted the differences between Shiites and Sunnis. Speaking with me at a west London hotel, he said: "There are many differences between Sunnis and Shias in the way they are organized. The Shiite have a very tightly knit and disciplined organization, starting with a base and finishing with Grand Ayatollah Sistani at the top. The Sunnis don't have this kind of organizational structure—there is no Ayatollah, no main leader. The Sunnis don't have any ambitions beyond the country, although they feel part of the greater Arabic world; they have always belonged to nationalist and pan-Arab movements. Shiites, because of where the base of their faith is rooted, have strong ties with Iran. The many Shiite political organizations are mostly religious organizations. Sunnis only have a couple of parties, the Association of Muslim Scholars, of which I am a member, and the Islamic Party. We have never been interested in building a strict and specifically Sunni religious organization. If you visit any Shia religious leader, within two minutes he will start talking about the Shia and their religious problems. If you visit Sunnis, we don't talk like that. A Sunni will always say, 'I am Muslim first and foremost.'

The inhabitants of Fallujah and other cities in Al Anbar province within what the Western media describe as the Sunni Triangle have always been a very conservative people. In the late 1960s they resisted attempts by Baath leaders to open entertainment facilities in the city, and when the Baath invited senior tribal members to attend one of their functions, at which they had arranged for ten voluptuous Egyptian belly dancers to perform, the evening ended with deaths and injury. Fighting broke out when the tribal leaders remonstrated the organizers that this display of bare flesh was an insult to their customs and religion. The next day, in retaliation for the previous night's violence, the *mukhabarat* arrested most of the Imams of Fallujah's mosques, including Ibrahim Al Qadi, Imam of the Grand Mosque in Fallujah.

By the 1980s, attempts were made to open theaters, but all were destroyed by locals who planted explosives. The following decade saw many young Fallujans imprisoned and tortured by Saddam's regime. Shops selling alcohol were bombed, nightclubs were attacked. With the innovations of satellite technology, information from other parts of the world were made more readily available inside Iraq; thus, more literature and publications were smuggled in, and the government lost its tight control over what its public could see or learn. Pressure on the Iraqi government by the United States forced the country to follow a different direction, and it appeared more Islamic than ever before. Many intellectuals, students, and professors at Iraq's universities emphatically declared their Islamic beliefs, while their liberal and socialist views went into retreat. Mosques became active, and this reached its height during the trade sanctions imposed on Iraq by the United Nations in 1991.

Many Islamic movements grew around the Middle East at this time, and the secular government followed step by permitting religious programs to be broadcast on state radio. This further encouraged religious groups to flourish and gave them confidence to openly pursue such activities as the Muslim Brotherhood and the Salafi movement.[5]

Saddam Hussein had witnessed the spread of Islamic extremism in the Arab world, and in the latter years of his power, he began to use Islamic rhetoric in his speeches in order to maintain the support of the religious groups. He was paranoid that his popularity might be threatened, and nipped in the bud any signs that either Sunnis or Shias were forming a cohesive group of support. In 2001 he added the phrase *"Allah Akbar,"* or "God is great," in his own handwriting to the national flag in order to garner support from the Islamic world in a united front against America. After Saddam's regime was overthrown in 2003, those Sunnis who were persecuted during his time in office decided to capitalize on the new situation. They began by reorganizing the Islamic Party, which had a strong base among the Sunnis.

The Islamic Party (of Iraq) is the Iraqi branch of the Muslim Brotherhood, led by Mohsen Abdul Hamid, a prolific writer about the Koran, and a member of the Governing Council. The party was officially established in 1960, but by 1963 it was put on ice by its rivals in the Baath Party. Even when they resumed their activities during the presidency of Saddam Hussein's predecessor, Abdul

Salam Arif, the Baath Party continued to kill and imprison many members of the Islamic Party. Nazem Kazzaz was then head of intelligence and shared the sadistic tendencies later exemplified by Saddam Hussein. I remember hearing about one of Kazzaz's victims, whose fingers had become gnarled and shriveled because of the harsh treatment he had received. One day his torturers allowed him to have a bath with hot water. He was surprised at this apparent luxury, but as he lowered himself into the bath, he found that the water was scalding. "They kept on adding boiling water containing concentrated salt, which stung every tortured wound in my body." Other Islamic organizations suffered similarly, but they continued to operate as an underground movement.

By 1989 the Islamic Party openly began offering courses in reading and interpreting the Koran in various mosques both within the capital and outside, taking advantage of the more relaxed attitude shown by the government toward Islamic activities. This provided the party with an opportunity for recruiting large numbers of young people into their organization.

Even though Saddam mistreated many of his own Sunni supporters, for many of them it was a case of "better the devil you know." So while some of his Sunni generals plotted to overthrow him, the majority of the Sunni population continued to support him. They feared that a regime change would lead to Shiites governing the country and depriving them of the privileges they had enjoyed for decades. In fact, the American-led administration was even more responsive toward leaders from the Shia sect. This was highlighted when the Governing Council was predominantly composed of Shia members.

It goes without saying that Sunnis resented the American plan, which favored better representation for the Shia under the U.S. formula for post-Saddam Iraq. This is not necessarily because they objected to the formula per se, but because it was American-imposed and not elected upon by the people. Many Sunni elders

I spoke to expressed no objection to a Shia or Kurdish-led government as long as it was voted for by Iraqis and not forced on
them by outsiders.

Sunnis claimed that the strong membership and influence of
Shia and Kurds in the U.S.-backed Governing Council was due to
their close cooperation with the Americans during the Saddam
era. Shia Governing Council members, on the other hand, hit
back, saying that Sunnis did not form a strong enough organizational structure, because they didn't feel it was necessary in a
Sunni-dominated Saddam regime.

The Iraqi government thus had no alternative but to adopt a
balanced approach when dealing with the Sunni religious groups.
Dr. Iyad Allawi, the first prime minister in the new Iraqi era and
a former Baathist himself, was one step ahead of any other Iraqi
political leader in expressing sympathy toward the Baathists. He
allowed them to return to their jobs, which the American-led
administration had forced them to abandon because of their connections with the former regime. Allawi was particularly keen to
support those Baathists whose hands were not bloodied during
Saddam's killing sprees. "This country needs every single citizen,"
he said "and we should not repeat the policies of Saddam Hussein, who favored some while excluding most of the population."
Allawi hoped that his conciliatory action would diffuse the
swelling ranks of the insurgency. The United States attempted to
follow his lead by making a pact with the Sunni insurgents, who
have inflicted heavy losses on the American military. Al Sharif Ali
bin Al Hussein, the head of the Constitutional Monarchy movement, told me of meetings and mediation efforts between different
strands of insurgents in Fallujah, Al Ramadi, Mosul, and the
American forces in Iraq in the summer of 2003. He tried to reach
an agreement between the parties concerned to end the blood-
shed. Al Sharif Ali's efforts were complemented by Dr. Iyad
Allawi's views against de-Baathification and his open criticism of

Paul Bremer's decision to dissolve the Sunni-dominated army, a move that led to anger among its ranks.

Dr. Iyad Allawi was born in 1944 into a well-educated and wealthy family from the Al Amiriya district of Baghdad. His father and twin brother were both doctors, and Iyad followed them into the profession, studying medicine and training as a neurologist in Baghdad. He joined the Baath Party in the early 1960s at a time when Baathist slogans called for Arab nationalism and anticolonialism, and before Saddam Hussein's rise to prominence. His rivals describe him as having a tough-man image in those days, when he was a student activist rallying support in his university campus on behalf of the Baath Party. Allawi left Iraq in 1974 after a dispute with the government, but returned in 1976 and stayed nearly a month before he realized that his differences with the leadership meant the best option for him was to head toward London, where he remained active in Iraqi politics. However, he soon turned against the Baath Party and its new leadership and began working strenuously for their removal. An angry Saddam Hussein sent his agents to London in 1978, where they attempted to assassinate Allawi in his London home with knives and an axe, leaving him seriously wounded. This was to be the first of more than a dozen assassination attempts on his life, which continue to this day. In the space of ten months after taking office at the end of June 2004, he has survived at least five assassination attempts.

Allawi, together with Salah Omar Al Ali–the former Iraqi ambassador to the UN, from the 1970s until 1982–founded the opposition group known as the Iraqi National Accord (INA) in 1991, but their partnership collapsed when Al Ali accused Allawi of establishing back channels to the CIA without his knowledge. Allawi has always defended this accusation by saying that his main goal was to get rid of Saddam and that he called in the help of several intelligence organizations, not just the CIA, to reach that objective.

As head of the INA, Allawi is considered a political moderate with liberal views. He maintained close relationships with the governments of the United States and the United Kingdom, and was appointed as a member of the Governing Council, with responsibility to oversee the Security Committee.

Allawi's position stands in noticeable contrast to his political rival Dr. Ahmed Chalabi, from whom the Americans distanced themselves because of his criticism of White House plans toward Iraq and its future. Chalabi became more vocal in his condemnation of Bremer's handling of Iraq, and in May 2004, Iraqi police, backed by U.S. soldiers, raided his home and offices in Baghdad. They seized computers, files, and dozens of rifles after claims were made that he had passed information to an Iranian official about the United States having broken the secret communication code of Iran's intelligence service, thus betraying one of Washington's most valuable sources of information about Iran.[6] Chalabi vehemently denied such claims. The chilly climate between Chalabi and the U.S. government thawed after the January 2005 elections in Iraq, when Chalabi found himself appointed as deputy prime minister. He received congratulatory phone calls from both Vice President Dick Cheney and Secretary of State Condoleezza Rice on his appointment, leading many commentators in Baghdad to remark upon this curious twist of events.

Allawi, on the other hand, while always remaining on good terms with Washington, has also forged long-standing relationships with other Arab governments, particularly the countries that neighbor Iraq. He made regular visits to Egypt years before the demise of Saddam Hussein, and with the sanction of King Hussein, his opposition group was the only one to establish a base in Jordan.

After a brief, secret ceremony by the outgoing American civil administrator Paul Bremer, the fifty-nine-year-old Dr. Allawi was appointed Iraq's interim prime minister on June 28, 2004. He concentrated on strengthening the country's security organizations —the police, the army, and government institutions. Not long after his appointment the *Sydney Morning Herald* quoted witnesses who claimed that Dr. Allawi had executed prisoners in cold blood in the Al Amiriya security center just days before Washington handed control of the country to his interim government. Dr. Allawi has denied such claims and described them as rumors fabricated by the enemies of the interim government who are keen not to see Iraq making any progress toward the future. Dr. Allawi has faced challenges every step of the way. Insurgents targeted his newly built army and police force, and the mass killings of police and army recruits were regular news. Special targets were raw recruits heading to their training camps for the first, and last, time, many of whom were slaughtered like sheep. I interviewed a group of insurgents who had been arrested in Baghdad in February 2005. One of them, a twenty-year-old, acknowledged that he had killed five policemen in Mosul, including some Peshmerga. He described the killings as if he were talking about beheading chickens.

Iyad Allawi had an interesting perspective on the motives of the insurgency. After casting his vote in the convention center in the early afternoon of of January 30, 2005, he talked to me in his well-guarded office in Baghdad's International Green Zone: "The leaders of the insurgents don't want the Americans to leave the country. That's why they are targeting the police and the army." Allawi believed that announcing a state of emergency in the country, soon after his appointment, was necessary to stem the spread of violence at a time when multiple daily attacks, including suicide missions, were derailing the process of rebuilding the country and allowing its institutions to stand on their feet. "Sunnis, Kurds, and Shia should work hand in hand," he said, "to rebuild this country and return it to the days when all the parties in Iraq worked in unison."

Allawi was very critical of the support Grand Ayatollah Sistani expressed toward the Shia-led coalition and his ordering of a fatwa to Shia voters just prior to the elections. Allawi told me he considered it wrong for the religious leadership to get involved in politics by manipulating the voting in this way, "because it appears he is taking sides in the election." His criticism is all the more pointed because the Shia-led coalition is used by his archrival Dr. Chalabi, who, according to his inner circle, is prepared to do anything to prevent Allawi from remaining in power.

* * *

During the first month of the American presence in Ramadi in April 2003, not a single shot was fired throughout the Sunni Triangle. But then the atmosphere changed. A doctor from the town, Dr. Omer Atiyah, recounted an unpleasant experience: "I was driving my car from my clinic in Ramadi to visit a patient when I was stopped at a checkpoint. While I was waiting for my turn to be searched, I was pulled out of my car and forced to the ground by a soldier. As he tied my hands behind my back, I asked him what I had done, and with that he put his boot on my neck, and once his colleague had finished searching my car, he shouted into my face that 'these were orders.' I wondered from whom these orders were given and why this kind of attitude was emerging. This kind of thing played a big role in changing people's attitudes toward the occupation."

Hard-core Sunnis believe that the United States will not be able to remain in Iraq as an occupying force and that those Shia who strongly support the U.S. presence in Iraq make up less than one hundred thousand people of the country's entire population, which is estimated to be around 25 million.

Sunnis believe the chalice presented to them is a poisoned one. Ninety-nine per cent of them are against the occupation. This is the conclusion that one makes after touring the country—in specific, Sunni-populated areas—and talking to people, including intellectuals and tribal leaders, not all of whom supported Saddam Hussein's regime. To them, both the American occupation and Saddam Hussein have treated Iraqis badly. Atiyeh accused the Americans of trying to create the impression that Sunnis are a very small minority in the country, which, he says, is not true. "Take a tour of the country and you will see. Estimates of the population figures are based on cards given to citizens to receive discounted food. Sunnis Arab make up forty-five percent of the population, and if we want to add the Sunni Kurds to that number, then the Sunnis in Iraq will exceed fifty-eight percent of the population. There has never been official statistics to support U.S. figures that the Shia are in the majority, yet Shias are able to occupy the majority of seats in the government and parliament on the basis of these American figures."

Salah Omar Al Ali, who fell out with Iyad Allawi over his alleged CIA connections, was a minister of information in Saddam Hussein's cabinet and a member of the Baath Central Command. Like Saddam, he hails from Tikrit, and as a Sunni, he and his party shunned the elections, because he felt that rushing to hold elections in the climate of the time was an attempt "to legitimize the occupation."[7]

Speaking to me in London on a visit from Iraq, Al Ali told me: "When it came to the elections, the Sunnis mostly boycotted them, while the majority of the Shia took part in the political process, with a few notable exceptions, including Muqtada Al Sadr. It is very important to understand, and this is how we feel in my party—that we Sunnis are Muslims, but when we are working in the political field, our faith doesn't come into it. We are a national organization prepared to work with Muslims, Christians, and all the different religious groups.

"The two Sunni organizations are the Association of Muslim

Scholars [AMS] and the Islamic Party. The Islamic Party, who previously held two ministries, lost most of its popularity because the head of the party, Mohsen Abdul Hamid, a Kurd, agreed to be a member of the Governing Council formed by Ambassador Bremer, unlike the AMS, despite being under a lot of pressure to join. Many members of the AMS were killed by Americans, and others were threatened if they didn't comply. Large numbers of them are in prison. Western ambassadors, including the assistant to U.S. Ambassador Negroponti, tried to convince our party head, Hareth Sulayman Al Dari, to form a part of the government, but he refused. We stuck to our guns. If there was no schedule for an American withdrawal, then end of story."[8]

* * *

The situation in Iraq both before and after the toppling of Saddam made it clear to me that the Kurdish issue was potentially the most explosive. The main goal of all Kurdish political parties is to establish some kind of autonomy within the Kurdish north of the country, which some hope will be the starting point in establishing a greater Kurdistan.

Seven decades of Kurdish struggle, together with the occupation of Iraq, have prepared the ground for the Kurds to achieve their nationalist dream. All parties inside Iraq describe the Kurds as the main winners and the most influential group in the establishment of the new Iraq. They have succeeded in forcing the Shia to accept their point of view concerning federalism and the right of veto on any law the new constitution draws up after the election. They also succeeded in taking a large share of posts in the government led by Dr. Iyad Allawi after the handing over of power to the Iraqis at the end of June 2004.

The first test of Kurdish influence came when Dr. Allawi announced the dissolution of militias after insisting that security and restoring law and order were uppermost on his agenda. This move was met with fierce opposition from Kurdish leaders, who command eighty thousand to one hundred thousand Peshmerga militia. The Peshmerga are well equipped and well trained, and their numbers exceed the current number of British army soldiers in Iraq.

Another setback for the Allawi government came during the Security Council discussions in June 2004, when the Kurdish leadership opposed the draft resolution, which failed to mention the temporary constitutional law giving the Kurds the right of veto over any decisions. This led the Grand Ayatollah of the Shia in Iraq, Sayed Sistani, to write a letter to the secretary general of the United Nations, Kofi Annan, warning him of the implications of such a step. This unprecedented confrontation between the leaders of the Kurds and the Shia spiritual leader forced Dr. Allawi to make new promises to the Kurds that their rights within the constitution will not be altered.

The Kurdish leadership was unhappy that the U.S. government in 2004 opposed their demands to hold two of the highest posts of power in Iraq—the presidency, which Massoud Al Barzani, leader of the Kurdistan Democratic Party, had coveted, and the premiership, which Jalal Talabani, leader of the Kurdish Patriotic Front, had set his sights on. This led to criticism of the United States by the Kurdish prime minister, Nechirwan Al Barzani, who warned them not to indulge other groups in Iraq at the expense of the Kurds. He was worried that such tactics by the United States might force others to take a stand against its policies and oblige the Kurdish leadership to reveal some of the commitments, offered to them in secret, by the American leadership. In the end, there was a U.S. policy change, and a Kurdish president was elected for the first time in Iraq's history.

The bargaining that followed the January 30, 2005, election between the Kurdish leadership and the Shia, who gained the majority of seats in this election, led me and others to speculate what kind of hidden promises were given to the Kurds on the eve of the U.S. invasion. Was it to create an independent homeland, announce separation, or give them a federal status? We still don't know.

The Kurds are trying to impose conditions that they believe will maintain their strengthened position without fear of losing their rights or their identity. The big test will be whether the new politicians in Iraq, especially those within the Shia sect, will accept these terms, particularly when it comes to federalism in the way the Kurds understand it. The Kurds want a share of the country's wealth and its resources and special security arrangements for their areas. Interestingly, Dr. Jaafari, the first elected prime minister, who represents the Shia-led coalition, carefully avoided the word "federalism" in his swearing-in speech, knowing the sensitivities of the issue. He later included it in a subsequent speech when he declared his thirty-six-member cabinet on May 9, 2005, after angry complaints from the Kurdish leadership and parliamentarians.

The Kurds live in the autonomous mountain region in the north, in an area the size of Switzerland. They are gradually distancing themselves from their Arab roots, with Kurdish being the only language spoken in schools and universities, apart from religious classes, which are conducted in Arabic. The Kurdish city of Kirkuk is described as "The City Built on a Sea of Black Gold." Sixty percent of Iraq's oil reserves are in the surrounding area, and the city has now become a threat to Iraq's unity. The Kurds see the city as the jewel in their crown that should become the capital of their dream homeland, Kurdistan. An added complication is the city's involvement in a historic dispute with Turkey. Turkey claims that it was forced to hand over Kirkuk to the British after the fall of the Ottoman Empire following World War I. Things have been further complicated by the intensity of fighting that Kirkuk has experienced since Saddam's regime collapsed, which has made the city synonymous with the bitter dispute between Turkomen, Arabs, Kurds, and Assyrians.

Massoud Al Barzani, the political leader of the Kurdistan Democratic Party, has been a central figure in the Kurdish movement for more than two decades. He is a conservative figure with a shy smile. His forces control the northern and northwestern area of Iraqi Kurdistan along the borders with Syria, Turkey, and Iran. I have known Massoud for nearly two decades and have had several interesting encounters with him, both in London and at his home and party headquarters in Salah El Din and Irbil. On those occasions he has insisted that the main condition to seek alliance with any party in Iraq is that the identity of Iraq should be based on a federal, multiparty system with proportional representation. He was surprised by the fact that some Iraqis have questioned why the Kurds should get one of the main leadership posts in the country, including the presidency and the head of parliament, as Jalal Talabani did before he was appointed as the first Kurdish head of state in Iraq since the country was established. The Kurds are part of Iraq, he says, and they assume they are entitled to any post they seem fit to have.

Massoud is the son of the late Mullah Mustapha Al Barzani, the most prominent Kurdish national leader in its history, who was greatly revered by his people. When he died on March 1, 1979, hundreds of thousands of Kurds mourned his death. He was the military commander of the Soviet-backed Kurdish Republic of Mahabad that was declared in Iranian Kurdistan. When the republic fell in 1947 after fierce fighting with the forces of the Shah of Iran, Mullah Mustapha, together with five hundred of his Peshmergas and devoted followers, fought their way through Iran, Iraq, and Turkey, finally seeking refuge in the Soviet Union. Massoud, along with the rest of his family members and thousands of the Al Barzani tribe, returned to Iraq, followed by his father, eleven years later.

Deeply influenced by the bravery and leadership skills of his father, Massoud was somewhat shocked when U.S. Ambassador Paul Bremer, during a tour of the local government offices in Irbil, remarked upon a prominent portrait of a proud-looking Mullah Mustapha wearing his signature turban and with a bullet belt fastened over one shoulder. Bremer asked his host, "Who is this guy?"9 Massoud speculated on Bremer's ability to run the affairs of such a vast and culturally rich country like Iraq if he hadn't even taken the trouble of finding out the history of the most loved spiritual leader of the Kurdish movement.

Al Barzani said that the absence of the Sunnis at the January election was more because of the security situation rather than the political process itself. "It is true that some of their organizations called for a boycott, but still, no one should ignore the Sunnis' participation in building the 'new Iraq.'" Al Barzani reminded me that he himself called for a "conference of reconciliation" and invited Baathists to take part in the political process. He was adamant that he would "pursue my efforts to make it work without ignoring the voices of those who have criticized my views. It is very important to differentiate between the ones who were just political activists and those who committed crimes against the Arabs and the Kurds of Iraq."

Massoud Al Barzani says he was "born under the shadow of the Kurdish flag in Mahabad" and is "ready to serve and die for the same flag." With a fighter's physique, dressed in his usual uniform of khaki-colored overalls, he almost cried when I asked him if a Kurdish politician occupying the seat of the presidency would spell the end of the Kurdish dream to have their independent state. His strongly worded reply was: "An independent state is a legal right and desire that the Kurdish nation will fight hard to establish. That presidential post in Baghdad has nothing to do with this or the rights of the Kurds for self-determination." He referred to the referendum held in Kurdistan in January 2005 when a large majority of Kurds voted for independence, describing this popular vote as "reflecting the mood of the Kurdish population in this part of the world."

Fears of a civil war or sectarian war in Iraq "are baseless," according to Al Barzani. "There are challenges ahead, and there is competition between the different parties, but at the end of the day this is part of the democratic process which we are starting to put into practice."

The opening session of Iraq's first freely elected parliament in half a century took place on March 16, 2005, and was inevitably accompanied by explosions targeting the fortified Green Zone, where the state-of-the-art convention center was hosting 275 deputies. As they took their seats, this eclectic gathering of men and women demonstrated the different dress codes of this Byzantine society. Men in Western-style suits conversed with women wearing the traditional hijab, the black robes and turbans of the Shias, and rubbed shoulders with the proud and baggy-trousered Kurds; and unveiled women in smart business dress chatted with Arabs in sand-colored dishdashas and white headdresses encircled by a black *ekal*. All were united in their determination to prevent insurgency attacks from derailing the political process. They were embarking on a journey that would culminate in choosing a government and writing a constitution that would form, they hoped, the basis of a new era in Iraq's modern history. The lawmakers listened to verses from the Koran while U.S. helicopter gunships hovered overhead.

Before the elected deputies went to take the oath, the Kurdish leaders–Jalal Talabani, Burham Saleh, Hoshyar Zebari, and Fouad Massoum–expressed their delight in participating in such a historic occasion, which, ironically for them, coincided with the anniversary of the chemical attack on the Kurdish town of Halabja by Saddam Hussein's forces in 1988.

A turning point that day was when the speaker, opening the

proceedings in Arabic, was interrupted by one of the Kurdish deputies asking for a simultaneous translation in the official Kurdish language. According to new legislation, Iraq is dually Arabic and Kurdish. The request was granted despite the fact that the translator who was present wasn't capable of providing a full translation. Nevertheless, a summary of proceedings was duly delivered.

The differences of opinion between the main parties in this coalition are very clear. Especially between Jaafari's organization, the Al Da'awa Party, and that of Al Hakim, the Supreme Council for the Islamic Revolution in Iraq, and the same is true between these two organizations and that of Dr. Ahmed Chalabi.

While the Supreme Council has maintained a very close relationship with Iran, Al Da'awa maintained its religious independence. But the influence of the Marjaeyeh, the spiritual leader, has played a big role in keeping this alliance together. Sistani himself intervened to convince the members of the coalition to put forward a name for the premiership after they failed to approve one name between the three candidates—Chalabi, Jaafari, and Al Hakim's choice (Adel Abdul Mahdi, the minister of finance in Iyad Allawi's interim government). Sistani told the three Shia candidates to concentrate more on the program than on the person. The three candidates finally agreed on Jaafari, who later visited Sistani to get his blessing.

When Achraf Qadi, the UN representative to Iraq, was granted the opportunity to meet Sayed Sistani in Najaf, he spoke of his admiration for Sistani, who had expressed every interest in seeing Iraq return to stability and allowing the Iraqi people to exercise their political rights. Sistani told Kofi Annan's representative that he is a man of religion, not politics, and he interferes only when there is a crisis. This was clearly a reference to his role in solving the previous year's Al Mahdi army crisis without the intervention of U.S. forces or the combined forces of the Iraqi police and army, who would inevitably have stormed and damaged the sanctity of the Imam Ali Mosque, the holiest site in Iraq for the Shiites.

Yet Sistani had apparently made a statement that had put other Iraqis–Sunnis, Kurds, Christians, and Turkomen–on red alert. In February 2005 he was quoted as saying that he would like to see Islam as the root for legislation in Iraq. I was in Baghdad at the time, and many eyebrows were raised at his words; people felt their fears were justified, as they knew the intentions of the two main religious parties–the Islamic Dawa Party (IDP) and the Supreme Council for the Islamic Revolution in Iraq (SCIRI). This panic did not last long, however, as Dr. Jaafari and Sayed Abdul Aziz Al Hakim made statements denying any such revolution was being considered. The situation was further diffused when a subsequent statement put out by Sayed Hamed Al Kaffaf, Sistani's spokesperson, said that reports made in the last two days quoting Sayed Sistani were not only untrue, but Sistani hadn't even made a statement at all.

Arriving at Dr. Ibrahim Al Jaafari's residence in the fortress-style Green Zone, I wondered what kind of reaction he gets from his religious visitors when they are greeted by his ever-present sniffer dogs. The use of these dogs for security has caused uproar and has resulted in deaths in some parts of the country. Their presence appeared particularly incongruous as Jaafari, the first elected prime minister in Iraq, is also the head of the Al Da'awa Party, an extremely religious and conservative Shia organization. The only time he has ever been known to shake hands with a woman, something the ultraorthodox avoid, along with eye contact with the opposite sex, was when Hillary Clinton visited Iraq in November 2003. Thus it was a surprise when Jaafari appointed seven women to be in his cabinet, four of whom were Kurds.

Dr. Jaafari, who occupied the post of vice president in the interim government led by Allawi, was the candidate named by the Shia-led coalition to lead the new government. All his diplo-matic and negotiating skills had to be brought into play to fairly allocate posts among such a wide spectrum of complex political, religious, and ethnic sensibilities.

When I asked him about the religious tensions in Iraq and the possibility of civil or sectarian war in Iraq, he said, "The mixture of religions, cultures, and traditions which exist in Iraq, together with the experience they have shared together, will make it diffi-cult for people like the Al Qaeda–linked terrorist Abu Musab Al Zarqawi and his followers to increase his support. It is a challenge the Iraqi people are facing at present among many challenges." While the coffin makers of Iraq like Ali Hussein Mohammed are seeing a dramatic upturn in their fortunes, it would be a truly sad state of affairs if the only entrepreneurs flourishing after the down-fall of Saddam Hussein are those involved in the death trade.

NOTES

1. Agence France-Presse, April 24, 2005.
2. *The Guardian,* April 24, 2005.
3. *Al Hayat,* April 18, 2005.
4. Middle East On-Line, April 11, 2005.
5. The Muslim Brotherhood is a religious and political organization opposed to secular tendencies. It was founded in 1928 in Egypt to foster a return to the original precepts of the Koran. The Salafi movement is often referred to as Wahabbism, the Salafis' aim to return Islam to its purist roots.
6. *Newsweek,* June 2, 2004.
7. Round-table discussion with *Al-Ahram Weekly,* headed by Salah Omar Al Ali, December 22, 2004.
8. Salah Omar Al Ali, interview with the author, April 22, 2005, London.
9. Massoud Al Barzani recounting story to author on February 10, 2005.

CHAPTER SEVEN

IRAQ AND ITS NEIGHBORS: SAUDI ARABIA, SYRIA, JORDAN, IRAN, KUWAIT, AND TURKEY

During Saddam's years in power, Iraq posed a threat to its neighboring countries and to the region's stability. This was highlighted during Saddam's wars with Iran and Kuwait and his targeting of Saudi Arabia and Israel with long-range Scud missiles. These threats were used by the United States as a justification to launch their war against Saddam's regime. Ironically, after Saddam's fall and the subsequent occupation by the American-led coalition, Iraq continues to be a source of danger to its neighbors. Syria and Iran feel particularly vulnerable and fear being invaded by the United States. For Turkey, because of the Kurds, Iraq continues to be a thorn in its side, while the Gulf States of Saudi Arabia and Kuwait fear the impact of the political vacuum in Iraq, particularly the lawlessness and chaos, which could spill over their borders and threaten the security and stability these countries have traditionally enjoyed.

* * *

The discovery that a son has disappeared from the family home in the Royal Kingdom of Saudi Arabia to travel across the desert to Iraq to join their fellow jihadis follows a familiar pattern. The family first learns about their mission via two telephone calls. The first, from an anonymous caller, reassures the parents that their son is in Iraq and that he is fine and well. The follow-up caller identifies his military group and tells the family that their son has died for the cause and that they should prepare to celebrate his departure to heaven as a martyr.

This story has become a source of great anxiety for Saudi parents, who wait in dread for that second telephone call as the number of suicide missions in Iraq has escalated. Hardly a week goes by in Saudi Arabia without families being informed by telephone of the death of a son or a brother, despite the efforts being made by the Saudi government to prevent its citizens from entering Iraq via neighboring countries. Counterterrorist experts in Saudi Arabia have calculated that the number of young Saudis who participated in Iraq's jihad between 2003 and 2004 exceed twenty-five hundred fighters. Five hundred of these were killed, and about one hundred were arrested by Iraqi authorities.

"The Saudis of Iraq" is the term coined to describe these jihadis, just as the Arabs who fought in Afghanistan were called "Afghani Arabs." This new phenomena has prompted some political analysts in the kingdom to warn of the dangers these "Saudis of Iraq" might pose to the future security of the country, which could exceed the threat that was posed by the Afghani Arabs when they returned from their jihadi tours of Pakistan and Afghanistan. There isn't much to distinguish between the Jordanian Abu Musab Al Zarqawi's group and the Saudi-born Osama bin Laden's Al Qaeda network, even though bin Laden's followers in the early 1980s used to only attack Soviet military conveys in Afghanistan, while the Iraqi insurgents are killing Iraqi civilians.

Saudi religious leaders are working day and night with the support of the royal family to curb the brainwashing carried out by the leaders of extreme religious groups and to create more space for the moderate religious leaders to maneuver and play a more influential role in guiding the youth of Saudi Arabia. A few well-known religious scholars went one step further and issued a fatwa banning Saudis from jihad in Iraq and declaring it illegal according to Islamic Sharia laws.

The return of two Saudi brothers who snuck into Iraq via the Syrian-Iraqi border a few days after their arrival in Iraq in April 2005 is one example of the kind of encounter some of these foreign fighters meet on the road to potential martyrdom. The two brothers, who had been following the activities of the insurgents on the Internet and Arabic news channels, managed to make contact with Iraqi insurgents close to the border with Syria. When the brothers asked the emir of one of the Islamic cells fighting the American forces if they could get a ride to Fallujah, he declined, saying it was too risky a mission these days. However, his alternative unnerved them. He told them that there were cars already rigged with explosives and they were welcome to take one of them. The young men were shocked at his readiness to pack them off to their death. "We hardly know Iraq," they told him, "yet you want us to go on a suicide mission straight away?" The emir's reply was that this was his offer, and if they weren't happy with it, they had better look for another militia to join. The brothers, who refused to disclose their identity, resigned themselves to returning across the desert to Saudi Arabia and abandoning their idea of becoming jihadis in Iraq.

The rulers of Saudi Arabia welcomed the overthrow of Saddam Hussein's regime but remain fearful about its consequences for regional stability. There are many Shiites living in the oil-rich eastern province of the Saudi Kingdom, but they are treated with great condescension by the Sunni elite. The rise in

Shia prominence in Iraq after the fall of Saddam Hussein and the subsequent election of Iraq's Shia-led government has already encouraged the Shia in Saudi Arabia to demand to play a bigger role in their Kingdom. This has galvanized the Saudi royal family to become more outward-looking in its politics in the region.

The Saudi leadership, however, has been unable to prevent its Islamic militant groups from crossing the Saudi-Iraq border, after it became clear that the Sunni-led resistance in Iraq proved popular among their young generation. This has created a schism between the mainly youthful Wahhabi population and the more elderly Wahhabi—namely, the ruling royal family, known as the House of Saud.[1]

The Saudi leadership faces new challenges as a result of the increased activity by Al Qaeda. Fifteen out of the twenty-one September 11 hijackers were Saudi nationals, not forgetting Osama bin Laden, who was born in the kingdom's capital, Riyadh. The goal is to marginalize those extreme elements in Saudi society to prevent the country from becoming another battleground, while at the same time kick-starting a process of reforms to help to restore the stability the kingdom has enjoyed in the past. Most importantly, Saudi Arabia must review its relationship with the United States, where trust and confidence has been damaged following the role played by Saudis in the 9/11 disaster. The country has been accused by many U.S. politicians of contributing to the spread of extremism by funding terrorist groups in other parts of the world.

The frequent attacks carried out by Al Qaeda followers in Saudi Arabia reflect the influence the organization has in the kingdom since the Baathist regime of Saddam Hussein was brought to an end. Extremist or idealistic young Saudis are filtering through the porous border into Iraq, where they receive military training before returning back to the kingdom to participate in attacks similar to those that happened in Al Khobar on

May 29, 2004. Al Khobar is one of the main centers of Saudi Arabia's oil industry and employs many Western workers. In at least three attacks spread over two days, twenty-two people lost their lives. Places of economic importance where large numbers of foreigners are known to work were deliberately selected with the purpose of frightening off Westerners, destabilizing the Saudi government, and damaging the world economy by driving up oil prices. Most of those killed were foreign workers. In one incident, the assassins attempted to separate Muslims from non-Muslims in order to emphasize who their desired targets were. A week later, Al Qaeda issued a statement via two Islamic Web sites warning Muslims in Saudi Arabia to steer clear of Americans and other Westerners to avoid becoming victims of their attacks. "All compounds, bases, and means of transportation, especially Western and American airline companies will be a direct target for our coming operations in the near future." It also warned "security forces and guards of Crusader compounds and American bases" and "those who carry weapons on behalf of the Crusaders and the covert agents of the Saudi government." Thirty-five thousand Americans live and work in the Saudi kingdom, providing the terrorists with a large and visible target.

The most important event in Saudi Arabia will be the election and appointment of the Shura council in the kingdom. Even though no date has been set for this, many suspect it will happen in the very near future. Half of the members will be elected, and the other half will be appointed by the king. The introduction of new laws are expected to give the Shura council the power to legislate in order to hold ministers or government officials accountable.

The Saudi government probably faces no alternative but to support America's efforts in Iraq and to help root out terrorism. Security forces in the kingdom have succeeded in rounding up many of the cells and arresting active members, but in terms of ideology, the government needs many years to reprogram the brainwashed elements that have benefited from the stifling religious environment that is intrinsic to the Saudi system.

* * *

It was late afternoon on election day 2005, and the polling station in the convention center inside Baghdad's Green Zone was about to prepare for the count. I came across Hazem Al Cha'alan, the defense minister in Dr. Iyad Allawi's interim government, and asked him for an interview. He invited me to join him in his office at the Ministry of Defense, once his arranged meeting with Dr. Ibrahim Al Jaafari, the leader of the Al Da'awa Party, had finished. Cha'alan explained that his forces had arrested many Iranians that day who had been involved in terrorist activities and that he would make them available to me to interview. Cha'alan, who was disliked by many pro-Iranians in Iraq for his vocal criticism of Iran, seemed very keen for me to accept his invitation. He was adamant that Iran was intervening surreptitiously in his country, including financing Shia groups or sending in their intelligence teams. Statements such as these by Cha'alan were usually met with condemnation by the Iranian government, but many in the Iraqi capital and abroad used them as a means to highlight the influence Iran is wielding in Iraq. Shortly after Cha'alan had concluded his meeting with Ibrahim Al Jaafari, his private secretary found me in the convention center and told me that the interview with the Iranian prisoners was now off. It appeared that Dr. Jaafari, the spokesperson for the ultraorthodox Shia Al Da'awa Party had mediated between Cha'alan and the Iranians. When I later asked Jaafari what he thought about Cha'alan's statements concerning Iran, his response was, "each one is entitled to his own opinions. This is Iraq, a new democracy."

After the fall of the Iraqi regime, Iran's influence has become more obvious. Before the dust of war had settled, I was on my way back to Baghdad from Tikrit, accompanied by a friend who told me that large amounts of weapons from the disbanded Iraqi army were being amassed and sold to the Iranians via armed groups. A recent-model Soviet-built Iraqi tank, the T-72, my friend informed me, was sold for just five thousand U.S. dollars.

Twenty-five years ago, Iraq feared the contagious spread of the 1979 Iranian Revolution, which saw the transformation of its neighbor from an autocratic, secular monarchy under Mohammed Reza Pahlavi, the Shah of Iran and friend of the United States, into an Islamic theocracy ruled by Grand Ayatollah Ruhollah Mousavi Khomeini, an avowed enemy of the United States. The stony-faced ayatollah's credo was, "There is no room for play in Islam. It is deadly serious about everything."[2] The revolution was divided into two stages. The first saw an alliance of liberal, leftist, and religious groups that ousted the shah. The second stage became known as the Islamic Revolution, which brought the radical Shiite ayatollahs to power, where they remain today.

As Iran's immediate neighbor, and with an estimated 60 percent Shia population, Iraq appeared ripe to receive this Iranian-style religious revolution. Ayatollah Khomeini's condemnation of Saddam Hussein as secularist, pro-Western, and worse can hardly have placated the Iraqi leader, especially as Khomeini had once taken up residence in Iraq's holy city of Najaf after he had been ordered out of Iran by the Shah in 1978. "He ate Iraqi bread and drank water from the Euphrates," Saddam declared, "but he was ungrateful."[3] He is also known to have derisively referred to the ayatollah as a "shah in a turban."[4] Saddam eventually threw him out of Iraq, and the unwanted ayatollah found a home in a Paris suburb until he seized his moment to return. Before the euphoria of the Iranian revolution had a chance to die down, Saddam launched his offensive against Ayatollah Khomeini, who declared: "This is not a war for territory. It is a war between Islam and blasphemy."[5]

Iran is enemy number one according to the former Iraqi defense minister Hazem Al Cha'alan. "Its [Iran's] interference will kill democracy and support terrorism, encouraging the enemies of Iraq to cross over its borders after gaining control of its border posts. This would allow agents to penetrate the new Iraqi ministries and even the newly appointed government." His comments coincided with a U.S. campaign accusing Iran of continuing to rebuild its nuclear program while ignoring the advice and warnings given by the International Atomic Agency to cease work on the program and allow international observers to inspect the country's nuclear facilities. Iraq's pro-U.S. government, together with American forces in Iraq, will do their utmost to prevent Shia Islamist groups known for their sympathetic views toward Iran from working against the interests of Iraq—especially in the south of the country, where the majority of Iraqis belong to the Shia sect.

Saddam Hussein fought a long and costly war to prevent Iran from spreading its influence across the border and to sever any possible connection between the Shia in Iraq and those in Iran. As is the case with Syria, a speedy American success in Iraq was not in the ruling elite of Iran's interests. There are reformist elements in Iran that now influence policy. Many Iranians have tired of the consequences of its global isolation, and some sections of the country's repressive regime are resented by moderate sections of the society. This is true despite the continued dominance of Iran's conservative Guardian Council led by Ayatollah Khameini, whose decisions are based on religious law (Sharia) and override those of the Iranian Parliament.

Despite its standoff with Washington over its nuclear program, Iran appeared to take a moderate position. It refrained from expressing resentment about the American presence on its borders with Afghanistan and Iraq, and even played a mediation role between the U.S. administration and Sayed Muqtada Al Sadr. At Washington's request, an Iranian diplomatic delegation visited

Baghdad on April 15, 2004, to halt Al Sadr's armed resistance against the American-led coalition. Kamel Kharazi, the Iranian foreign minister, made it clear that it was the United States who asked Iran for help in calming down the explosive situation. Washington's request to the Iranian leadership was handed over by Swiss diplomats in Tehran, who have looked after American interests in Iran since the American embassy was closed after the 444-day hostage siege in 1980.

The toppling of Saddam Hussein and his eventual capture provided Iran with a precious opportunity to have a greater influence in Iraq. Iran has strong ties with the Shia majority in Iraq and with their principal Shia political parties. It is anticipated that the Shiites in Iraq will have the upper hand in ruling the country, which would lead to the formation of new alliances in the area. Iran has proved in the past that it is capable of benefiting from alliances with new groups such as Hizbollah in Lebanon without compromising its international role.

* * *

Even leaders in politically dangerous country of Syria manage to enjoy a relatively normal social life. Syrian president Bashar Al Assad is regularly spotted accompanied by his London-born wife, Asma, going to the movies or enjoying a meal or drink in one of the many lively restaurants and coffee shops in Damascus, albeit with bodyguards in tow. Baria Yagi, a journalist friend in Damascus, told me of an outing she made to the theater on September 30, 2004, to see a critically acclaimed political satire, *The Rule of the Shepherds*. She paid for the best seats in the front row of the stalls only to discover that Bashar had spontaneously chosen the same night to take his wife. He clearly hadn't made reservations, and my friend found that her expensive front-row seat had been reassigned to Bashar and his wife. After arguing with the box office, she was given a seat in the second row, alongside one of Bashar's bodyguards and directly behind the young leader and his wife.

The play, delivered in a local dialect, made frequent caustic references to autocratic rule, and Bashar was observed attempting to keep his wife abreast of the plot by translating the colloquial Arabic. Before the play began, my friend Baria had struck up a conversation with the bodyguard. When the curtain calls were over, the bodyguard took a call on his cell phone. The voice on the other end of the line was the president's mother, asking for her son to return home soon, as she was concerned for his safety. In the meantime Bashar and his wife were happily mingling with the theatergoers and posing for photographs.

This relaxed attitude reflects the lifestyle of a man who chose an academic and civilian life, becoming an eye specialist with no intention of going into politics. But Bashar's older brother, Basil, who was heir to the presidency, was killed in a car crash. So on the death of his father, Hafez Al Assad, the young doctor was left with no choice but to inherit a complex political role at a time when the Arab-Israeli conflict, the volatile situation in Lebanon, and the implications of a regime change in Iraq were at the heart of Middle East politics.

From day one after the collapse of the rival Baath Party in Iraq, America accused Syria of harboring senior Iraqi Baath leaders and turning a blind eye to the insurgents who crossed its borders into Iraq to participate in the resistance against the U.S.-led forces and the newly formed army and police force. Unconcerned by any reproach from the American superpower, in a televised interview the Syrian leader described the Iraqi resistance as "legitimate." Syria has nothing to gain from an Iraq ruled by a pro-U.S. government. President Bashar fears that if the American plan succeeds in Iraq, the regime-change model will be replicated in other parts of the region, which could compromise Syria. Syria's official support for the Iraqi resistance at some stage was an attempt to cushion the internal anger of its people, who were brought up on a combination of nationalistic slogans and Islamic sentiments.

Prime Minister Iyad Allawi and Interior Minister Falah Al Naqib told me in early February 2005 that they had concrete evidence of Syria's support for militant activities in Iraq against the coalition forces. This was confirmed when I was given access to militants who had been arrested by the Iraqi government and who confessed to receiving training and financial support in Syria before joining insurgency groups in Iraq.

Saddam Hussein's half brother, Sabawi Ibrahim Al Hassan, was captured on February 27, 2005, in Hasakah in northeastern Syria, thirty miles from the Iraqi border, and was handed over to Iraqi officials. Al Hassan was one of the most wanted men in Iraq. His role as head of the general security directorate put him at number thirty-six on the American list of the fifty-five most wanted members of the overthrown regime. He is suspected of financing and directing insurgents from exile in Syria. Dr. Allawi's government confirmed that Al Hassan was handed over together with twenty-nine other members of Saddam's collapsed Baath Party, whose Syrian branch has been in power in Damascus since 1963. This overture toward America on Syria's part is seen as a response to increasingly hostile pressure by both the American and the Iraqi governments, who have accused them of harboring key insurgency leaders and former regime members.

In the early days after the deposing of Saddam, Syria feared that Iraq might be used as a base from which to attack its regime. Even worse, the Americans might consider occupying Syria. The United States has carried out many incursions into the country, one of which came on June 23, 2003, when U.S. troops crossed into Syria as far as Ghob El Deeb, 33 miles from the border. Syrian soldiers–who were accused of turning a blind eye toward the foreign fighters crossing Iraq's border or knowing their identities and the places they were coming from—were arrested and interrogated for almost two weeks to determine whether they were acting in an official capacity and where their orders came from. "Thus far, the Syrians have been willing to expel fugitives only after presented with incontrovertible evidence that a particular official has been given sanctuary. . . . the fact that the captured Syrian soldiers were held for nearly two weeks (ostensibly for "medical treatment") is a pretty strong indication that the Pentagon believed that Syrian forces deliberately assisted the escape of the Iraqi fugitives."[6] Syria wisely refrained from publicly denouncing these activities.

As a result, the following day U.S. Secretary of Defense Rumsfeld made an announcement praising the Syrian government for not highlighting this incident and for its cooperation. This atmosphere of bonhomie with the Americans gave Syria the leverage to adopt new policies.

Syria's laissez-faire policy toward Arab fighters entering Iraq through its borders, even before the fall of the regime, was not well known.

The joint Syrian-Iranian interest in Iraq is trying to keep one step ahead of America's next move toward them. While Iran has concentrated its activities on the Shia in the main and on the Kurds in part, the Syrians have devoted their attentions toward the Sunni areas, especially in the provinces that run alongside their border.

Iran hopes for political stability in Iraq, while, ironically, Syria feels more secure with the continuation of instability. This calculation has proved to be disastrous. Many in Washington began speaking of passing laws in Congress related to Syria, similar to the one that the United States adopted against Saddam Hussein's regime in 1998, which will open the doors to finance some of the growing Syrian opposition. The U.S. administration has held meetings with Syrian opposition figures in Washington to discuss the future of Syria. It was the first high-profile meeting that the White House highlighted.

Syria together with Egypt and Saudi Arabia used to be a political force to be reckoned with in the Arab world. But Syria recently lost its ranking when other countries began to mistrust it, thanks to Syria's policies toward Lebanon and Palestine.

Despite the signals given out by the regime about promised reforms in Syria, it is difficult to see this happening in the immediate future because of the strong grip the internal security agencies have on its people. There is no one on the political scene who can provide an effective opposition to the regime at a difficult time in its history, when Syrian forces have returned to the country and a power struggle is already brewing.

* * *

The last contact that Jordan's late King Hussein established with Saddam Hussein occurred toward the end of 1990 during the Gulf War, after a French-led initiative that was designed to convince Iraq to withdraw peacefully from Kuwait. On August 9, 1995, Hussein Kamel, Saddam's son-in-law, defected to Jordan with his brother and their wives who are Saddam's daughters. At the time, few were aware that the sudden defection by Saddam's right-hand man was arranged secretly a few months before. Senior Jordanian and Iraqi officials confirmed to me that a few months before Hussein Kamel's defection, he traveled abroad for medical treatment via Amman, the Jordanian capital. While in the Jordanian capital, he held a secret meeting with King Hussein, during which he received the king's approval to defect to Jordan in the near future. King Hussein was buoyed by the idea of Kamel's future arrival in Jordan, which was clearly expressed in statements he made during 1996 when he alluded to Saddam Hussein's fate and how his days were numbered.

It appeared that King Hussein had overestimated the influence Hussein Kamel wielded in Iraq. The night before Kamel left Amman, he called me. Over the telephone, Hussein Kamel told me about the assurances he received from Saddam Hussein that if he went back to Iraq, he would participate in the changes Baghdad was about to initiate. During our evening conversation, which lasted an hour, Kamel sounded frustrated about not being taken seriously after his rebellion against his dictator father-in-law. He had expected to receive red-carpet treatment and support from the West, which had been calling for someone within the regime to lead the vanguard on any power change in Iraq. But Kamel was clearly not the person they were prepared to back. His frustration began when he requested a visit to Washington after sending two envoys–Mishan Al Jabouri and Saad Al Bazzaz–to establish contacts with the American administration concerning a future visit by him. Washington's curt response, as Al Jabouri told me, was that they suggested if Hussein Kamel had any new evidence concerning Iraq's nuclear or chemical capabilities, the best thing for him to do was to contact the U.S. embassy in Amman and discuss it with diplomatic officials there.

Kamel was also made to feel persona non grata when he attempted to contact neighboring countries–Syria and Kuwait. The Kuwaitis, who politely refused to invite him, advised his intermediary to get in touch with the Khaled Al Dowisian, the Kuwaiti ambassador to London, if he had any information concerning Kuwaiti prisoners in Iraq. Damascus likewise shunned him. Instead they relayed a message through General Wafiq Al Samarrai, head of military intelligence, who had defected from Baghdad a few years earlier, saying that Syria would talk to him on the condition that he passed on information concerning individuals or organizations in Iraq who were collaborating against Syria. To add further insult to injury, Kamel learned that he was to face a civil court in Jordan for using abusive language against a

Jordanian journalist during a telephone conversation. Kamel, who had believed he was enjoying royal, kid-glove treatment in Jordan, was dismayed when he heard that a date had been set for his trial–in other words, he was being treated as a commoner. When he approached the royal court in Amman to contest his treatment, the reply came back that court orders cannot be overturned. These compounding factors made up his mind for him: Kamel decided to return to Baghdad, where he met his fate, a few days later, on February 23, 1996. Together with his brother and their two wives they were met at the Jordanian-Iraqi border by Uday Hussein. Uday ordered his two sisters to travel with him and told their husbands to follow separately. Both were killed during a thirteen-hour firefight at a safe house in Baghdad, having been denounced by Saddam and his tribe as traitors.

Unlike his late brother, King Hussein, who chose to work for a regime change in Iraq through plans set up in Amman, Prince Hassan found a more effective partner to plot with after his brother's death. He decided to travel to Washington, where a series of secret meetings took place. Plans were hatched by Prince Hassan, the former Crown Prince of Jordan; President Bush; and Donald Rumsfield to amalgamate Iraq with Jordan and create one large Hashemite Kingdom.

This came to light a few weeks later during an unusual conference held in Kensington Town Hall in London on July 15, 2002. The conference was attended by Crown Prince Hassan, former Iraqi military officers in exile, and a large gathering of opposition members of the Iraqi National Congress, led by Ahmed Chalabi. Prince Hassan's contribution to the event was seen as his own expansionist plans to enlarge the Hashemite Kingdom and didn't have the approval of his nephew, King Abdullah, back in Amman. Fearing that Prince Hassan had ambitions for his throne, the audacious plan, which Washington had hoped would provide an ideal scenario for a stable postwar Iraq, was swiftly thwarted.

Considering the large-scale terrorist attacks that Jordan has recently managed to curb, the country has demonstrated sufficient control to maintain stability within its current borders. Cross-border penetration to and from neighboring countries is also providing more challenges for King Abdullah. Jordan is not concerned with democracy being established in Iraq, but fears a prolonged period of anarchy and lawlessness while being troubled by the Palestinian-Israeli confrontation.

Jordan was the first Arab country to invite Prime Minister Dr. Ibrahim Jaafari and President Jalal Talabani. Jordan had many concerns—mainly that Sunnis in Iraq might be excluded in the formation of a new Iraq. Also there were, and still are, concerns about growing terrorism in Jordan as a result of activities by its homegrown Abu Musab Al Zarqawi. Many Iraqis believe that the Jordanian government and even the Jordanian public are fully behind what remains of Saddam's old regime, including the insurgents, but the facts on the ground tell a different story.

Jordan's main concern is how to bring the Sunnis back into the fold. The roads leading to Baghdad from Amman pass through the restive Sunni towns of Fallujah and Ramadi. Jordan has lobbied Washington to convince the administration and decision makers that dissolving the Iraqi army was one of the biggest mistakes committed by the U.S.-led administration and must be reversed. There is no possibility of normalization between these two countries while the insurgency is flourishing and the roads are unsafe.

The Salafi religious revival in Fallujah in the Sunni Triangle happened because the trucking trade from Jordan passed through the city on the way to Baghdad. This form of Sunni Islam is theologically similar to the Wahhabi movement, which is predominant in Saudi Arabia. Using the tenth-century scholar Ibn Taymiyyah as their theological guide, Salafis strive to return Islam to its purest roots and emulate the Prophet Mohammed in every aspect of life. Al Qaeda and the Islamic Brotherhood are linked with both the Wahhabi and Salafi movements. Salafism has become popular in the smaller cities of Jordan such as Maan and Zarqa, the hometown of Abu Musab Al Zarqawi.

Jordan maintained contact with senior Iraqi opposition leaders during Saddam's years. Jordan's King Hussein was well respected within the Shia community of Iraq to the extent that before the fall of the regime, many were hoping that the Hashemite royal family would restore the throne in Iraq to ensure the country remained united. The Hashemites, or "Bani Hashem," are direct descendents of the Prophet Mohammed through his daughter Fatima and her husband, Ali bin Abi Talib. On the death of King Hussein on February 7, 1999, the Hashemite crown was passed down to his son, King Abdullah bin Al Hussein.

King Abdullah surprised many in the Arab world with his out-spoken comments before an audience with George Bush at the White House on March 15, 2005. He warned about the dangers of an emerging Shiite Crescent extending from Iran via Iraq to Lebanon and Syria. Advisers close to King Abdullah explained that his concerns were exacerbated by the tens of thousands of Iranians who had entered Iraq, taking advantage of the overall chaos in the country, where the loss of public records, including identification papers, meant that no one could question their iden-tity. This influx is bound to increase the Shia influence in Iraq, which Tehran is already exerting on some of Iraq's religious organizations and parties.

There is a saying in Arabic about divorce between two people that could be applied to two countries that live side by side: no matter how bad things get between them, they will still need each other. Whatever the outcome of the relationship between Jordan and Iraq, many believe that for economic, geographic and demo-graphic reasons, they have to remain on good terms. Jordan is preparing itself for the challenges ahead. In 2007 the country must pay its debts toward the Paris Club, an informal group of official creditors that was established in 1956 when Argentina agreed to meet its public creditors in Paris. Time is running out for debt restructuring by Jordan, which is no longer in a position to pay off its loan interest. Unemployment figures in Jordan are officially 15 percent, but actual rates are thought to be more in the region of 30 percent. Also at a time when oil prices are soaring above fifty U.S. dollars a barrel, Jordan, which formerly received discounted oil from Iraq, will no longer enjoy this privilege, and the country expects to face an oil bill estimated at $2 billion U.S. a year. Jordan's external debt was $7.683 billion, and the outstanding domestic debt was $2.40 billion in October 2004.

Jordan hoped that a peace agreement with Israel would transform and revive Jordan's economy and create more jobs, but the fact remains that the chances of this are very slender. The Iraqi imbroglio only further complicates the Hashemite Kingdom's precarious position, thus making Jordan a potential flashpoint in the near future.

* * *

The small but wealthy, oil-rich country of Kuwait was the first of the Gulf States to give its female citizens the right to vote, after years of opposition from the conservative male-dominated leadership.

Iraq has a long-standing territorial dispute with its southern neighbor Kuwait that extends back to the Anglo-Ottoman Empire, when Kuwait was considered to be an autonomous zone while geographically being within Ottoman Iraq. Following World War I, Kuwait fell under British rule, and in 1961 Britain granted the country independence when it became an independent monarchy. Iraq never accepted the legitimacy of Kuwait's newfound independence but was indebted to Kuwait for supporting it in its war with Iran, which resulted in an estimated $14 billion debt to the country.

More than ten years after the Gulf War, Kuwait was still ridding itself of the stain left by Saddam's invasion. This created a climate of fear that was erased only after Saddam was removed from power. With the stigma removed and with renewed confidence, Kuwait has begun a new era with different political parties.

Kuwait was financially behind many of the groups who opposed Saddam Hussein before the war, and it opened its borders in welcome to Iraqis wishing to do business with Kuwaiti civil society and politicians. There are many projects in Iraq's private sector that are being financed by Kuwaitis—in particular, media organizations, oil companies, and building projects. Large sums of money have already been spent to encourage Iraqis to expand their business connections with Kuwait. Many more projects are in the pipeline, waiting for the appointment of a long-term government in Iraq that will enable Kuwait to establish proper contracts. In common with Jordan and Saudi Arabia, one of Kuwait's main concerns is the rise of the Shia influence in Iraq—especially the parties that have connections with Iran. Kuwait has a historical fear of Iranian influence, and many believe that this fear prompted Kuwait to finance Saddam during his war against Iran. The Kuwaiti government is also apprehensive that the Shia in Kuwait, seeing their newly empowered Shia brothers and sisters to the north, might equally strive for greater influence in the country.

The worst-case scenario for Kuwaitis is how to manage the thousands of jihadis from Kuwait, Saudi Arabia, and other Gulf States who have traveled to Iraq and can easily slip back into Kuwait through the long border. Kuwait has already experienced attacks carried out by these extreme elements that targeted American forces based in Kuwait. There have also been confrontations between Kuwaiti jihadis who were influenced by bin Laden and

Zarqawi. When Kuwaiti security forces tried to arrest them, there was an exchange of fire. The Kuwaiti government has tried to stem the tide of insurgents infiltrating its border with Iraq, but these young Kuwaitis, who are prepared to join the ranks of Al Qaeda, are using all means available to reach Zarqawi's generals in Iraq, including traveling via Syria and Jordan. Some of these Kuwaitis were arrested en route by the Syrian government as they approached the borders that have experienced the fiercest battles between U.S. forces and Al Zarqawi fighters—in particular, the Iraqi city of Al Qaem, close to the border with Syria.

*   *   *

The sound of screaming fighter jets fills the air around the NATO military airbase in Dyarbakir, the largest city in the Kurdish part of Turkey. A Turkish immigration officer checks the passport of a Kurdish passenger newly arrived from Sulaymaniya in Iraq and exchanges a few words in Kurdish within earshot of his Turkish soldier colleagues. Until recently, Kurds were forbidden to publicly express their ethnic identity, whether it be in word or deed. If caught, they would be punished by the Turkish military junta. The spring of 2005 was the first time that the Kurds of Turkey could openly celebrated their Norooz, an ancient festival symbolizing death and rebirth, to welcome the first day of spring.

Wearing colorful traditional costumes, they danced and sang, accompanied by tambourines and an assortment of instruments. Carnival-like parades filled the streets while elderly men watched from the street bars, drinking raki, the Turkish anisette. On the eve of Norooz, I was traveling through the Kurdish areas in northern Iraq. As I drove through the towns and villages along the border with Syria and Turkey, I noticed that the sky was lit by hundreds of bonfires, and I could sense an atmosphere of excitement on this eve of war.

In the presence of Turkish officials, some people dared to burn the Turkish flag, yet no one was arrested. Turkey is under tremendous pressure from Europe because of their human rights violations and questionable democracy, and this visible relaxation of their hold on the Kurds is the beginning, they hope, of their journey to Europe.

I was in Brussels in February 2005, attending the European summit, which was designed to discuss Turkey's future membership to the European Union (EU). As the session drew to a close, it became clear from statements issued by various European politicians that Turkey has to make concessions toward the Kurds and other minority groups and must treat them according to the human rights and democracy standards set by the EU for all member countries. By fulfilling the requirements necessary for EU membership, Turkey would have the added benefits of diffusing any underlying tension that has been bubbling under the surface among what is the largest concentration of Kurds in the region. If the Kurds are given the right to express their own personal identity, including speaking their own language, they must also receive help to put an end to the deprivation in their minority areas.

Just one week before the beginning of the war, on March 14, 2003, Rajib Taib Erdogan, the leader of the Conservative Justice and Development Party, or the AKB, became the new prime minister of an Islamic-led government. He refused to join the American -led coalition in its war against Iraq or to allow their airspace or military bases to be used in this war.

The more flexible and relaxed internal policies that the Turkish government has adopted have also been reflected in their foreign affairs. This became evident when Erdogan made a high-profile round of shuttle diplomacy to neighboring countries, including a visit to Syria, which must have been a further annoyance to the United States, having recently snubbed the superpower by not joining the Iraq war coalition. The Turkish leadership felt it was more important to establish good relations with the neighbors than to bow to U.S. demands so that they could contain any developments in Iraq.

Turkey's main concern is the Kurdish situation in Iraq. The country's administration fears that the strong cross-border ties that have been developed between the Kurds of Turkey and Iraq might encourage a situation whereby Kurds inside Turkey would also make demands for federalism or an independent state. While preferring to handle this sensitive issue diplomatically, Turkey is also losing sight of its historical claims to Mosul and other parts of Iraq. Turkey is exerting pressure on different Iraqi political groups, particularly concerning the rights of the Turkomen, with whom they have a close bond, in order to justify its interference in Iraqi affairs.

Other Iraqi political parties have supported the views of their fellow Kurds and adopted them because they felt that the intervention of a neighboring country, like Turkey, would open the doors for other countries in the region—especially those sharing their borders with Iraq—to intervene. As a result, an understanding has been reached with Washington that the United States can ask for help from any force in the world to participate in its coalition efforts in Iraq, except those from neighboring countries.

For the last decade, Turkey has gone to great lengths to establish an intelligence station in the north of Iraq to keep an eye and ear on Kurdish separatist Turks who have found refuge in the Kurdish areas of Iraq. These groups have traditionally supported Abdullah Ocalan, the leader of the Turkish Kurdish separatist organization, the Kurdish Workers Party. Turkey realized that any direct military intervention in north Iraq would be neither wise nor useful and preferred to coordinate with neighboring countries, especially Syria and Iran. The sole purpose of this coordination was to overcome their concerns about Kurdish ambitions. They opted not to allow an independent Kurdish state to spring to life, because it would threaten the stability of the countries concerned.

Turkish officials were reassured during the first visit to Ankara by the American foreign secretary, Condoleezza Rice, on February 5 and 6, 2005, that Washington would not support any Kurdish ambitions to establilsh an independent state in Turkey and that the U.S. administration will always encourage the Iraqi Kurds to adjust to the fact that they can be most successful by being part of Iraq as one state. Massoud Al Barzani, the leader of the Kurdistan Democratic Party, described the frustration of the Iraqi Kurds with those who write for the Turkish press and make statements concerning their political affairs in Iraq: "The subject of Kirkuk is an internal Iraqi issue, and Turkey should leave it to us to handle it with our partners in this country. We have agreed on measures to solve this issue in our constitution, and there is a special paragraph–number 58–which is specifically about this, so there is no need for foreign interference. We are willing to have good, friendly relations with Turkey as well as our other neighbors." Turkey's application to join the EU will make a difference to the lives of the Kurds. Many for the first time feel there is a future for them in Turkey, and are scaling down their ambitions of forming one entity with their fellow Kurds in Iraq, Iran, and Syria.

NOTES

1. Wahhabism, an orthodox version of Islam, was established in the eighteenth century by Mohammed bin Abdul Wahhab, who felt that Islam had lost its purity and wanted to interpret the Koran and practice its teachings as it was written in the seventh century, during the time of the Prophet. Inspired by the puritanical teachings of the fourteenth-century theologian Ibn Taymiyyah, the Wahhabis forged an alliance with Ibn Saud, the ruling family of the time. The Sauds remain the ruling family in Saudi Arabia today.

2. Speech at Qum, reported in *Time,* January 7, 1980.

3. Quoted in David Reed, "The Unholy War between Iran and Iraq," *Reader's Digest,* August 1984, p. 39.

4. Ibid.

5. Ibid.

6. "Is Syria Harboring Saddam?" Middle East Intelligence Bulletin, vol. 5, no. 6 (June 2003). Available at www.meib.org/articles/0306_s1.htm.

CHAPTER EIGHT

THE PALESTINIAN CONNECTION

J ust after 4:30 PM on Tuesday, August 19, 2003, Baghdad's working day was beginning to wind down. The recently opened Internet café at the United Nations headquarters, a popular haunt among the city's NGO community, was serving the first of its evening e-mail customers. A UN news conference was under way, detailing the organization's efforts to deactivate the dangerous landmines that were buried across the country. At around 4:45 PM a cement truck drove along a service road leading to Qanat Al Jaish Street, better known as Canal Street, and exploded into a concrete wall of the former Canal Hotel. Sergio Vieira de Mello, Kofi Annan's highly respected special envoy, died of his injuries, along with several of Annan's staff and employees of the World Bank who shared the four-story building. The Internet café was destroyed, and more than one hundred people, some with horrifying injuries, were reported wounded by the massive fifteen-hundred-pound bomb.[1]

Ten days later, two car bombs exploded outside the Imam Ali Shrine in Najaf, resulting in 125 fatalities. In October there were further attacks on international organizations—first the Turkish embassy in Baghdad, then the International Red Cross offices. In November, a number of Italians and Iraqis were killed in a suicide attack on the Italian Carabinieri (military police) training center in Nassiriyah.

These suicide bombings signaled a clear change of tactics by Iraq's growing resistance movement. The U.S.-led coalition forces, frustrated by their inability to control the situation, blamed foreign infiltrators, emphasizing the similarity between these new tactics and those used by Al Qaeda and other militant groups in the Middle East. Few seemed to realize that these Iraqis, who are well trained militarily, have learned from others' experiences and executed these attacks themselves. Meetings are known to have taken place in the Jordanian capital between elements of the Iraqi resistance and high-ranking members of Hamas. Thus, the Iraqi resistance forces have benefited from the expertise accumulated by the military wing of Hamas, which is notorious for its suicide bomb attacks against Israel.

The Western media, too, was quick to plant blame squarely on the shoulders of foreign fighters who had arrived to fight in Iraq from countries such as Jordan, Syria, Saudi Arabia, and Palestine, claiming that it was not in the psyche of the Iraqi people to use this method of destruction. While suicide bombings have proved an effective weapon in these countries, notably in Palestine during the country's long intifada with Israel, it was actually Iraqis who were the first to use human bombs in the Middle East, as far back as the 1970s.

The thousands of Iraqis who were expelled from Iraq for opposing Saddam Hussein's regime and the Baath Party arrived in Lebanon or Syria, where they joined the PLO or its various factions, playing an active role in military and political campaigns.

Ironically, while Saddam had expelled them for opposing his Baathist government, he was indirectly supporting them through his financial and military backing of their newfound allies among the Palestinians.

The first attacks carried out against the Israeli settlements that line the northern border with Lebanon were carried out by Iraqis. One of these was on a settlement known as Kiryat Shimona, on April 11, 1974. Three commandos from the Popular Front for the Liberation of Palestine–General Command (PFLP–GC), led by an Iraqi named Yassin Moussa Hazza'a, crossed the southern border of Lebanon and made their way into Israel's Upper Golan region under cover of night. At dawn they slipped down the mountain slope that forms the backdrop of this pretty border town in the Hula Valley and entered an apartment building, taking eighteen residents, including nine children, hostage. They holed themselves up in one of the apartments while demanding the release of Palestinians jailed in Israel. Their demands were not met, and the commandos detonated their explosives, killing themselves and their Jewish hostages during a failed rescue attempt by Israeli authorities.

Two months later, on June 13, 1974, a similar suicide attack was made on a settlement known in Arabic as Umm Al Akareb, or Kiryat Shamir in Hebrew, the home of mainly Russian Jews. This, too, involved Iraqi suicide bombers from Ahmed Jibril's PFLP-GC, named Amer Baqer Al Saadi and Salah Abdul Hamid Muza-affar. Following this lead, other Palestinian guerrilla organizations, including the Democratic Front for the Liberation of Palestine, led by Nayef Hawatmeh, and the Popular Front for the Liberation of Palestine (PFLP), led by George Habash, undertook cross-border missions, which eventually provoked Israel's invasion of Lebanon in 1978.

I grew up in a Palestinian refugee camp in Lebanon, and part of my education and upbringing was my exposure to the many

Palestinian social and political organizations, which put me in good stead during my early years in journalism in the mid-1970s. Even then I became aware of a growing Iraqi connection to Palestine, but little did I realize the future global impact this connection would have.

My first journalistic assignment, in November 1978, was for a Palestinian magazine. I traveled to Baghdad to cover the Arab Summit, which was to be hosted by Vice President Saddam Hussein, the de facto president until his official appointment as president of the Republic of Iraq on July 16, 1979. Egypt boycotted this gathering, having signed the Camp David Accords with Israel just two months before.[2] Arab countries at that time were opposed to any peace agreements with Israel unless it recognized UN Resolutions 242 and 338.[3]

The reception dinner for visiting heads of state was held at the presidential palace, and it was my first introduction to overstated opulence and luxury. Under the dazzling glare of an elaborate chandelier, I found myself face-to-face with Saddam. Our meeting didn't last more than a few minutes, during which the notorious Iraqi leader reinstated his government's position toward the Palestinians, which was that no peace agreement with the "Jewish State" would be acknowledged unless the Palestinians achieved their rights according to UN resolutions.

The history of Iraq's involvement in Palestine goes back to the 1930s, during an uprising in Palestine against the British Mandate that became known as the "Great Arab Revolt" of 1936–1939. The British were accused of turning a blind eye to the influx of Jewish immigrants from all over the world, especially from Germany and Eastern Europe, who were arriving in British-mandated Palestine at that time. A close relationship was established by Haj Amin Al Husseini, the Grand Mufti of Jerusalem, and Dr. Rashid Ali Al Kilani, the vociferously anti-British, Iraqi prime minister. Al Husseini was the leader of the so-called Arab Higher Committee, which was responsible for co-coordinating the Arab rebellion in Palestine. The Grand Mufti was forced into exile after the British government outlawed the committee. His arrival in Baghdad on October 16, 1939, opened a new chapter in pan-Arabism in Iraq. Along with Al Kilani, he provided the leadership and inspiration to the ultranationalism that had been incubating during the previous two decades of British rule in the Arab world. In this atmosphere of nationalism and anti-occupation militancy, the Iraqi army gained strength. It was composed of officers who believed that an army-led regime was imperative if Iraq was to take control and unite all Arabs in their fight against imperialism.

This united front with Palestine continued when the State of Israel was declared by its first prime minister, David Ben Gurion, in May 1948, leading to the eruption of bitter fighting between Israel and the Arabs. Iraq placed itself at the center of confrontation with the new Jewish State. The cemeteries in Jenin and Nablus in the West Bank are marked with the headstones of thousands of Iraqi soldiers, providing ample evidence of the extent of Iraq's willingness to die for the Palestinian cause.

At the start of the Six-Day War in 1967, when Israel launched its offensive against Egypt, Syria, and Jordan—which ended with the occupation of Egypt's Sinai Desert, the West Bank from Jordan, and the Golan Heights from Syria—the Iraqi army offered assistance to Jordan to prevent an Israeli incursion into the West Bank. But by the time the Iraqi army had rallied its troops and arrived in the Jordan Valley, the Israelis had already seized the West Bank and a cease-fire agreement had been reached between the two countries. The now redundant Iraqi army, under Jordanian supervision, withdrew from the Jordan Valley and set up military camps bases in Al Zarqa and Al Mafrek and other parts of the Jordanian desert.

This Iraqi military presence continued during the early days of the Palestinian Liberation Organization (PLO), which emerged as a more significant entity after the 1967 war. The head of the Iraqi forces in Jordan at that time, Lt. Gen. Hassan Naqib, established both a working and personal relationship with all the different Palestinian factions. The largest of these was Fatah, which was under the umbrella of the PLO and was formally launched in 1965 with Yasser Arafat as its leader. General Naqib was known to have supplied these various Palestinian groups with weapons and support under orders from Baghdad. When confrontations between the Jordanian army and the Palestinian military groups began in earnest in the 1970s, the Palestinians were hoping that Iraq, whose support they had come to rely on, would back them up with their strong military presence in Jordan and help them to overthrow the government of King Hussein. When this didn't happen, it led to a temporary rift in the Palestinian-Iraqi relationship, which was healed only by further injections of financial and military support from Iraq once the Palestinians were thrown out of Jordan and moved to new bases in Beirut and Damascus.

By the early 1970s, Iraq was gaining a reputation for its extreme and bellicose views toward Israel. The country was against recognizing UN Resolutions 242 and 338 because it believed the resolutions were slanted in Israel's favor, particularly in their official description of Israel as a State within the region. Even Yasser Arafat, who was by now executive chairman of the PLO based in Beirut, accepted these resolutions as a basis on which to reach a solution with Israel. To counter this, Iraq began courting and financing leftist factions within the Palestinian organizations.

At its twelfth annual meeting, the Palestinian National Council (PNC) reached an agreement with the PLO to craft a political solution by establishing a national authority to take control over any territory that Israel withdrew from. This "Phased Plan" was adopted on June 8, 1974. Prior to that meeting, the PLO's position was that it would accept nothing short of the immediate destruction of Israel. When the PLO announced its preparedness to solve the Israeli conflict and accept Resolution 242 and any Israeli withdrawal from any piece of land, Iraq pulled together the different Palestinian factions who opposed Arafat's moderate stand and invited them to Baghdad. These were the Popular Front for the Liberation of Palestine, led by George Habash; the Palestinian Liberation Front (PLF), headed by Samir Gousha, Ahmed Jibril's PFLP General Command, and the Arab Liberation Front's Iraq faction, led by Abdul Rahim Ahmad.

During their first meeting with Saddam Hussein, in his office at the presidential palace in Baghdad, I was told by Khaled Abdul Majid, spokesman of the Palestinian Popular Struggle Front (PPSF), one of those attending the meeting, that Saddam illustrated his ambitions using a large framed map behind his desk. The map highlighted the disputed area between Iran and Iraq that he called "Arabistan," or Al Ahwaz, meaning "Arab Land." This disputed area, 263 miles long and 238 miles wide, is southwest of Iran and southeast of Iraq and is bounded on the north and east by the natural barrier of the Zagros Mountains. Arabistan has a predominantly Arab population of approximately five million but is now part of Iran, having been given to Persia by the British in 1925. Saddam told his assembled guests that Iraq intended to liberate every single Arab territory that was under occupation. This included Arabistan, Palestine, the Golan Heights, and Iskandaroun Sanjak, a Syrian territory that was annexed by Turkey in 1939, calling it "Hattai." (Damascus clings to the idea that the territory belongs to Syria, and Syrian TV channels still show Iskandaroun as part of Syria when giving the area's weather forecasts.)

The intention of this coterie of leftist Palestinian groups, courted by Saddam, was to oppose the PLO's peace efforts led by Fatah and its leader, Yasser Arafat. They formed an umbrella group called the Rejection Front in Baghdad in late 1975. The group was financed by the Iraqi government, which also supplied it with munitions, and set up a media operation from where they printed many publications. During my first year as a journalist, I was given a job on a newspaper called *Al Somoud,* which was financed by the Rejection Front. This was a daily newspaper published from Al Fakhani Street in Beirut, just a few hundred yards from Arafat's headquarters. It was the height of the Lebanese civil war, and I remember feeling quite shocked at the amount of money that was being poured into this mouthpiece for the Rejection Front, whose sole purpose was to criticize Arafat's policies. The stupendous amounts of money that came in from the Iraqi government were superfluous to the costs of running the newspaper, and many bags that were bulging with U.S. dollars could be found behind the desks of the senior executives.

By the time Syrian forces intervened in Lebanon in May 1976 to put an end to the country's civil war between Christians and Muslims, Saddam Hussein, who was at odds with Syria, started pumping in even more money and weapons to support these groups and keep them as allies. These included not just Palestinians and Lebanese but Christians, too, who later opposed Syria's presence. On the face of it, the situation appeared to be an odd equation: a triangle of enemies, financed by the same source, while fighting against one another in the fifteen-year civil war. Saddam's ulterior motive was to weaken Syria.

One of the first Iraqi opposition leaders I was introduced to in Beirut back in 1979 was a high-ranking officer from Samarra—Lt. Gen. Hassan Al Naqib—who had formerly been the commander of the Iraqi forces based in Jordan after the 1967 war. When he returned to Iraq in April 1970, he was promoted to deputy chief of staff of the Iraqi army. Saddam, who harbored suspicions about Al Naqib's loyalties, transferred him to a diplomatic post and sent him to Madrid as Iraq's ambassador. In 1976 he was posted to Stockholm, where he remained for two years until defecting, becoming one of the first to oppose Saddam Hussein's regime in its early days in power. He went first to Beirut, where he worked closely with the late Palestinian leader Yasser Arafat as his military adviser. Arafat at that time was waging a verbal war against Saddam for having assassinated some of his prominent PLO representatives in Europe—Naim Khader, the PLO representative in Amsterdam; Issam Sartawi, Arafat's advisor in Lisbon; Ezz Al Din Al Qalaq in Paris; and Salah Khalaf and Hayel Abdul Hamid, members of Al Fatah's central committee, who were killed in Tunis.

Khalid Abdul Majid who happened to be in Baghdad then for meetings related to the Palestinian Rejection Front, met with Iraqi foreign minister Tariq Aziz in an attempt to complain about the negative impact of assassinations committed against moderate, intellectual Palestinians by a group supported and financed by Iraq. Abdul Majid told me that when he referred to the recently assassinated head of the PLO in Paris, saying, "He was a good person and totally dedicated to the cause—why was he assassinated?" Tariq Aziz's response was, "We are not involved with such things. That is a matter for you Palestinians."

These men were all assassinated by Sabri Al Banna, whose nom de guerre, Abu Nidal, was legendary during his worldwide reign of terror, which was at its height during the 1970s and 1980s. Abu Nidal held the card as the most wanted terrorist along with the Venezuelan "Carlos the Jackal" (Ilich Ramírez Sánchez) before Osama bin Laden arrived on the scene. Abu Nidal's most high-profile mission was masterminding the Black September organization's assassination of Israeli athletes in the Munich Olympic Stadium in September 1972. He was also the brains behind several plane hijackings and assassinations of ambassadors, including an attempt on the life of the Israeli ambassador to London that prompted Israel's second invasion of Lebanon in 1982. Abu Nidal became head of the Palestinian Fatah Revolutionary Council, a splinter group from Fatah, which was financed and supported by Saddam Hussein, together with other far-left Palestinian organizations. Fatah-RC had the same associations with terror as Al Qaeda has today. Its campaign was to overturn Arafat's moderate stance toward Israel. This was another odd strategy devised by Saddam–giving full support to Abu Nidal and his Fatah-RC while keeping a back door open to Arafat. Extremely militant in his views, Abu Nidal's hit list included the names of every moderate Palestinian he thought would establish a dialogue with Israel.

In the summer of 2002, Abu Nidal crossed the border from Iran into Iraq, using a false Yemeni diplomatic passport. According to a Palestinian source with whom I spoke, Abu Nidal revealed himself by paying a surprise visit to Barzan Al Tikriti, Saddam's half brother. He walked into his office in the Directorate of Intelligence in Baghdad to inform Barzan of his presence in town. Barzan's immediate reaction was disbelief that a wanted man such as Abu Nidal had managed to enter the country and remain in Baghdad for weeks, undetected. Shortly after Abu Nidal left, Barzan placed a call to Saddam to inform him of the meeting that had just taken place with the unwelcome guest. Saddam's immediate response to his brother was to get rid of Abu Nidal at any price.

On Barzan's instructions, Abu Nidal was placed under house arrest. Saddam had long suspected that this master of fickle allegiances was fraternizing with enemy governments in order to overthrow him. Abu Nidal was finally murdered by the dictator's death squad when it was determined that he had become a liability. Saddam invented a cover story for Abu Nidal's death, saying that he had committed suicide when confronted with evidence of his alleged crimes. However, Abu Nidal's body was discovered in his Baghdad apartment in August 2002 riddled with bullet holes.

Another Palestinian who found refuge in Baghdad was Wadi Haddad–the master planner of the airplane hijackings of the 1970s. Haddad belonged to the PFLP and believed that hijacking planes in Western capitals was a show-stopping way to highlight his cause. Unlike Abu Nidal, Wadi Haddad was liked by many Palestinians—even those who thought his vision and methodology of promoting their cause was extreme. His modus operandi was to make life difficult for Israelis by showing them what it was like to suffer and be shown no mercy. He didn't carry out jobs on behalf of any other governments, Iraq's or otherwise. The banner of his organization read, "We Must Seek our Enemy Everywhere."

One of the most audacious attacks attributed to Haddad's group involved the hijacking of four airliners in a single day— September 6, 1970. This came during a month of skyjacking and hostage taking that sparked bloody fighting between Palestinian organizations and the Jordanian army. The resulting fatalities, which ran into the thousands, led to this dark period in Arab history becoming universally referred to as Black September.

More than four hundred passengers were held hostage over several days. Three of the airliners were blown up at Dawson Field, a former Royal Air Force airstrip in the Jordanian desert, while the fourth landed in Cairo and was blown up after the passengers and crew were released. The object was not to kill people—the only fatality was a hijacker—but the events were enough to cripple the airlines and create panic among the governments of the United States, Britain, Jordan, and Israel.

In 1976 Wadi Haddad left Lebanon after splitting from the PFLP when the former mainstream organization embraced Marxism as its ideology. This was contrary to everything he believed in when he first joined the PFLP's nationalist pan-Arab movement. He chose Baghdad as his base from where to mastermind his particular specialty—airplane hijackings.

The kind of blackmailing deals Wadi Haddad was able to strike with Western governments in those days were described by Khalid Abdul Majid. Haddad's group hijacked a Lufthansa 737 jet, the "Landshut" on October 13, 1977, en route from Palma de

Mallorca, Spain, to Frankfurt, Germany. Their demand was to secure the release of Palestinian and Baader-Meinhof guerrillas who were being held in custody. After several days, during which the plane was ordered to fly to Italy, Cyprus, Bahrain, Dubai, and South Yemen with its terrified passengers strapped to their seats and doused in flammable liquids, the pilot was killed en route, accused of attempting to summon help. The copilot eventually landed the aircraft in Mogadishu, where a team of West German special forces stormed the plane with stun grenades, freeing the eighty-six passengers and killing three of the hijackers. The Germans subsequently negotiated a deal whereby in exchange for a lump sum of five million dollars paid into a Beirut bank account, Wadi Haddad and his group would not target the German national airline.

Wadi Haddad died under suspicious circumstances in a Berlin hospital in 1978. While he officially died of a severe blood disorder or cancer, there are rumors that he was poisoned by either the Mossad or agents of Saddam Hussein.

Muhammad Ahmad Fahd Abbas/Zaydan, more commonly referred to as Abu Abbas, was the leader of the Palestinian Liberation Front and had been brought up in the largest refugee camp for Palestinians in the Arab world—Yarmouk, in Damascus, Syria. His group became known for their ingenious incursions into Israel, including flying hang-gliders over the border from Lebanon, and landing rubber dinghies unnoticed on Tel Aviv beaches. On March 5, 1975, after one such beach landing, eight Palestinian guerrilla fighters entered the Savoy Hotel in Tel Aviv, taking dozens of hostages in return for the release of their fellow Palestinians held in Israeli jails. After Israel refused their demands, the hostage takers blew themselves up, killing all but one of their group and eight of the hostages as commandos from the Israeli Defense Force broke into the hotel room.

The role for which Abu Abbas is best remembered was that of

instigating the hijacking of the Italian cruise ship *Achille Lauro* in the Mediterranean in October 1985. Four Palestinian hijackers from the PLF had hijacked the ship to demand the release of fifty Palestinian prisoners in jail in Israel. Abu Abbas was in Tunisia at the time and was asked by the head of the PLO, Yasser Arafat, to travel to Egypt, where the ship was docked in Port Said, to help bring the negotiations to a peaceful conclusion. After two days, the hijackers agreed to surrender in return for a safe passage.

Assuming all was well, Abbas left Cairo to Tunisia on board an Egypt Air flight from Cairo to Tunis, but his plane was forced to land in Sicily after being intercepted by fighters from the American navy. According to his wife, Reem, the Italian authorities were very careful not to allow the Egyptian civilian plane land at a nearby American military airbase so they could prevent Abbas's arrest. Abu Abbas was able to leave Italy under an assumed name and travel to Belgrade because of its proximity to Rome and because of the relationship that existed between the Palestinian leadership and the Yugoslavian leader, Slobodan Milošević.

Following this episode, Abbas chose Baghdad as his headquarters, and for the next seventeen years he remained beyond the grasp of American and Italian officials. Abbas's wife, Reem Al Nimer, who is the daughter of a wealthy Palestinian banker, told me that both she and her husband enjoyed a very special relationship with Saddam and his wife, Sajida Tilfah, and family, including their two sons, Uday and Qusay.[4]

Before the fall of the regime, Reem Al Nimer described how sincere the Husseins were toward the Palestinians' plight, to the extent that when they felt her husband's life was in danger, they arranged for him to be taken to various safe houses in the Kurdish area in northern Iraq in order to protect him from Israeli agents. Even Abbas himself remained in the dark about where he was being hidden. He was on the U.S. terror list after the *Achille Lauro* incident, and tried to flee Iraq after the fall of the regime.

Attempting to pass through the Syrian border, he was stopped despite holding an Iraqi diplomatic passport. Syria by then had given America assurances that it would not allow any Iraqis to cross their border. After two days on the border, where he tried to negotiate with high-ranking Syrian officials and Palestinian leaders based in Damascus, they remained unmoved, and Abbas was forced to abandon the idea of going to Syria, where he grew up, and returned to Baghdad. He was arrested a few weeks later on April 15, 2003, after American forces succeeded in pinpointing his location via his regular use of a Thurraya satellite telephone.

According to U.S. officials, Abu Abbas died in a Baghdad prison cell of "natural causes," or a "heart attack." His wife told me that her husband had lost weight dramatically in the last weeks of his life, and she suspected that he had been mistreated. She planned to take the Americans she claimed were responsible for his death to court in the United States.

Saddam Hussein, who was a master at using the Palestinian cause for his own interests, had given the Palestinian leadership refuge and freedom to organize the second intifada against Israel, from Iraq. Khalil Al Wazir, known as Abu Jihad, the second in command of Fatah and the commander of the first intifada, was a regular visitor to Baghdad. The PLO had chosen Tunis as its head-quarters after evacuating Lebanon in 1982, and although they were tolerated by Tunisia, they were restricted to political and diplomatic negotiations only. Saddam Hussein allowed them a platform from where they could plan their military operations.

From November 1987, the beginning of the first Palestinian uprising, Abu Jihad used to call me regularly from Tunis or Baghdad to update me on the operations of the intifada in the Occupied Territories. He would express his confidence that this uprising, the first of its kind in the Palestinians' recent struggle against Israel, would not rest until a Palestinian state was declared. On April 15, 1988, Abu Jihad called me to say that he was leaving the next morning for Baghdad and that he could be reached at his Iraqi telephone numbers if I had any questions about the intifada. A few hours later he was assassinated by Israeli commandos led by former prime minister Ehud Barak, who was then the deputy military chief. Barak oversaw the operation from a navy missile boat off the shore of Tunis. The body of fifty-two-year-old Abu Jihad, who had been working late at his residence, was reported to have been riddled with seventy-seven bullets. He was killed in the early hours of April 16 in what was claimed to have been a coordinated attack by Mossad, the air force, navy, and the Sayeret Matkal commando unit.[5]

Both Islamists and Baathist have exploited the oppression and suffering experienced by the Palestinians to bind supporters to their cause. Saddam Hussein and his regime, when planning their invasion of Kuwait in August 1990, became more involved in the Palestinian cause, hoping to benefit from the sympathy Palestinians received in the Arab world and elsewhere. In addition, Saddam began supporting the victims of Israel's response to the intifada. Payments were made by the Baath Party to the families who had been directly affected by the Palestinian armed struggle. Payments were handled by the Arab Liberation Front—the Palestinian faction of the Al Baath Party in Iraq. The membership of this organization was tiny, but when the few Scud missiles launched by Saddam Hussein's regime targeted Tel Aviv and other Israeli cities, many Palestinians, especially in the Occupied Territories, welcomed this support. Iraq was the first Arab state to launch an attack against Israel since October 1973.

Many Iraqis involved in the Palestinian struggle became very influential. Mohammed Rachid, an Iraqi known as Khaled Salam, was Arafat's most senior financial adviser, lived in Gaza, and was responsible for Palestinian investments. Another adviser is Qais Al Samarrai, known as Abu Leila. He is number two in the Palestinian Democratic Liberation Front (PDFLP) and lives in

Ramallah in the West Bank. Those Iraqis who became part of the Palestinian struggle were treated with the same respect as Palestinians within the PLO organizations. They could join the union of writers, vote in elections, and become involved and accepted in all walks of Palestinian life. When I visited Yasser Arafat in 1994 at his headquarters in Tunis, a few weeks before his heralded return to Gaza, he was busy negotiating for these key Iraqis to go with him to Gaza and the West Bank. As a result of the Oslo Accord, the Israelis were determined to prevent the return of anyone other than Palestinians.[6] Arafat told me that he made it a condition that if Abu Leila and Khaled Salam were prevented from going with him, he would not return to his homeland.

Prior to Iraq's first elections, President George W. Bush and his new foreign secretary, Condoleezza Rice, received requests from Iraqi politicians urging the U.S. government to turn their attentions toward solving the Palestinian-Israeli conflict. The first interim Iraqi prime minister, Dr. Iyad Allawi, told me that he was one of those politicians, along with his foreign minister, Hoshyar Zebari, and interior minister, Falah Al Naqib. Zebari promised future support for Palestine, saying, "I can assure all my brothers"—who included the head of Palestinian diplomacy, Farouk Qaddoumi; President Mohmmad Abbas; and Mohammed Dahlan, the minister for civil affairs in the Palestinian government—that Iraq will always support their cause." Although sincerely spoken, Zebari's assurances did not reflect the views of the majority, as some Iraqis believe that the Arab world, including the Palestinians, did not care about their sufferings and oppressions at the hands of the previous regime.

Iraqi politicians realized that achieving a just peace for the Palestinians would satisfy the Sunni Arabs in Iraq as well as the Shiites, and would convince them that U.S. policy is not there just to support Israel, but to implement UN resolutions. Most Iraqis are furious that Iran has been ordered to dismantle its nuclear program while a blind eye is turned toward Israel's nuclear capabilities at the Dimona plant in the Negev Desert, which were exposed in 1986 by the Israeli whistle blower Mordechai Vanunu.[7]

Tens of thousands of Iraqis poured into the streets of Iraqi cities, brandishing Palestinian flags, after the Israeli army assassinated the Hamas leader, Sheikh Ahmed Yassin, in Gaza in March 2004. They were calling to avenge his death in a climate already tense from the heated confrontations between the American-led coalition forces and Iraqi resistance groups. The intensity and scale of these demonstrations highlighted the empathy felt by Iraqis toward the Palestinians. After Saddam's downfall, the power balance was tipped between Israel and the Arab world as the Palestinians found they had lost essential financial support given by the former regime to casualties of the intifada. It is unimaginable that the Iraqi masses will accept the United States having a central role in post-Saddam Iraq until America adopts a more evenhanded approach in resolving the Israel-Palestine conflict.

Some of the resistance groups are now aligning themselves to Islamist organizations such as the Egyptian-founded Muslim Brotherhood. Meetings have also been held in the Jordanian capital of Amman between high-ranking members of the Palestinian group, Hamas, and the Iraqi resistance groups who are seeking to learn from the experiences of the military wing of Hamas and its suicide bomb tactics against Israeli targets. Muqtada Al Sadr has vowed that his Iraqi army, Jaish Al Mahdi, will follow the path of Hizbollah in Lebanon and Hamas in Palestine.

Saddam Hussein has used and abused the Palestinian cause. While his own people were suffering under sanctions, he sent large sums of money to the Palestinian leadership to donate to the victims of the Israeli occupation. He established a new army in Iraq, calling it Jaish Al Quds (Army of Jerusalem), to be used for propaganda and demonstration purposes, and forced Iraqis to enlist. Before the American-led invasion, popular opinion among many Iraqis was that the Palestinian cause was detracting from their own plight while Saddam Hussein was using it to increase his waning popularity in the Arab world. After the fall of the regime, Palestinians living in Baghdad were targeted and large numbers were evacuated from the homes they had lived in since they arrived as refugees in 1948, and once again they found themselves living in camps. I visited one such camp in early July 2003 that had taken over the former football ground of the Palestinian team they called the Haifa Club. Many families complained to me about the treatment they received, which has forced them to live in tents supplied by NGOs just as they had almost sixty years before. The small clinic, which was run by doctors and nurses from the Palestinian Red Crescent, was full of patients–many suffering from the heat, which that day was a suffocating 140 degrees Fahrenheit. They have no travel documents, money, or passports, so they are purely and simply stuck. Those who decided to leave for Jordan had to camp out on the border between the two countries for many months before they were finally permitted into Jordan following the intervention of aid organizations.

In Iraq, the Kurds believe that the Palestinians stole the limelight from their own struggle, and in general the Kurds never felt they had any political or moral commitment toward them. The Kurds were first to establish contacts and open channels with the Israeli state, according to Mahmoud Othman, a well-known Iraqi politician and former member of the Iraqi Governing Council, whom I interviewed at his home in London. Their relations go back to the 1960s. Othman, who was very close to the late Mullah Mustapha Al Barzani, the veteran Kurdish politician, told me that in the mid-1960s Levi Eshkol, prime minister of Israel, sent David Kimchi, a former Mossad, to meet Mullah Mustapha. A few years later Othman accompanied Mullah Mustapha in secret visits to

Israel, where the Kurdish leader was hoping that the Israelis would assist the Kurds in having an open dialogue with Washington. Kamran Karadaghi, a Kurdish Iraqi political commentator, remarked, "Most Kurds consider Israel as a friend, and paying visits to Israel is something normal. Kurds are not allergic to the Israelis."[8]

On an international level, Iraqi diplomats feel that the Palestinian issue is detracting from their own cause and has compounded the negative attitude some in the new Iraq express toward the Palestinians. They need the American administration's full attention to be focused on their concerns and receive more help from the international community. Others believe that the growing Shia influence in Iraq will downplay the importance of the Palestinians to Iraqi diplomacy to the extent that some Iraqi politicians are willing to open a dialogue with Israel and contribute on a party level or even on intelligence sharing. They anticipate that such a dialogue would be welcomed by Washington.

One can conclude that the Palestinian issue is no longer an ingredient in Iraqi diplomatic negotiations, although it is still an important priority for every other Arab government.

Notes

1. Figure estimated by the U.S. Federal Bureau of Investigation (FBI).
2. The first peace deal between Israel and an Arab state was signed in September 1978 by Prime Minister Menachem Begin of Israel, President Anwar Sadat of Egypt, and President Jimmy Carter of the United States.
3. UN Resolution 242 stated that Israel would give back occupied territories in exchange for normalized relations with the Arab states desiring the land. UN Resolution 338 called upon parties to cease all firing and terminate all military activity immediately and no later than twelve hours after the moment of adoption of the decision.

4. Yasser Arafat in an interview with the author, December 26, 1998, Ramallah.

5. *Maariv,* July 4, 1997.

6. The Oslo Accord was the declaration of principles on interim se government arrangements. On September 13, 1993, in Washington, D.C., it was signed by Yasser Arafat and Yitzak Rabin and witnessed by the United States and the Russian Federation.

7. Mordechai Vanunu exposed his story to *Sunday Times* journalist Peter Hounam, and it was published in October 1986.

8. *Daily Star,* Lebanon, August 4, 2004.

CHAPTER NINE

THE FUTURE

There was still a slight chill to the dry, winter Baghdad dawn when at 7:00 AM on Thursday, January 30, 2005, the Palace of Conferences in Baghdad's protected Green Zone promptly opened its heavily guarded doors as a polling station. Sheikh Ghazi Ajeel Al Yawer, the interim president, was one of the first dignitaries to cast his vote. The most recent of his three wives, Nisreen Mustafa Barwari, the Kurdish minister for municipalities and public works, followed her husband in her own bid for reelection. Ghazi, sheikh of Iraq's largest and most powerful tribe, the Shammar, cut a distinguished figure, wafting through the VIP area in his traditional long black tribal cloak, edged with gold, which signifies his tribal rank, and his snowy white headdress. The Shammar tribe numbers one and a half million people in Iraq (five million total), and the tribe has branches stretching across the Arabian Peninsula from Iraq in the north to the southern tip of Yemen.

Security was inevitably tight. The CIA, Iraqi police, and Iraqi intelligence officers had taken up sniper positions overlooking the entrance to the two-story center. A rope cordon was in place, filtering the voters into single file. The intermittent throbbing of helicopter blades was the only sound interrupting a Thursday morning made eerily quiet due to the twenty-four-hour curfew that had been imposed on nonofficial road traffic.

Around 11:00 AM, Dr. Iyad Allawi, cocooned by a ring of armed bodyguards, arrived through the VIP entrance in what was to be his failed bid to retain his position as prime minister of the country. Illuminated by the flashbulbs and camera lights of the world's press as he negotiated his way through the throng of journalists to place his historic vote, Dr. Allawi spotted me and joked, "Let me vote for Zaki Chehab—an old friend of both myself and Iraq—before I cast my own vote!" I felt strangely touched to have been singled out like this on such a momentous day in Iraq's history by its first interim prime minister.

Up to fifty Iraqi citizens were killed that day in hundreds of attacks that erupted all over Iraq as insurgents targeted voting centers in their attempt to throw the political process into disarray. In case voters thought twice about voting because of such attacks, the Shia clergy intervened and warned the Shiite electorate that they would "go to hell" if they didn't vote for the Shia-led coalition. Uneducated women were particularly pressured by threats that their husbands would divorce them if they didn't vote likewise. The insurgency had its strongest effect on Sunnis. Large numbers of them failed to register their vote either through fear of reprisals from the insurgents or as a stand against an election that was unlikely to give them power in any significant measure. But eight million brave and determined citizens did cast their votes in the country's fifty thousand polling stations for a choice of more than seven thousand candidates.

On election day daily life for the average Iraqi was more difficult than one could imagine. Electricity and water supplies to homes and businesses was sporadic and unpredictable. The situation begged the question: how could a country like Iraq, called "The Land of Two Rivers," after the mighty Euphrates and Tigris Rivers that flow through it, be struggling for water? And how could a country that has the richest oil reserves in the world lack power? When voters raised this issue, government officials passed the blame onto the insurgents for causing these shortages by blowing up oil pipelines on a daily basis and attacking oil tankers as they traveled from the oil fields of Kirkuk in the north and Basra in the south to merge in Baghdad. With world oil prices soaring ever higher, the insurgents would siphon off the oil to sell on the black market. Under cover of night, smugglers with motor boats loaded with stolen oil would slip quietly out of the Shatt Al Arab delta, past the British army posts, and off-load their lucrative cargo onto oil tankers lying in wait in the safety of international waters in the Arabian Gulf.

With all of these ups and downs and questions about whether it represented a truly democratic process, the election nevertheless gave Iraqis their first opportunity in over thirty-five years to select their own elected assembly.

There were complaints of irregularities. Sharif Ali Ibn Al Hussein, the head of the Iraqi Constitutional Monarchist movement and aspiring king of Iraq, complained of many alleged wrongdoings, including the removal of ballot boxes from certain voting centers long before the 5:30 PM closing time. Calls were made by his supporters to the Iraqi Electoral Commission to inform them about suspicions of ballot rigging, but these reports were not acted upon. Party agents of Al Hussein were attacked and beaten, and according to Sharif Ali, ballot boxes disappeared for nearly three days in Baquba, thirty-five miles northeast of Baghdad: "We still don't know if the recovered ones were the original ballot boxes or if they were exchanged for tampered ones." Sharif Ali, who is a direct descendent of the Hashemite dynasty, has harbored a desire to restore a throne that has remained empty since 1958, when his royal forebears were murdered. His party did not get a single seat in the assembly.

The results produced a multiparty cabinet led by Shia prime minister Dr. Ibrahim Al Jaafari (the spokesperson of Al Da'awa Party), together with Kurdish president Jalal Talabani (the head of the PUK) and Sunni and Shiite vice presidents Sheikh Ghazi Al Yawer (the Iraqi Party) and Dr. Adel Abdul Mehdi (Supreme Council for the Islamic Revolution in Iraq), respectively. The new and oil-rich Iraq will be mainly governed by Shia Arabs for the first time in centuries, making Iraq the only Shia-led Arab government in a region traditionally ruled by Sunnis.

Three months after the elections, time was running out for Dr. Jaafari to form his new cabinet. After weeks of hard bargaining and wrangling between the different Iraqi groups—mainly between Dr. Iyad Allawi, the head of the Al Iraqia list and the leader of the Iraqi National Accord (INA), and the Kurdish Alliance, led by Massoud Al Barzani (KDP) and Jalal Talabani (KUP), concerning the share of power and the conditions for their participation in the government—the situation was close to chaos. Jaafari's cutoff point was May 7, 2005; otherwise his government would be deemed null and void.

Under Iraq's Transitional Law—drafted by selected Iraqi leaders who were members of the Governing Council and supervised by the occupying power led by Ambassador Paul Bremer—Jaafari would automatically lose his position if he didn't form his cabinet by that date. It was already the end of April, and there was no solution in sight.

The impasse was being watched nervously in the United Kingdom and America. Britain was about to hold its own general election. Prime Minister Blair was depending on a timely and positive outcome concerning the formation of Iraq's government to bolster his own image with voters, especially with his party's liberal base, many of whom were skeptical about the whole Iraq enterprise.

During a surprise visit to Baghdad on April 11, 2005, Donald Rumsfield warned Dr. Jaafari and the Kurdish leadership against political purges and cronyism in forming the cabinet. He also reiterated that the United States opposed any move to delay the political schedule, including the drafting of a new constitution. As April drew to a close and with no cabinet announced, President George Bush and Condoleezza Rice piled on the pressure. In late April and early May, they initiated a series of telephone calls to Dr. Jaafari, Dr. Allawi, and the Kurdish leadership, urging them to put their differences aside and form a government so that it could help British prime minister Tony Blair, who, in allying so closely with the Americans, had gambled his political career.

The United States was not particularly interested in interfering in the actual selection of the would-be cabinet ministers but insisted that a government had to be formed by May 5.

With his own deadline just four days away, and two days before the British general election, Jaafari finally declared that he had completed his cabinet selection and his government was formed. Coincidentally or not, the announcement fell on Saddam Hussein's sixty-eighth birthday. Bakhtiar Amin, the human rights minister at that time, told me over the telephone from Baghdad that he didn't want Saddam to miss out on this historic occasion on, of all days, his birthday, and sent a television set to his prison cell close to Baghdad airport. According to American sources in the Baghdad Airport jail, where Saddam is held in renovated soldiers' lavatories, Saddam watched the broadcast, a privilege not accorded to other high-level inmates. My source would not go far as telling me his reaction, but one can only imagine.

It is difficult to say whether this American politicking helped Blair, but he was reelected for a historic third term of office with a much-depleted majority, as many of Labor's traditional voters stayed at home or defected to the Liberal Democrat party in protest at Blair's pro-war position.

* * *

Safieh Al Suhail, a Baghdad-based human rights activist, told me of the fascinating behind-the-scenes political maneuvers that led to the formation of the new Iraqi cabinet.[1] She played hostess to Ahmed Chalabi and Iyad Allawi in her Baghdad villa, a house in which she was not entirely comfortable. It used to be a grace-and-favor home of a former Saddam acolyte. At the time, Chalabi and Allawi were being portrayed by the press as nonspeaking rivals. Nevertheless, they met three times at Safieh's villa to discuss the formation of Jaafari's coalition government. It was clear that Chalabi and Allawi would be the power base in the formation of any future government, and they realized they had to iron out their differences to allow the formation of a coalition government, using Al Jaafari as a figurehead. As happens so often in history, the two powerful men, for pragmatic reasons, agreed to unite behind a leader who needed their support for the immediate future, which also suited them. Chalabi and Allawi essentially agreed to postpone their fight for another day.

This might seem to be an incongruous coupling. In the run-up to the election, Chalabi, who was well known for his liberal and secular views, had allied himself with the coalition of religious Shia organizations. Before then he had been the darling of the Pentagon; then, once the Pentagon got him into Iraq, he fell out with those supporters and rebranded himself as an Iraqi patriot. He was a founding member of the deeply religious Shia coalition, answerable to Ayatollah Sistani, who received him on many occasions as his new best friend. I was therefore surprised to learn that in his latest role as a senior figure on the Shia religious list, which got him elected as deputy prime minister, he was meeting the quiet man of Iraqi politics–Dr. Iyad Allawi–who wished to remain influential regardless of which government came to power.

But I realized that to feel surprised by this volt-face was to forget everything I know about Chalabi, who did his utmost to oust Saddam and was the most successful politician-in-exile from any continent to manipulate the American government to his goal. Chalabi, after all, is a master manipulator, who would give Machiavelli a run for his pasta.

The American government, particularly the CIA, wrote Chalabi off and did everything to stop his rise within the Iraqi government, but it seems that however long their acquaintance with this wily character, they did not really know Chalabi. Despite American efforts against a man they came to view as a traitor, he nonchalantly waltzed back in to what the Americans saw as their dependent government to the powerful job as deputy prime minister. One can imagine the private fury and curses that were muttered inside Washington's beltway. It must be said that a lot of American bitterness toward Chalabi–which is spelled out in the State Department's ABC policy, meaning "Anyone But Chalabi"– has a lot to do with anger and humiliation at being outfoxed by an exile with no known following and few resources.

The moment he was elected on a religion Shia coalition ticket, it was clear that Chalabi had used it to defeat his main rival and fellow secular Shiite, Dr. Iyad Allawi. But just as transparent was that Chalabi felt no more obligation to the Shia religious coalition than he had to any of the others. He had used both it and the American government, purely as a means to his own ends. From my acquaintance with Chalabi, I realized it was inevitable that the moment he came to office, he would slide away from the religious coalition and begin forming an alliance much closer to his own beliefs and to what he foresees will favor him in the next ballot. Chalabi is archly aware that the next election is more important than that of January 2005. The initial election selected an interim government, while the next vote will produce the internationally recognized government of Iraq.

Evidence that the Americans have reluctantly accepted that at least for now they can't put a brake on Chalabi came on the day he was elected by way of congratulatory telephone calls from both Dick Cheney and Condoleezza Rice. A new chapter may be about to unfold in Iraqi politics. The Americans are desperate for a positive outcome for their venture in Iraq, and are keen to put aside vendettas and deal with anyone who can further their aspirations for a democratic regime. Both Chalabi and Allawi fit the bill.

Most interesting is the alliance Chalabi and Allawi forged in mid-2005 with the real power brokers in Iraq. Over the years, Chalabi in particular has formed strong ties with the two rival Kurdish leaders, Massoud Al Barzani and Jalal Talabani, knowing very well that any government that will rule a united Iraq will need the blessing of these two Kurdish leaders.

The future of Iraq will not be determined by last January's much-hyped and propagandized election, which was orchestrated by and insisted upon by the Americans. Iraqi political figures accepted such U.S. "assistance" because they were not yet ready to operate in such an unstable environment. Iraq's future will be determined by a new alliance that I believe will emerge out of a partnership between Chalabi, Allawi, and the Sunni leader, Al Yawer, together with the Kurdish leadership, which will sideline religious groups and bring enough disaffected Sunnis back into the mainstream to defang the insurgency. This will create a powerful, moderate, and pragmatic government that the Americans might not like, since it won't be their puppet government, but such a government is more able to rule a fractious country like Iraq.

The journey ahead for any Iraqi government is bound to be difficult. Writing a permanent constitution, deciding on whether Iraq should be a secular or a religious state; establishing rights for minority groups and women; agreeing on whether Iraq should be a federal or unified state; deciding upon the future role of both foreign forces and Iraq's internal militias are among the topics that confront the new Iraqi political class. With or without an insurgency, these complicated and combustible issues threaten to throw Iraq into further chaos.

There have been six constitutions in the modern lifetime of Iraq. The only permanent constitution to date was drawn up in 1925, followed by five subsequent temporary constitutions. Under Saddam the constitution was written to suit his own ends, which he either embraced or flagrantly ignored at will. The challenge for the fledgling Iraqi government is to come up with a modern and enduring legislative framework that will be sensitive to Iraq's potent mix of cultures and religions and steer the country in a more harmonious direction.

The Transitional Administrative Law (TAL)—known as the Interim Constitution—was delivered on March 8, 2004, by Paul Bremer's now disbanded Coalition Provisional Authority, and the Interim Governing Council. It was designed to support the new government until such time as it held a referendum on a permanent constitution, scheduled for October 15, 2005. While controversial in some aspects, the interim constitution made unprecedented provisions for women in the new parliament.[2] At least 25 percent of the General Assembly had to be composed of women, and this was enforced on all the parties. Many women activists have exhaustively lobbied both inside and outside Iraq to convince tribal leaders, political party leaders, and American administrator Paul Bremer to create a larger role for Iraqi women in politics. I was invited to an early dinner hosted by Safieh Al Suhail at her uncle's home in Baghdad. Safieh was the daughter of Sheikh Taleb, the head of the influential Bani Tamim tribe who was assassinated in Beirut in 1994 by Iraqi agents.[3] Her Kurdish husband, Dr. Bakhtiar Amin, is known internationally for his work on human rights, crimes of war, and genocide. The couple had recently moved back to Baghdad after living in Washington for some years, in order to pursue their political ambitions. Dr. Bakhtiar, a minister for human rights in Dr. Iyad Allawi's interim government, and his wife had invited senior figures in the Coalition Provisional Authority and many political party leaders, including Jalal Talabani. It was a typical Iraqi occasion—the first meal held to celebrate Safieh's return. Everyone who had a connection with her came and feasted on dolmas, lamb, rice, salad, sweets, soft drinks, and fruits.

I was seated next to Safieh and her cousin Ghaleb Al Tamimi and was surprised to hear him say to her that now that she had settled in Baghdad, she should exercise her responsibilities as the head of her tribe. I was taken aback because it is almost unprecedented for a woman to be offered the role of a tribal leader. But Safieh is no ordinary woman. An imposing figure with a strong character, she is known for her flamboyant tastes and a thick mane of hennaed hair. She had met with George W. Bush and his wife, Laura, on two occasions, as well as with the British prime minister Tony Blair with his wife, Cherie, at 10 Downing Street, when she headed a delegation of Iraqi women just a few months before the fall of the Iraqi regime. Her cousin suggested she should follow the path taken by Leila Charaf, a Lebanese woman who became Jordan's first woman minister, serving as minister of culture and information in 1984 and 1985.

In the end Safieh accepted the post of Iraqi ambassador to Egypt, one of the most important Arab postings, and on January 30, 2005, after casting her vote, she announced her ambition to one day become the first female president of Iraq.

While many Iraqi women have climbed their way to the top of Iraq's professional career ladder, many of those who have become involved in politics are paying the ultimate price. Dr. Aqila Al Hashemi, a member of the dissolved Iraqi Governing

Council, held a doctorate in French literature and had previously worked in Saddam Hussein's foreign affairs ministry. She was shot in the stomach, shoulder, and leg when her convoy, which included her driver and brother, was ambushed by six men in a pickup truck close to her home in western Baghdad. In her mid-forties, Aqila was a champion of women's causes and was described as a "Babylonian Moon Goddess." She died five days after the shooting, on September 25, 2004.

Dr. Sawsan Al Sharifi, the minister of agriculture, lost two members of her family who had been targeted by insurgents who wished to force her out of office. Her cousin Taleb was murdered while driving to the market on March 22, 2005, followed three days later by her brother Ahmed, who was killed in his coffee shop. Dr. Al Sharifi has since survived a suicide bomb attack against her ministry on April 9, 2005. I found Al Sharifi mourning yet another life lost when I spoke to her a few weeks after the opening of the first elected parliament. She had spent the day in parliament with her friend and fellow lawmaker Lamia Abed Khadouri, who was a member of the outgoing interim prime minister Dr. Iyad Allawi's list. Lamia was shot later that day, on April 27, 2005, after she returned home. She was killed on her doorstep by insurgents as she answered the door of her home in east Baghdad. She was the first Iraqi legislator to be assassinated.

Given the patriarchal nature of this and any Arab society, women involved in politics are likely to face a rough ride. If they prevail, it will be because of their toughness and their high educational level. Iraqi women, after all, have always played a visible role in Iraq. But other battles will be far more difficult and the outcomes less predictable. The framers of the new Iraqi constitution will have to deal with issues that are fundamental to what will be the new Iraq.

The Transitional Administrative Law states that Islam is to be the official religion of the Iraqi State but also guarantees citizens the freedom to practice other faiths. The TAL also states that Islamic law, or Sharia, is defined as "a source" of legislation but not the primary source.[4]

Any discussions on the role of Islam must take into consideration the background of the Iraqi population. While the majority are of the country's people are Muslims, what binds all Iraqis together is their history, which predates Islam, going back to Mesopotamia, the oldest known civilization and the land of the legendary Garden of Eden.

Even under Saddam's dictatorship there was tolerance among the different Islamic sects. Shiites in Baghdad could freely marry Sunnis without an eyebrow being raised. Observant Iraqi families dined next to men who would be drinking the afternoon away.

Iraq, though deeply religious, is also a secular society. Religious groups, liberals, and intellectuals have all indicated to me their determination not to allow any conflict to arise over Sharia law, which is the legal system adopted in next-door Iran. The impression I gleaned from my many trips to Iraq is that the average Iraqi simply wants to go about his life, working for his family and going to the mosque on his own volition rather than by dictation. Most Iraqis seem to realize that the imposition of this purist version of Islam would mean the end of a cohesive, united Iraq.

Dr. Abdul Al Hussein Cha'aban, an Iraqi human rights activist and political analyst from the holy city of Najaf, spoke of his fears if Iraq were to become another Iran. "Islam must stand for democracy and human rights," he says. "What is the meaning of Sharia? Nobody knows. No one can say Sharia should be administered by a religious man or ayatollah with the authority to hand out fatwas—this is a huge obstacle." Iranians themselves, after less than thirty years of their Islamic revolution and the introduction of Islamic Sharia, are struggling to find a way of extricating themselves from a system they locked themselves into. For this reason, many of the Iraqi Shiites in the Shia-led coalition have tried to distance themselves from this issue, including making several trips to Washington, to give assurances that the idea of Islam being the only source for law is a minority one, something only the ultrareligious organizations are promoting, and will not be carried out.

The Kurds especially are likely to resist the creation of an Islamic state. I have heard both Massoud Barzani and Jalal Talabani in their respective offices and homes opposing a religious state. They are interested in two things: (1) making sure that all Iraqis, whatever religion they belong to, are given the freedom to exercise their religious duties; and (2) ensuring that Iraq will always preserve the unique mixture and color of the different religions and ethnic backgrounds of its people.

The Shiites for their part—and by this I mean the religious leaders such as Grand Ayatollah Sistani—feel differently. They will do their utmost to make Islam the sole source of legislation in spite of reassurances made by influential figures of the Shia-led coalition like Dr. Jaafari and Abdul Mahdi. Many Iraqis believe that the Shia religious leaders will not succeed, and they are predicting that "there will be a consensus that Islam will be *a* source but not *the* source for law."

One of the Shiites' main problems was that they were never able to talk about their grievances as Shiites. They had no external Shia identity. It was always a feeling that was internalized. They were afraid of freedom of expression, because they have been a minority in the wider Muslim world and in Saddam's Iraq were discriminated against and murdered because of the targeted sectarianism of the dictatorship. In order to protect themselves, they invented a concept that they call *taqiyya*, which is not lying exactly but is rather hiding your true feelings to avoid persecution. Finally, after two years of discussion and deliberation, the Shiites published their "Declaration of the Shia of Iraq" in June 2002.[5] This was signed in London by four hundred men and women from all walks of life: writers and scientists, members of the business society, religious leaders and social activists, military personnel, and tribal leaders from the Iraqi Shia communities of America and Europe. The twenty-page document detailed their demands for the abolition of the dictatorship and its replacement with democracy; the abolition of ethnic discrimination and its replacement with a federal structure for Kurdistan; and the abolition of the policy of discrimination against the Shiites. This public declaration enabled them to talk about a Shia identity for the first time.

Most Christians in Iraq are ethnically Assyrian and lay claim to being the first Christian nation in history, many still speaking Aramaic, the language of Christ. The community of one million people is predominantly based in the northern cities of Mosul, Qal'aat Sharqat, Khursabad, and Nimrod, the four ancient capitals of the former Assyrian Empire.[6]

Shortly after the Baath regime was overthrown, Assyrian families all over the country began receiving threatening letters with instructions that if disobeyed would expose them to "Killing, Kidnapping, Burning the house with its occupants or exploding it." The letters, one of which was signed, "From the leadership of Islamic troops of 'Al Bader,'" were worded similarly: "To this noble family," one began. "We hope that the head of this family will stand with the 'brothers of Muslims' group and follow basic Muslim rules of wearing the veil and possessing honorable teaching of Islam that Muslims have continued from old epoch." "If not," it threatened, "we will take [action]."[7]

Another warning letter was sent to a Christian storekeeper who sold alcohol and was signed: "Harakat Ansar al-Islam," the Partisans of Islam movement. "We are warning you, the enemies of God and Islam, against selling alcohol again, and unless you stop we will kill you and send you to hell where a worse fate awaits you." At the storekeeper's home, his five-year-old son, Aziz, was enjoying a glass of milk while his fourteen-year-old sister, Raneen, was trying on a new outfit. A car drew up and, thinking that it was her father returning home from his store, Raneen opened the windows of their home in welcome. Four men shot her and her young brother dead.[8]

With frequent attacks against churches and the rise of radical Muslim clerics, the situation has become serious. There has been a dramatic exodus of these once large, indigenous Christian communities. Church officials estimate their numbers to be around two and a half million Assyrian Christians. The real figure is thought to be closer to one-third of that.

Saddam Hussein's alcohol rules were flexible when they applied to himself, but they were strictly applied when it came to his people. Only Iraqi Christians were permitted to sell alcohol on the street, although Muslims were allowed to buy from their stores. These liquor shops were especially well patroned by day-trippers from nearby Kuwait, where there is a total ban on alcohol. In Basra it was a common sight to see Kuwaitis passed out in hotel lobbies, having drunk too much. After sleeping it off, the next day they would drive back to their homes in Kuwait across the border.

Since the war, Shia clerics have become increasingly vocal against this trade. Two Christian liquor sellers were shot dead in the southern Iraqi city of Basra in May 2003, and over a hundred liquor stores have been burned down. Even hairdressers are receiving death threats. Several have been killed because their salons offered "un-Islamic" services such as beard trimming and Western haircuts, particularly marine-style cuts. Ultraorthodox Muslims believe that men should follow Prophet Muhammed's hadiths on the subject: "Amongst the fitraat (Deen) of Islam is the cutting of the moustache and the lengthening of the beard for surely the Majoos (fire worshippers) lengthen their moustaches and cut their beards so oppose them by cutting your moustaches and lengthening your beards."

During the 1970s and 1980s Iraq was one of the few places in the Arab world where drinking was part and parcel of proving one's manhood. When I used to go out drinking with my Iraqi friends during my trips to Baghdad, I was amazed by their capacity for beer. As the evening wore on, our table would gradually disappear under a clutter of empty beer bottles, cigarette stubs, and drained glasses. The bartender, anxious to restock his depleted glass supply was invariably turned away, because the number of bottles and glasses that covered the table served as visual evidence of the virility of the drinker. It was common knowledge that Saddam Hussein was partial to Scotch whisky at that time. His favorite brand was "Silver Label," which nobody else could afford.

Al Nidal Street, a back street in Baghdad's Al Waheda neighborhood, provided the nighttime atmosphere of what Baghdad was really like in those days. There was a much frequented bar called Al Gareeb, which translates as "The Stranger." I enjoyed going to this bar because it was a place where poets, artists, and musicians would congregate and show off their talents to the customers.

That was Baghdad before Saddam launched himself as a born-again Islamic leader at the beginning of the 1990s, riding on the crest of the wave of Islamic revivalism and adding *Allah Akhbar* to the national flag. This was not what Iraq wanted. This was what Saddam Hussein wanted. Drinking bars were suddenly banned now that Saddam had become reborn as a pseudo-religious man, except of course in his palaces, where he continued to receive (and consume) obscene amounts of Silver Label and Johnny Walker Black Label in a time of stringent economic sanctions against his country. During a briefing with Peter Hain, the British minister of state for the Foreign and Commonwealth Office in October 2000, he quoted to me staggering figures provided by the UN Security Council. The figures, calculated over a six-month period, showed that Saddam smuggled in on a monthly basis

"38,000 bottles of whisky, 115,000 litres of beer, 40,000 litres of vodka, and almost 19,000 bottles of wine" across various frontier posts.[9]

At the start of Operation Desert Storm in 1990, many Baghdadis fled their capital amid rumors that the American's were using "smart bombs," the precision-guided munitions designed to be laser-controlled and pinpoint-accurate. This was the first time Iraqis had heard of these bombs, but when news got around that the bombs really did turn right at the corner of the street and dive straight into their preprogrammed target—the defense ministry, for example—while avoiding their homes, they accepted that the bombs really were as smart as the Americans claimed. Reassured, they returned home to Baghdad and continued their illicit street trade of Johnny Walker Black Label whisky and Marlboro Red cigarettes. That was back then.

On my subsequent trips to Baghdad following Saddam's fall, I watched the atmosphere becoming increasingly Islamic. Recently Mohammed Sarraf, a men's hairdresser, was pulled out of his barbershop in Al Jadiriyah, a suburb of Baghdad, yelling, "No! I don't do Western haircuts! I don't do marine-style haircuts! I don't cut beards!" Despite his protestations, he was dragged down the steps from his hairdressing shop, bundled into a car, and was never seen again. When I first heard the story from my driver, I was shocked. It was an indication of where Iraq might be heading unless moderate Iraqis joined together in force and raised the alarm against the biggest danger their country was facing—a danger that could lead them back toward a place that was no less dark than the one from which Iraq has recently emerged.

Yet there is an encouraging consensus among Iraqis from all backgrounds to prevent the issue of Islam from dividing the country. Hoshyar Zebari graduated from the University of Jordan and lived in exile in London, from where he traveled all over the world championing his cause. He was the main negotiator for

Massoud Al Barzani's Kurdistan Democratic Party to help settle differences between the Iraqi opposition in exile and foreign governments. During an interview in his Baghdad office just a week after the elections, I broached the thorny subject of Iraqi identity. Zebari replied that he has never argued against Iraq having an Islamic identity: "Iraq is a founder member of the Arab League, and I have no intention of pulling out of this league of Muslim nations. But," he added, "Iraq is a liberal country and should remain so in the future. We will not promote a religious regime in our constitution, and the Iraqi people will also have their say on this issue."

On his appointment as oil minister in May 2005, Ibrahim Bahr Al Oloom vowed to boost Iraq's oil production to 1.75 million barrels per day and said that the ministry's motto would be to "fight corruption and boost production."[10] Iraq's oil-rich provinces are mainly near Basra, in the south, and account for more than 80 percent of the country's discovered oil reserves; the remaining oil is near Kirkuk in the Kurdish north. It is these provinces that are making the strongest push toward autonomy and provide us with an optic to view the question of the future political structure of Iraq—namely, the question of federalism and autonomy. If the Kurds are given the right of self-rule, this will mean they would form a federation of provinces in the north to include Kirkuk, Sulaymaniya, and the current provincial capital, Irbil, as well as a southern federation, which would comprise the Shia provinces of Basra, Missan, and Diqar.

Saddam used the years he was in power to Arabize what were defined as Kurdish areas to restore the balance of Arabs in the north, and this is why the issue of federalism is most important to the Kurds. They suffered for many years after Saddam's troops pushed them out of their villages and into the semi-autonomous mountain region. While officially remaining under the control of the Baathist leader, a strong Kurdish fiefdom grew up away from

Saddam's direct interference and gave them fifteen years of experience in which they got used to running their own affairs.

As far as the emergence of a future Kurdish state is concerned, the January 2005 election of a Kurd as the president of Iraq will not directly affect the Kurdish dream for statehood one way or the other. Dreams remain dreams. Even before it became clear that a Kurd would become president, a very large majority of Kurds officially voted for self-determination. There are two ways of looking at what this would mean. One is that by electing a Kurd as president, Kurdish aspirations for independent statehood might diminish because the Kurds would then be too busy running the country as a whole. But equally, a Kurdish president based in Baghdad could consolidate Kurdish aspirations and their demands for a federal state within Iraq while still nurturing the peoples' dreams for a separate state.

Geographically, Kirkuk is part of Iraqi Kurdistan, but it is not purely a Kurdish province. Although Kurds make up the majority of the population, Turkomen, Christians, and Arabs add to the complexity.

Talabani insisted to me that the Kurds had no complaints in negotiating with the Shia-led coalition over their joint desire for federalism. He agreed that while the Kurdish dream for their own separate state continues, at the same time Kurds have become more mature and realistic that this dream is unlikely to manifest itself in the short term, because neither the regional nor international environment is conducive. "I am an Iraqi democrat," Talabani proudly declared, "and believe in a federal but united Iraq both within the government and outside."

The Shia are not seeking federalism along ethnic lines–they are mostly Arabs. What they desire is a federal structure based on administrative and demographic criteria. According to their "Declaration of the Shia of Iraq," their proposed federal system "would grant considerable powers to the regions, including legislative, fiscal, judicial and executive powers, thereby removing the possibility of the centre falling under the control of a dominant group which would extend its hegemony over the entire country."[11] The Kurds disagree with this. They argue that *they are different* and that federalism has to be based on ethnicity as well as geography.

But poor communications between the different sects and groups in Iraq means that more time needs to be spent explaining each other's point of view. For example, the Kurds should explain to their fellow Arabs why they need the Peshmerga and Federalism, and why Kirkuk should become the capital of Kurdistan. Other Iraqis don't necessarily understand why the Kurds are so passionate about these things. The Kurds associate the Iraqi army with devastating the countryside and using chemical weapons and have an almost allergic reaction when they see them in the streets. The same goes for the police force that is currently patrolling in the same khaki uniforms they wore under Saddam. "That color," said Mohammed Hamid Saleh from Sulaymaniya, "reminds me of the injustices done to the Kurds. It reminds me of mass graves." Mohammed Ali, a grain store owner in the same town, agreed, saying, "It is the uniform of the Baath Party and Saddam Hussein. We hate Saddam and we don't want anything that reminds us of him."[12]

The Kurdish Peshmerga was formed by the late, legendary Kurdish leader and fighter Mustapha Al Barzani in 1946, and it has become almost mythical place in the Kurdish psyche. There are an estimated one hundred thousand people in this militia, including a strong women's force. Kurdish women have a long tradition of fighting alongside their menfolk, and their toughness and independence, honed by years of hardship in the Zagros mountain range, has earned them respect on a par with their fellow male fighters. At an academy in Sulaymaniya run by the PUK, women are being trained in the art of combat using Soviet-era weapons. Although the older warriors are still armed and dressed like their founder, in baggy Kurdish trousers and a turban, and armed with rusty Kalashnikovs and AK-47s, there is an elite team of young, fit soldiers called the Kurdish Special Forces, who are kitted out with smart combat khakis, peaked caps, and automatic weapons, who have been working together with America's Special Forces in the region.

Of all the people in Iraq, the Kurds are the most reluctant to allow a national army and police back to their areas. There are two reasons why the Peshmerga are so important for the Kurds. One is purely practical, and the other is psychological. It is within the Kurdish psyche that they have been able to keep their movement going only with the backing of the Peshmerga. The Peshmerga for the Kurds mean those who face death against "the bad guys"–the bad guys being the Iraqi army, Arabs, Iranians, or Turks. Within this group of bad guys, the really bad guys are the Iraqi regular army. So it is very important for the Kurds to preserve their viable and organized Peshmerga. They need them not purely for their protection but also as a powerful tool with which they can strike a bargain among other Iraqi groups. These groups would have to sit up and take notice of the Kurds, with their hundred-thousand-strong army to back their political demands. Their army is one of the main reasons they have political clout in Baghdad.

I visited Kirkuk for the first time less than few hours after the fall of the city, and despite it being considered one of the wealthier parts of the country, thousands of families who were forced to leave the city by Saddam Hussein's Arabization process had started to return, only to find many of their homes had been repossessed, thus leaving them refugees in their own hometown.

A Christian family I encountered in the city invited my driver and me for a glass of tea. Abu Bashar and his son are traders and have lived all their lives in Kirkuk. I was interested to speak to the elders and intellectuals of the city, and they recommended names representing Sunni, Shia, and Kurds, Turkomen, Kildans, and Assyrians. Abu Bashar and his sons accompanied us on our tour of Kirkuk to meet some of them, and I was heartened by the way they were respected by everyone we met. During my second trip to Kirkuk, less than a week later, I made a return visit to Abu Bashar. He was welcoming and this time insisted my driver and I stay for lunch. After accepting his hospitality, I noticed that beginning to creep across his face were the first signs of unhappiness about the way things were going wrong in Kirkuk. He told me that the situation was not promising and that ethnic rifts were opening. Ripples of discontent had started to build that first week after the fall of Kirkuk, when the city was still in turmoil and homes and property were being looted. A Turkoman was randomly killed by Kurdish Peshmerga from Talabani's militia, and his family and friends, as is the Turkomen custom, wanted to keep him in the house until they could take their revenge on his killer. Many communal efforts were made to try to convince the family to take the man's body to his village and bury him there, and only after the intervention of an elder did the family agree. This was the first incident to spark a series of ethnic clashes since the liberation of Iraq from Saddam Hussein.

Abu Bashar was anxious to explain how Kirkuk was being administered. The two main parties led by Massoud Al Barzani and Jalal Talabani had distributed the allotted seats in the town council among the Sunni, Shia, and Kurd while totally ignoring the Christians, who have been in Kirkuk for centuries. I returned back to Irbil, where I had based myself, a curious moundlike town that is built on top of one of the oldest settlements in the world in the foothills of the mountains. I was interested to discover that in Assyrian times, Irbil was a religious center for the chief goddess, Ishtar, goddess of hunting and war.

I had an appointment with Massoud Al Barzani in his office in the nearby mountain-top town of Salah Eldin, which is a pleasant summer resort inhabited by wealthy Kurdish politicians. As Al Barzani was confidently explaining the efforts he was making to keep the town under control, he described his joint council running the affairs of Kirkuk as being "representative of all the inhabitants." When I told him of my recent encounters in the town and the complaints being raised by the Christians who were not represented in his council, he appeared genuinely surprised and assured me that he would personally look into the situation. On my third visit to Kirkuk, I found a much happier Abu Bashar. But the fate of Kirkuk in the long term is still undecided. Many foresee that Kirkuk will have some kind of special status, which means it will have a relationship with both Irbil and Baghdad.

How Kirkuk can work as an administrative and financial capital while at the same time having ties to both Irbil and Baghdad will provide an interesting puzzle for the government to solve. Massoud Al Barzani recently made a statement, saying, "Kirkuk must be part of Kurdistan but will not be the capital–the capital will be Irbil." Yet the city's concerns are not just ethnic issues, but economic ones, too. Kirkuk is sitting on oil. The Kurds claim they should have the lion's share of input in the financial distribution of their natural resources. They believe they should either receive a percentage of the oil revenues or should be in charge of administering it, because it is on their land. Behind closed doors, some Kurds are demanding they receive a percentage of oil revenues from Iraq as a whole proportionate to their numbers. This will amount to even more than Kirkuk's oil revenues, because its output is dwarfed by the oil extracted in the south.

Another important issue regarding Kirkuk is the deportation of Turkomen. During Saddam's Arabization policy in 1991, many were forced to leave their towns and villages. The Turkomen population either went to Turkey or to Baghdad, where they became urbanized professionals.

Descendants from the Turkish-speaking Oguz tribes of Central

Asia, Iraq's Turkomen are the third largest ethnic group after the Arabs and Kurds. Thought to number around 2.5 million in Iraq, the majority of Turkomen share the northern city of Kirkuk with the Kurds. Although they consider Kirkuk to be their capital and have ambitions for an autonomous Turkomen area within a federal Kirkuk, the Kurds are reluctant to accept Kirkuk as a Turkomen city. The relationship between Turkomen, Assyrians, Kurds, and Arabs was severely tested and disturbed in the past thirty-five years of Baath rule and the Arabization policies adopted by Saddam. Kirkuk, which many describe as a melting pot of rival communities reflecting in miniature Iraq's turbulent makeup, will sorely test the government, which will need to bolster the relationship between these groups, recognize their rights, and frame them in the constitution, while avoiding referring to them as "minorities."

The Turkomen didn't have as much impact as they anticipated in the elections, and the result was a huge setback for them. The Turkish capital, Ankara, bet on their Iraqi allies gaining several seats, but the Turkomen Front won only three seats, although there are altogether fourteen Turkomen in the current assembly. The remaining eleven were part of other political party lists.

Diplomatic sources in Ankara and Kurdish leaders have told me that a joint plan for administrating Kirkuk was discussed in Turkey between Jalal Talabani and Turkish officials prior to his appointment as president. The plan as disclosed to me calls for an independent administration for Kirkuk on the basis of equal representation for Kurds and Turkomen, while the Arab and Assyrian representation will, proportionate to their population in the city, match that representation. Other ideas were explored, such as detaching Kurdish districts and subdistricts that are currently attached to Kirkuk and reattaching them to either Sulaymaniya or Irbil. The majority of the population in these areas are Kurds, but all the signs lead to adopting a Brussels-style solution where Kurds, Turkomen, Arabs, and Assyrians can live and rule together in Kirkuk in a similar way as is found in the bilingual home of Brussels, which is made up of both French and Flemish speakers.

Mixed marriages, mixed workplaces, and the many activities that Iraqis have jointly enjoyed over the years have brought them closer together. But the political disputes and the opposing views as to the American-led occupation and the distribution of power after the fall of the regime are affecting this unity. The manner in which people voted was based on their religious and ethnic background more than on national issues and views concerning the future of the country.

Even the Iraq-Iran War of the 1980s, which was fought by Shia and Sunni Arabs against a Shia-Persian force, emphasized the unity of Iraqis as Arabs rather than the divisions of Sunni and Shiite religious differences.

The ultimate priority for Sunnis in the new Iraq is for a scheduled withdrawal of American coalition troops within the foreseeable future. Under Saddam Hussein, Sunnis were the absolute elite. Those who were members of the most influential Sunni tribes were rewarded with pinnacle positions in the military, government, and business institutions. Now, along with everyone else, they are having to jostle for position among the flotsam and jetsam of all the ethnic, religious, political, and secular groups that are vying for space in the vacuum left by the enforced departure of the one-party Baathist state.

When I asked Kurdish president Jalal Talabani to describe the portion of the cake the Sunnis would enjoy in the new government, he reminded me of the common misconception that Kurds are neither Sunni nor Shia: "We Kurds are Sunni, too, so you can say Sunnis occupy the posts of both the presidency and the head of the parliament. But if you are talking about Sunni Arabs, they have both an instrumental and an historical role to play." He described Sunni Arabs and Sunni Kurds as being an "important force to be reckoned with." "As Kurds," he said emphatically, "we will not ignore the Sunni Arabs. We sided with the Shia when they were ignored by Saddam Hussein's regime, and now—and I repeat—I will not allow Sunni Arabs to be ignored or sidelined, and if necessary, as Kurds we will defend them."

The problem for the Sunnis is that for sixty years they were associated with a centralized Sunni-backed government, and it wasn't necessary for them to set up decentralized organizations. Now, although Sunni Arabs mostly live in areas that can vaguely be defined as central Iraq, they have been dragged into a new, and to them scary, modern, political world, where they will have to organize and work like every other Iraqi. They can no longer expect that because they are Sunnis they will be guaranteed the best jobs or even the best table at a Baghdad restaurant.

To package the Byzantine composition of the people of Iraq into one neat box is impossible and unwise. The Arabs of Iraq account for 80 percent of the population. Kurds, Turkomen, Assyrians, and Kildans comprise the remaining 20 percent. If the population is to be divided along religious lines, 95 percent are Muslims and 5 percent are a mixture of Christians, Jews, Yazedis, and Sabe'ah. The Muslim population are adherents to either the Shia or Sunni doctrines, and within these Iraq's Shia Muslims can be Arab, Kurds, or Turkomen. Likewise, the country's Sunni Muslims are Arab, Kurds, or Turkomen. The overall historical identity of Iraq is as a supporter of the pan-Arab movement and the Muslim world in general. In other words, the identity of Iraq cannot be defined purely by religious, ethnic, or tribal generalizations: Iraq is Iraq.

Dual nationality is another topic that will emerge in the future. An estimated two million Iraqi people have second nationalities. Since the freeing of Iraq from Saddam's control, hopes have revived for compensation for Jews and other groups such as the

Kurds, Assyrians, and Shia, who were unfairly deprived of their property, their nationality, or both during successive Baathist regimes.

Tens of thousands of the once-flourishing Jewish community in Iraq were forced to leave or were expelled from the country after two years of growing anti-Semitic sentiment as a result of the creation of the State of Israel and the expulsion of hundreds of thousands of Palestinians from their homes. In 1948 Iraq amended its penal code, making Zionism a crime punishable by arrest, which in practice meant torture and a lengthy jail sentence. Those who are old enough to recall tell of Jews being hanged in Baghdad's Independent Square in 1948. Jews were also dismissed from government positions. They began to flee in vast numbers, smuggling out money and belongings where they could, but many were tricked, either because of the Iraqi authority's practices against them or because the Jewish organizations who were active then encouraged them to emigrate to Israel and to leave their assets frozen in the country. At the same time, Iraq revoked their citizenship. Iraq's Jewish population was the wealthiest and most highly educated in the Arab world. In an ironic twist to this exodus, the fledgling State of Israel, which badly needed this intellectual and business-savvy population, played a supporting role in galvanizing their flight to their new country. In what was called Operation Ezra and Nehemiah, approximately 120,000 Jews were brought to Israel over a two-year period. As Benny Morris, the Israeli historian, claimed in his seminal work based on the archives from early Israeli governments, it was Israeli agents, sent by their own government, who planted a series of bombs in Baghdad throughout 1951 that provided the impetus for this mass exodus.[13]

The Jews have lived in the region for twenty-six hundred years, ever since King Nebuchadnezzar, who built the hanging gardens of Babylon, captured Jerusalem in the seventh century B.C. and brought its Hebrew inhabitants in chains to Babylon. Their population has dwindled from almost 150,000 in 1948 to fewer than 40 today.[14] When I visited the now-decrepit synagogue in a Baghdad back street, I found only a few elderly Jewish men still attending Sabbath prayers. Their grandsons held no hope for the community's future, for one simple reason, according to one of the old men: the last Jewish wedding took place twenty-five years before, and there are no more women left to marry.

Since 2003 many stories have been circulating around Baghdad concerning Iraqi Jews returning to the city and trying to locate their former homes. Some have come accompanied by Iraqis whom they befriended while they were in exile, while others arrived with their American soldier friends of Iraqi-Jewish origin. Iraqis were puzzled about this trickling influx of Jews, saying that American forces were encouraging matters beyond their scope of their duties. Rumors being spread saying that Jews were planning to take back their former homes now occupied by Iraqis also caused panic.

I was in my office in Baghdad's Palestine Hotel in June 2003 when I received a hand-delivered statement from an unidentified group, threatening to blow up the nearby Baghdad Hotel. The stated reason for this threat was that the hotel was being used to house Mossad agents and Iraqi Jews who had returned to the country. (I could not confirm the presence of Mossad members, as the Baghdad Hotel was under strict security by U.S. forces.) A few weeks later the hotel was attacked by a suicide bomber, but it is unknown whether Israeli intelligence agents or Jewish returnees were inside. It is widely known, however, that the Mossad has set up clandestine offices in the main cities of Kurdistan. Since the summer of 2003, estate agents have reported sales of properties to Israelis of Iraqi descent, particularly in the north, where the security situation is safer. As a result of a general permit signed by Israel's minister of finance, Benjamin Netanyahu, authorizing trade between Israel and Iraq, Israeli companies can now trade and invest in Iraq without facing any sanctions from the government.[15] Israeli businessmen have subsequently been investigating Iraqi markets, obtaining licenses to operate in Iraqi Kurdistan and setting up utility businesses such as telephone and water supply companies.

It is too early to say whether Israel will succeed in a deeper involvement in Iraq. The consequences of ties with the Jewish state can be summed up by the experience of the first Iraqi politician to openly visit Israel, who called for peace: "I was calling for peace, and I will continue to call for peace—even [for peace] with Israel. . . . And may all the world hear that there will be no war if the Palestinians, Syrians, Egyptians, and Jordanians do not want war. I am not prepared to allow Iraqis to be turned into kindling for the flames of terrorists and ghosts of death."[16]

The politician was Mithal Al Alusi, founder and general secretary of the Iraqi National Democratic Party, which broke from Chalabi's INC. Al Alusi was expelled from INC after he visited Israel and played a significant role in the de-Baathification policy of the Interim Governing Council. Al Alusi accepted an invitation to attend a conference on the global impact of terrorism, which was held in Herzliya, Israel, in September 2004. On returning home to Iraq he discovered he was being charged with breaking a 1968 Saddamite law stating that visiting "a Zionist Entity" was a crime. Despite the fact that the former dictator was languishing in prison, his laws could still be invoked! Many attempts were made on Al Alusi's life, and in February 2005 he survived an attack that killed his two sons, Ayman and Jamal, together with a bodyguard. Despite this personal tragedy he bravely announced: "Peace with Israel is the only option for Iraq; peace with everyone but the terrorists."[17]

If the new Iraqi government does allow Jews to regain their nationality and their right to return, conditions will almost certainly be applied. For example, they must not have worked with the Israeli army or the Israeli secret services Mossad or Shin Bet.

That will be a problem, because Israelis are subject to compulsory national conscription. Every male and female must serve in the army, with the exception of the ultraorthodox. Salahaddin Mohammed Bahaddin, a former member of the Governing Council when it was weighing this very question, asked: "The previous Israeli Minister of Defense in Ariel Sharon's government, Benjamin Bin Aliazer, is an Iraqi Jew [who liked to be called Fouad by his Iraqi Jewish friends]. Should we let him return?"[18]

These questions of Iraq's identity and the role of religion will take years to resolve. For most Iraqis, however, the government must, first and foremost, deal with the issue that is having the most impact on their daily life—security. Under Saddam they may have suffered from repression, but there was almost no crime—burglaries were rare and kidnappings unheard of. While the Americans are worried by the politically inspired kidnappings and suicide bombings by the Jordanian jihadi Abu Musab Al Zarqawi, ordinary Iraqis are far more concerned about the explosion of domestic crimes and lack of security.

In an interview I conducted with prime minister Dr. Ibrahim Jaafari, he acknowledged the deteriorating security situation and admitted that this was due to internal disruptive elements as well as from foreigners. "We should allow the security situation to guide the way we are planning our Iraq," he said, "and it is very important that we should involve everyone—civilians, army and police force, and the government—to help us corner these terrorists who are trying to destroy the achievements we made since the fall of the regime."

Jaafari asserted that his priorities were "to secure Iraq's borders with neighboring countries by recruiting more people to join the police and the army, install better communication systems, fight unemployment, and allow a culture of forgiveness and cooperation to flourish between Iraqis." He ruled out future sectarian war in Iraq, however, and said that he intended to build on the experience his party had in opposition when they adopted practices to ensure that Iraq stayed united. He added, encouragingly, that there is a tighter bond between Sunnis and Shia than the terrorist Abu Musab Zarqawi had envisaged. "There are large tribes in Iraq with branches which are both Sunni and Shia, and there are many mixed marriages between these tribes. There is also the shared faith which makes it possible to unite them. We have the wisdom as Iraqis not to be drawn into a sectarian war. There are large areas of the country where Sunnis and Shiites live harmoniously together or they share the same neighborhood. Even Saddam Hussein's evil games to forge a sectarian divide failed because of the astuteness of his people as to what he was up to. It is true that terrorists are attempting to draw the country into a sectarian conflict, but I can assure you that it is not going to work."

The American occupation committed one of its gravest errors by inviting specially selected Sunnis back from exile and enforcing these handpicked representatives on the general Sunni population—people like Adnan Pachachi, for example, the former Iraqi foreign minister (1965–1967) who based himself between London and Dubai. Pachachi failed to gain one single seat in the election despite the financial and moral support he received directly or indirectly from the American administration. In May 2004 Pachachi was America's number one choice to be Iraq's new president, but came under strong opposition from the Shia organizations and political parties. The job went to Ghazi Al Yawer. I believe such support for Pachachi by the Americans gave the wrong impression to the insurgency and the resistance and supplied the extreme organizations "with a reason to flourish which has turned the whole country into a hell."

Al Sharif Ali, the would-be king, told me that during the summer of 2003 he personally met Ambassador Bremer and the commander of American forces in Iraq, Ricardo Sanchez, on many occasions. Ali was used in an attempt to broker an agreement between leaders of the Iraqi resistance and the American-led coalition. "Bremer, who was aware of my efforts and was briefed about it," said Al Sharif Ali, "has hinted that I should handle this issue with the commander of American forces in Iraq, Ricardo Sanchez." But the situation deteriorated as the conditions put forth by resistance leaders in Ramadi, Fallujah, Mosul, and other parts of Iraq were turned down by the Americans. These conditions were not altogether unreasonable. Some talked about American withdrawal from the populated areas in Iraq as a first stage, while others insisted on a scheduled withdrawal by the American forces in exchange for curtailing attacks targeting them.

Most Iraqis want the Americans to leave, with the exception of the Kurds, who feel that the American military presence will be a safeguard against any foreign interference or threats, especially from Turkey and Iran. As a long-term prospect, I anticipate that the Americans will maneuver to have some kind of permanent presence in the country.

But foreign troops will not be welcome forever. Sistani himself never gave the occupation a green light to stay indefinitely. He insisted on the United Nations playing an instrumental role in putting together a framework for the future of Iraq by dictating the conditions as to how long foreign forces will stay in Iraq, and admitted there was a need to review their presence. "We feel that the Iraqi security organization is capable of securing the country, and there are United Nations resolutions to support the way things will develop." But without question, it is in the hands of Iraqis to dictate how the country will be governed in the future. It is not in their interests or ours for foreign troops to remain in our new sovereign state. "We have made great progress, and Iraqi security organizations should now take charge."

There are wider concerns among Iraqis that the Americans are using their country as an experiment to gain control of the oil in order to influence the whole region. Certainly for Washington, the battle for Iraq is part of a wider international strategy. Success would mean eradicating the insurgency as a first step as well as the emergence of a stronger and more united democratic country, which hopefully will lean toward the West. They hoped that the creation of a new Iraq would have a ripple effect across the Middle East, encouraging democratization in a region predominantly ruled by dictators and autocrats. However, this is not being done out of the kindness of their hearts or for any true love of the Iraqis. Government policy makers believe that many of the more radical Islamic organizations that have attacked them amassed their membership from those who were forced out of their own countries because they had no opportunity to play any part in governments that brook no dissent. For the insurgents and the Americans the battle for Iraq is not for Iraq itself but as part of an ongoing international war. Success for the Americans would mean controlling the world; failure would give the world an opportunity to finally force the United States to review its foreign policies.

Iraqis want only one simple thing from the Americans–to regain their independence. They don't want to be at war with the United States, or any country for that matter. They have been through many wars and have seen their country destroyed and their people go hungry. Iraq needs to be rebuilt so that its people can begin to take things into their own hands. But first they need technology and a lot of help, and for now the United States is a resource to enable them to achieve this. Knowing the history of Iraq and the past experience the United States has in the region, I think that American military forces will remain in Iraq for at least five years, if not longer. The Iraqis know very well their political maneuvering is possible only while there is a strong military presence to keep order in the country. The Iraqi forces are not capable of that. Despite the fact that a new constitution will give an Iraqi government a veto on the presence of any foreign force, I think it will take more years than Washington realizes for Iraq to be restored to normal health, but the Iraqis—whom Arabs call the "Prussians of the Middle East"—will achieve this despite of, not because of, the Americans.

The American government shows signs of realizing it will have to compromise if there is any chance of withdrawing its forces and leaving behind a working Iraqi government. It does not want to repeat what happened in Vietnam when that government fell the moment American props were pulled from under it. This is not a rosy assessment, but one made in the light of a new pragmatic approach in Washington and Baghdad.

The Americans are suffering losses in Iraq far beyond their previous incursions, such as in 1982 in Lebanon, where they were forced to leave with their stated task unfulfilled. The stakes are much higher now, and I think they will stay the course this time or they will lose everything.

Foreign Minister Hoshyar Zebari has asked the United Nations to play a more influential role in the future of Iraq but believes that the United States, with its large number of troops in the country, will remain a force to be reckoned with. "The Americans have already helped us by eliminating the dictator and assisting us in going to the ballot boxes. In return I am sure they would say, 'We have helped you to go though all this because of the courage you have exercised, and it is up to you to decide what you want for the future.' That said, it doesn't mean their influence over events here is finished. My gut feeling is that they will intervene as they always have done in the past."

Others might take a less sanguine approach. For example, there are many people who are sympathetic to the Iraqi resistance and many voices from the Sunni camp who argue that if it weren't for the resistance, the United States would have succeeded in controlling everything. American commanders in Iraq conceded that the Iraqi army, and security forces in general, still need a strong chain of command, greater confidence, and a different attitude when dealing with members of the Iraqi public. The image of Iraqi police patrolling the streets of Baghdad, and even outside the capital, wearing balaclavas to conceal their identity, reflects their state of fear and worry. This kind of policing is also counter-productive; citizens are likely to feel even more insecure at the sight of policemen and soldiers covering their faces to survive. But the security forces face a catch-22 situation. Many, on being recognized by someone in their neighborhood, have been betrayed to the insurgents and murdered.

The ferocity of attacks against Iraqi police and army is reflected in their panicky behavior at checkpoints, where the slightest movement or hint of tension in their direction can lead to firing in the air or toward passers-by or cars around them.

The shooting of an Italian commando, Nicola Calipari, following the release of the fifty-six-year-old Italian journalist Giuliana Sgrena, of the communist *Il Manifesto* newspaper, reflects the tactics used by American and Iraqi police that were adopted to deter would-be suicide bombers. After twenty-eight days in captivity, Sgrena was released at the main American checkpoint about a mile from Baghdad International Airport on March 4, 2005. This incident was no different than what Iraqis encounter while going about their daily business since the fall of the regime. International interest in Sgrena's story was aroused as a result of the death of the Italian Calipari, who was accompanying her after kidnappers had negotiated her release from captivity, but also because Sgrena's country is one of the main pillars of the American-led coalition in Iraq.

The Italians were divided into two camps. One supported the government's views toward the war in Iraq, while the other—polls put the figure at 70 percent of the population—furiously demonstrated against the war in the streets of Rome and other main cities in Italy. Many questions have been raised about the shooting that rainy Friday evening, which left the rescued hostage wounded and her rescuer dead with a single shot to his head. Calipari was one of Italy's most skilled intelligence agents, with a record to be proud of in negotiating complicated missions, including the release of five previous Italian hostages in Iraq. American military officials in Baghdad claimed that his car was traveling at speeds of more than ninety miles per hour. The First Battalion, sixty-ninth Infantry Regiment of the New York National Guard, who were manning the checkpoint, also noted that the car lost control several times before the shooting took place. They claimed efforts were made to warn the occupants of the vehicle to slow down using flashing lights, waving, and firing warning shots. The Italian government gave a different version of events.[19] Gianfranco Fini, the foreign minister in Silvio Berlusconi's government at the time, claimed that not only were there no roadblocks, but no warnings were given, and he described the speed of the car as not exceeding 25 miles per hour. Fini also remarked that the Italian agent had made all the necessary arrangements in Baghdad before he headed toward Baghdad Airport with the former hostage to return her to Rome. Fini's claims were dependent on statements given by the surviving Italian agent who was driving the car. According to a CBS report, "Data from military satellites clearly showed the car traveling toward the checkpoint at over 60 MPH without slowing down at all, triggering the defensive response from the American soldiers."[20] Sgrena herself, a veteran of many conflict zones, including Afghanistan and Algeria, and having made seven trips to Iraq, refuted claims that they were speeding along the most dangerous road in Iraq: "As the car rounded a turn, driving no faster than thirty miles an hour, it was heavy gunfire and at the same time, bright light (sic). He [Calipari] pushed me down, and with this, the body covered me. . . . I realized that Nicola was dead, without saying anything, nothing at all."[21] In a subsequent television interview she dismissed as "lies" that warning shots were fired together with hand signal warnings.[22]

I first met Sgrena in the convention center in the Green Zone in central Baghdad on the afternoon of January 30, 2005, while we were lining up to interview a senior member of the Al Da'awa Party, Sayed Jawad Al Maleki. Sgrena, who was behind me in the line, asked me if I would mind if she had a five-minute interview with him ahead of me, which I agreed to. I had been in the Al Jadiriyah neighborhood on February 4, 2005, meeting Fateh Baban, senior adviser to the head of the monarchist movement, Al Sharif Ali. Returning to the Al Hayat–LBC TV office, which was close to the University of Baghdad, where Sgrena was last seen, my colleagues were discussing this latest kidnapping. Some of them had heard a few shots fired in the air by her kidnappers before they sped away, and they commented that Sgrena's visit to the university was a particularly unwise act by a Western journalist. Even Iraqis dare not go about the capital unless absolutely necessary since kidnapping became a lucrative business.

For a relatively small sum of money, hostages can be handed over by one kidnap gang to more serious gangs, where, if the hostage is of Western nationality, they can be used as political pawns by the various militant groups, with the added bonus of receiving a possible large ransom. Mohammed Kabbani, an LBC TV correspondent in Baghdad, told me that Sgrena was at least the third journalist to be kidnapped from the area surrounding the University of Baghdad. Foreign journalists would visit one of the colleges that houses refugees from Al Fallujah who have been occupying the premises since the first American offensive against their city designed to flush out insurgents. It is understood that certain elements among the refugees alert their fellows outside the university of the presence of potentially high-value hostages in the university complex.

Many Iraqis have joked with me about the different price tags attached to hostages. The value of an Iraqi hostage can vary between one thousand and fifty thousand U.S. dollars, calculated on the wealth of his or her family or their respective profession. An Arab can raise similar amounts or even more, depending on which field he works in and the company he belongs to. But the ultimate prize is the Westerner, who can be exchanged for millions of dollars if the country he belongs to is participating as one of the coalition forces. Italy sent three thousand troops to Iraq, and a ransom of six million U.S. dollars was allegedly paid for the release of Giuliana Sgrena.

I had a scrape on a far less dangerous scale when I found myself facing guns one day in February 2005, while being driven from Al Fardawas Square to Al Qadisiyah neighborhood in Baghdad. Approaching a traffic island, a police patrol came speeding in our path, sirens blaring, and forced us to stop. One of the policemen pointed his Kalashnikov barrel toward my chest while demanding the driver to clear the way. My short-tempered Iraqi driver was all fired up to answer back and made moves toward the pistol he kept. Thankfully, I was able to calm him down, and the Kalashnikov was returned to a safer position.

There is a consensus among many Iraqis that an American military presence will be sustained in Iraq one way or another. There is talk about agreements between Iraq and the United States that will grant the United States military bases. According to Iraqi and American sources, four bases will be maintained: one of which is close to Baghdad International Airport; one on the outskirts of Nasiriyah at Talil Air Base in the south; a third in the western desert, toward the border with Jordan and Syria; and a final one in Bashur, in the Kurdish-controlled areas in the north. The Talil Air Base, located in a sandy desert 186 miles southeast of Baghdad, now has a Burger King and a Pizza Hut to cater to the hungry service men and women. These eyesores clash with Iraq's most famous archeological site—nearby Ur, the earliest city in the world. The seven-thousand-foot runway of Bashur Airfield, which rips through a green valley in the northern end of the country, is strategically close to the Iranian and Turkish borders and the key oil fields of Mosul and Kirkuk.

Traveling across Iraq via its borders with Syria, Jordan, and Iran, I saw for myself how close to those borders American forces have established their checkpoints and bases. The U.S. presence here is bound to exert more pressure on Syria and Iran. U.S. officials expect a long-term defense relationship with Iraq, which will strengthen the American presence in the Middle East in order to compensate for the eventuality of their reduced presence in Saudi Arabia. This could of course provide a magnet for even more terrorist attacks.

Jalal Talabani gives this issue an optimistic spin: "If it wasn't for the American forces who removed Saddam Hussein, our people would still be suffering under his dictatorship today. The American-Iraqi relationship should build on establishing and preserving the modernity of our country and our mutual interests. There are a lot of areas in which we can cooperate that would benefit both the Iraqi and the American people. The United States is a super-advanced industrial power and has a great influence in the region. I feel our people still need America's help concerning gaining our independence, and I feel we still need the American forces in our country until such time as we can rely on our own security forces."

CONCLUSION

I have been following Iraqi politics for more than a quarter of a century since my debut journalistic assignment took me to Baghdad to cover the 1978 Arab Summit, held there following Egyptian president Anwar Sadat's visit to Jerusalem, which prompted the decision taken by Arab capitals to boycott Cairo. (Sadat was eventually assassinated by Islamic militants on October 6, 1981, while saluting troops at an annual military parade, almost three years after he made peace with Israel. He was succeeded by Hosni Mubarak, who remains the president today.) Since then I have been in touch with the different players on both sides–those from Saddam Hussein's regime and the Iraqi opposition in exile. Traveling all over the country and meeting the different factions, it became clear to me that Iraq's regional and international politics will be defined by its current and future relationship with America. Once the Iraqis are confident enough to run their own affairs, this will inevitably lead to requests for American withdrawal. But until such time, in order to strengthen the country's security organizations, they will still require American forces to remain in place to provide further training for the Iraqi army and police force and to improve security along the lengthy borders it shares with its not-always-friendly neighbors. While Baghdad still lacks the presence of a strong army, its next-door neighbors all have large and very well equipped military organizations.

Another security issue concerns the militias and how they can be incorporated into this new military structure. If the Kurdish Peshmerga, the Sunni-backed insurgents, and the two Shia militias–the Jaish Al Mahdi army and Al Hakim's Badr Brigades–are integrated in this, many believe that they will protect their own loyalties foremost in any conflicts that may arise. The esprit de corps of some of these groups cannot be compared with that of a disciplined and trained army, and it would be difficult to see how an integrated army could successfully function using these very disparate militias.

The Sunni Arabs are major components of Iraq, and the country cannot return to normality if they are not integrated into the political process. Sunni participation is vital in helping redress the balance within Iraq itself. Their involvement would also benefit Iraq's relationship with the rest of the Arab world, which is mainly Sunni. Saudi Arabia and Egypt in particular would have cause for concern if the government in Iraq struck a deeper alliance with Iran, as this would further destabilize an already unstable region.

If the Americans committed one fatal mistake, it was dissolving the Iraqi army and the predominantly Sunni Baath party. No consideration was given to the strength of the tribal roots that bound together the Baath Party or to the damage that would be wreaked if they were uprooted. Any possibility of establishing a dialogue between the Americans and the Sunni Arabs was thereby lost. This mistake has confirmed suspicions that the United States had no forward plan to replace the Baath regime, and this led to the power vacuum that was filled by the Shiites. At the same time, it has encouraged the militant Abu Musab Al Zarqawi and his band of foreign fighters to push the Sunnis toward further extremism and militancy. The Sunnis are now in the wilderness. Bringing them back into the new Iraq is dependent not just on the Americans but also on the will of the Shia to embrace them and open the way toward a national conciliation, which is vital to the renewed stability of Iraq.

Steps taken by the American administration to address the Sunni issue in Iraq were showcased during the brief visit made by Condoleezza Rice to Iraq in May 2005, when she urged the new leaders of Iraq to embrace the Sunnis as partners in any decisions they take relating to the rebirth of Iraq, referring specifically to the constitution. This statement, delivered by Rice during her first visit to Iraq, emphasized that force alone will not solve the volatile security situation in Iraq. Other means have to be employed. This was the first indication that Washington was seriously reconsidering how to handle the insurgency in Iraq, which was claiming American lives on a daily basis.

Rice's statement fell short of suggesting negotiations with those among the insurgents who are willing to talk or heads of tribes who are in a position to influence the insurgents to put their arms aside and take part in the political revival. Nevertheless, her challenge has raised the stakes of seeing Iraq back on track. Many of the elders whom I have met on many occasions in different parts of the country, but mainly in the Sunni areas in central Iraq, expressed nothing but sympathy with the resistance. If they didn't support them financially, these elders were sympathetic toward them, having felt humiliated by the treatment they had received from the American-led occupation.

Many tribal elders were staunch opponents of the Baathist regime, and not only their families but their tribes in general paid a heavy price for this. I was present when a group of leaders from the Sunni tribes met to discuss the security situation in Salah El Din province. They invited the commander of the American forces in their region to attend their meeting, but their request was turned down. Some of them asked whether Paul Bremer expected them to go and line up at the palace gates in Baghdad in order to beg him to solve their problems.

News circulating by early summer 2005 indicated that contact had been established between American officials and the insurgents. This was not the first of its kind, but many people hoped that this kind of diplomacy would be taken seriously in order to marginalize the extreme and foreign elements of the insurgency while convincing Sunnis in general that their contribution to the political process is vital.

The insurgency is flourishing and dominating the news from Iraq in such a way that its influence far outweighs its numbers. Iraq will be unable to function normally until this insurgency is brought under control. Zarqawi and his band of foreign fighters are not Iraqi and are widely despised, but they are profiting from the anger and frustration felt by Iraq's Sunni Arabs. Zarqawi and others like him will be defeated only after the local population and the government turn the tables on these terrorist militias and engage with the Sunni insurgents on a political level rather than as military enemies. It is true that the Americans have the capability to fight the insurgency more effectively than the current Iraqi security forces, but as history shows, a military can never defeat a guerrilla force without the support of the indigenous people.

NOTES

1. Safieh Al Suhail, in conversation with the author, May 5, 2005.
2. Article 30, chapter 4, "The Transitional Legislative Authority," Transitional Administration Law, March 8, 2004.
3. See chapter 3.
4. Article 7, chapter 1, "Fundamental Principles," Transitional Administration Law, March 8, 2004.
5. "Declaration of the Shia of Iraq," Dr. Mowaffec Al Rubaie, Dr. Ali Allawi, and Dr. Sahib Al Hakim, London, June 2002. Available at http://www.defenddemocracy.org/publications/publications_sho w.htm?doc_id=258915.
6. Frederick A. Aprim, *Assyrians: The Continuous Saga* (self-published, 2004).
7. Glen Chancy, "Christians in Iraq," Coptic Digest, September 15, 2003. Available at http://www.copts.net/detail.asp?id=472.
8. *Christian Science Monitor,* July 13, 2004.
9. "U.K. Briefing on Iraq," Foreign and Commonwealth Office, United Kingdom, October 23, 2000.
10. Reuters News Agency, May 9, 2005.
11. "Declaration of the Shia of Iraq."
12. Institute of War and Peace Reporting, Iraqi Crisis Report No. 85, October 20, 2004.
13. Benny Morris, *Righteous Victims: A History of the Zionist-Arab Conflict 1881–2001* (New York: Vintage, 2001).
14. *Banking on Baghdad: Inside Iraq's 7,000-Year History of War, Profit, and Conflict,* Edwin Black (Hoboken, NJ: Wiley, 2004).
15. This arrangement was coordinated on July 21, 2003, with Minister of Foreign Affairs Silvan Shalom.
16. Mithal Al Alusi, "Iraqi Official Mourns Sons, Vows to Fight 'The

Ghosts of Death,'" Radio Free Iraq, February 8, 2005. Edited transcript available at http://www.rferl.org/featuresarticle/2005/02/70bb0174-012b-483d-a708-467530aaa9ca.html.

17. Sawt Al Iraq, February 2005.

18. *New York Times,* February 28, 2004.

19. ABC News, March 8, 2005.

20. CBS, April 30, 2005.

21. Sgrena talking to Scott Pelley, *60 Minutes,* Wednesday, April 13, 2005.

22. Ibid.

INDEX